Rustics in Rebellion

RUSTICS IN REBELLION

A Yankee Reporter on the Road to Richmond
1861-65

GEORGE ALFRED TOWNSEND

With an Introduction by
LIDA MAYO

Chapel Hill

THE UNIVERSITY OF NORTH CAROLINA PRESS

Contents

v

Contents

Editor's Note

THE CIVIL WAR reporting of George Alfred Townsend first appeared in book form in 1866, entitled *Campaigns of a Non-Combatant,* and published under the imprint of Blelock and Company, New York. *Rustics in Rebellion* reproduces the material of this earlier edition, with the exception of an introductory chapter in which Townsend made some philosophical comments on his career as a newspaperman; a final and digressional chapter describing executions which he had witnessed; a chapter on his experiences in England, where he spent nine months in 1862-63; one on his impressions of Florence, Italy; and a chapter on Washington after the war. These have been omitted in order to present a continuous war narrative.

Few changes have been made from the original edition. Obvious minor errors in names, dates, punctuation, and spelling have been corrected. But Townsend's occasional lapses in reporting events of the war—only too understandable in "the fog of battle"—have been allowed to stand as they were written.

Rustics in Rebellion is Townsend's own title for Chapter VII. It was used for the book title of the present edition as representative of Townsend's characterization of the Southern people as he saw them—a people whom he liked and admired but whose cause he deplored.

Introduction

———

I

At two o'clock in the afternoon of a winter day early in 1862 a newly accredited war correspondent rode out of Washington into Virginia to cover the Civil War. He was the youngest of all the correspondents, only twenty-one years old, a stocky, rather handsome boy with thick brown hair, high cheekbones, and intelligent blue eyes. His name was George Alfred Townsend. Cheerful by nature, he was more than usually light-hearted at the prospect of adventure and excitement, but he was a little anxious, too. The Army of the Potomac was about to begin its long-anticipated advance and he expected to follow it into battle.

His expectation was not fulfilled; the advance turned out to be only a practice march toward Manassas; but in the three years that followed, he saw war at close quarters. Soon after his first assignment he was sent by the New York *Herald* to cover the terrible Seven Days' battles on the Virginia peninsula. He was with General Pope's Army of Virginia at Cedar Mountain. Later he rounded out the war with Sheridan at Five Forks, and was one of the first of the correspondents to enter captured Richmond.

The boy's dispatches covering the tremendous battles of 1862 were signed only "By a Correspondent," or "Correspondent's Account." It was not until 1865, when by-lines began to be used, that he received any personal recognition. His brilliant stories on Lincoln's assassination and the capture of Booth were widely acclaimed, and it was in the Reconstruction era that he began to be really well known. In the Gilded Age he became famous as a Washington correspondent and columnist. His by-line, "Gath," was known from one end of the country to the other, and he was regarded with the affection that people bestow on a columnist who becomes a part of their daily lives. Americans followed him through the scandals and excesses, the miseries and the gaslit splendor of his age, and even those who disagreed with him were captivated by his charm and impressed by his success. He became the prototype of the successful newspaperman. Post offices, race horses and jackknives were named for him, and even a cigar whose trade mark was a quill pen. Fabulous stories were told of his country estate, Gapland, in the Maryland mountains near Washington.

It is this "Gath" who is remembered by some of the older generation even now, and whose name is greeted by an affectionate and nostalgic smile.

In the course of his long and active life (he died in 1914), he wrote some twenty books, of which a few— *Washington Outside and Inside, Tales of the Chesapeake, The Entailed Hat, Katy of Catoctin*—are read by historians or students of American regional literature. Very few people, even among American historians, have ever heard of the book he called *Campaigns of a Non-Combatant*, which is here reprinted. It was written between 1862 and 1865, while the battle scenes he had witnessed were still fresh and vivid in his impressionable young mind. It is above all a personal narrative, more concerned with people than with battles, and its leading characters are not generals and statesmen but weary soldiers slogging along a muddy road or dying in a barn, runaway slaves, sutlers and skulkers, and the ruined Virginia people behind the lines.

II

His early life and the stock he came from peculiarly fitted George Alfred Townsend to understand and to portray the rustics in rebellion.

After the battle of Five Forks, he saw Federal and Confederate wounded laid out on the floor of a small Virginia church. At the back was a gallery for the Negroes, at the front a varnished pulpit. On the pulpit, underneath some torn blankets and stained uniforms, were the hymn book and the Bible, which was inscribed, "Presented to Gravelly Run Meeting House by the Ladies." The pulpit lamps shone down on the pale and dusty faces of the wounded, and outside under the stars fevered men lay where "the Methodist circuit-rider had tied his horse, and the urchins, during class-meeting, had wandered away to cast stones at the squirrels."

It was the familiar setting of his own childhood. His father was an itinerant Methodist preacher who travelled up and down the Eastern Shore of Maryland and the Delaware Peninsula; his family's roots on both sides were in the sandy soil of the Pocomoke River region of the peninsula, near the line of Virginia's eastern shore. It was a "little, lowly region" of small farms and courthouse towns in which the inn, jail, and shingle-boarded, dormered houses were grouped around a tree-shaded square. Creeks ran through the towns; in neighboring coves and inlets swung pungy boats and oyster canoes, and oxen grazed in the marshes. The people were never far from the smell of salt water and the feel of the open sea.

In such a courthouse town, Georgetown, Delaware, Alfred was born on January 30, 1841. His mother, who had been Mary Milbourne, was thirty-nine years old, his father, Stephen Townsend, was thirty-three, and his brother Emory was six. Three months after the baby was born, the family moved to Salisbury, Maryland, a hundred miles away; and by the time Alfred was sixteen, they had packed up their thin rag carpets, their blue earthenware and copies of Bunyan and Fox's *Book of Martyrs*, and moved eleven times. It was a life of poverty and deprivation. Alfred's memory of his mother was of her white, anxious face; of his father, his bent shoulders and the thin sinewy legs that testified to the hardness and steepness of his path. In the early part of his ministry Stephen

Townsend worked as a carpenter during the week; later the family, to which a third son had been added, got along somehow on three or four hundred dollars a year.

On Sunday morning by starlight the preacher would hitch his horse to his sulky, put Alfred on a carpet stool between his knees, and travel all day from one crossroads chapel to another, with a morning sermon at one place, an afternoon sermon at another, miles away, and an evening sermon at some point still more remote. Alfred's earliest and strongest memories were of these excursions down some sparsely settled neck of land where the narrow, sandy road led through sombre pine forests and the only sound was the solitary cawing of a crow or the tap of a woodpecker. In the bleak uncarpeted meeting-houses, where the men sat on one side and the women on the other, there were hymns sung with the aid of a tuning fork, and after the long sermon there were the "class meeting experiences," that stirred the boy's heart and remained with him all his life: "the pinched, hard faces of the older people telling their bitter trials in bereavement, misappreciation, and poverty ... the timid utterances of the younger converts, outlining the rebellious instincts of their tempted bodies."

This was the raw material of life. When Alfred began to write, he knew the troubles and longings of ordinary people just as Stephen Crane, who was also the son of an itinerant Methodist preacher, knew them; and some of the descriptions in this book have the insight and realism of *The Red Badge of Courage*. The class meetings, the changing scenes, the drama of revivals and conversions, and above all the reading of three chapters of the Bible every day, were invaluable equipment for a writer, far better training than anything he could get at schools in Delaware and Maryland and, finally, Philadelphia, where his family's wanderings took him in 1853.

There Stephen Townsend settled down at last. At the age of 48 this remarkable man (who received a Ph.D. degree at the age of seventy) took up the study of medicine and practiced in Philadelphia until the end of his life.

But the early itinerant life had affected his boys with wanderlust. Emory became a soldier of fortune and was killed fighting under General Walker in Nicaragua in 1856. Alfred, who was lucky enough to get a job with the Philadelphia *Inquirer* the day he graduated from high school in February of 1860, and competent enough to become city editor of the Philadelphia *Press* a year later, began to get restless when the war came; and before long he was on the road to Washington.

III

Young Townsend loved the life of a correspondent, "this roving commission, these vagabond habits, this life in the open air among the armies, the white tents, the cannon, and the drums," but he did not serve continuously throughout the war; very few of the correspondents did. In the early fall of 1862 the Chickahominy fever he had contracted in the Peninsular Campaign was succeeded by a fever to see Europe, and while the guns of Second Bull Run were booming he went to England. The British were eager for first-hand information about the great American war. He tried lecturing, but he was too pro-Northern to please his audiences. With writing he had better luck: articles such as "Richmond and Washington During the War," and "Campaigning with General Pope," appeared in the *Cornhill Magazine* and other English periodicals and brought enough money to enable him to spend a year on the Continent, leading what he considered a bohemian life with writers and artists. He came home in time to see the end of the fighting; and after the war he put together his first book, *Campaigns of a Non-Combatant,* using material he had written in England, his later dispatches to the New York *World,* and his reflections on aspects of life in Europe and America.

On December 21, 1865, Alfred married a Philadelphia girl, Bessie Evans Rhodes, and took her abroad for a year. This time he made a serious study of European governments; and when the young Townsends came home, bringing a baby born in Paris, Alfred decided to settle in Washington in order to study politics and government in America. The result of these researches was a ponderous book, *The New World Compared with the Old.*

It was dryly factual, but it sold more than 80,000 copies. People of the North and West felt new pride in their reborn nation. The growing interest in their government was manifest also in a demand for daily information from Washington: the Civil War had made Americans a nation of newspaper readers. This was an extremely fortunate state of things for a young man of Alfred's talents. In 1868 the Cleveland *Leader* took his first letters from Washington, then the Chicago *Tribune,* the Cincinnati *Commercial,* and the Missouri *Democrat;* and before long he was appearing in almost every newspaper of importance in the country. It was in the Chicago *Tribune* that he first used "Gath." As he told the story, at the end of the first letter for the *Tribune,* "I put 'G.A.T.' and then balanced my pen, and said, 'I'm tired of writing that.' So I tried to make some monogram of it, and the only consonant that would make a syllable with it was H, which I added. 'Hello,' said I, 'that's a Philistine city. Hello again,' I said, 'It's written in the scriptures, Tell it not in Gath. So I wrote Gath below the letter.'"

His columns were informative, independent, personal, and often witty. They caught on at once. In the seventies he wrote another long book, *Washington Outside and Inside,* the first book to have "Gath" on the title page. He became a Washington personage and other members of the press corps wrote about him for the edification of their readers. One of them, the female correspondent of a Boston paper, commented on his laughing eyes, his exceedingly pleasant mouth, and his charm, which so beguiled her that she found herself saying all sorts of things, forgetting that she was talking to a skillful interviewer who, in spite of the fact that he trifled with his cane and seemed to pay no special attention to what was said, was undoubtedly storing everything away in his active brain.

Behind the easy, genial manner of the man of thirty-two who sat chatting so agreeably, trifling with his cane, there was great drive, a high conception of his responsibility to his readers, and a consuming thirst for knowledge. In order to study the financial structure of America he moved his family to New York in the middle seventies—keeping, as he said, one foot in Washington. He made a great deal of money. He could give his wife diamond earrings on her birthday and could provide for her and his children all the elegancies of the age. Three children had been born in Washington, but two died as babies; there were left Genevieve, born in 1866, and George Alfred, Junior, born eight years later. The family lived in New York for the next fifteen years.

If New York was the financial capital of the country, it was also the literary capital, and it is probable that the friends Gath made during this period encouraged in him a half-buried longing to write fiction. Occasionally he had dashed off a poem or a story, but in the busy rush of his life, when he felt sometimes as if he were rushing toward oblivion down the groove of a steel pen, there had never been time for the historical novel he wanted to write. He was now approaching forty, and there was not much time left.

His thoughts turned to his youth and to the peninsula where he had spent his childhood. On an impulse one day he made a voyage by steamer down the Chesapeake Bay to Pocomoke, the region where his mother and father had been born. He had left the peninsula when he was twelve years old and had never returned. As the steamer glided past coves and inlets, its paddles starting the loons, past level shores shaded with water oaks and cypresses or fringed with marshy splutterdocks, he felt as if he were voyaging toward his own youth. He walked the tranquil streets of the little towns and the charm of the quiet region captured his heart, bringing painful reflections upon the "fever and errantry" of his "vain career."

The result of this pilgrimage to the peninsula was a small volume called *Tales of the Chesapeake,* published in

1880. Its reception was enthusiastic. Reviewers applauded
the venture of a brilliant and popular newspaperman into
the field of literature, and were deeply interested in a
region hitherto unexplored by any American writer. They
were reminded of Washington Irving, Bret Harte, and
George W. Cable. Leading literati of the day, Mark Twain,
Henry W. Longfellow, and Oliver Wendell Holmes, were
generous in their praise.

Inevitably there was another and longer visit to the
Eastern Shore. Gath went to his birthplace in Delaware
and retraced the wanderings of the circuit-rider's family,
of which he was now, except for his father, the only sur-
vivor. He talked to old people and rummaged through
yellowing wills and deeds in village courthouses. At the
courthouse in Snow Hill, far down on the peninsula near
the border of Virginia, he found the will of a maternal
ancestor of whom he had heard tales from an aged relative, and in it, dated February 12, 1800, was a provision
that at once seized his imagination: "I give and bequeath
to my son, Ralph Milburn, my best hat, to him and his
assignees forever...."

At that moment there was born the idea for *The
Entailed Hat,* a historical novel laid in the Peninsula of
about 1828. It began as the story of Meshach Milburn,
who inherited the fateful Puritan hat; but as the author
progressed with the writing, immersing himself more and
more in the history of the region, stories told him by his
mother and father of the time of their youth rushed into
his mind, and a wicked old woman marched into the novel
and took it over. Her name was Patty Cannon. In the
novel, as in life, she headed an infamous gang who kid-
napped free Negroes in Delaware and sold them into
slavery in Virginia, and she had actually died in the jail
of Townsend's native town. When the novel was published
by Harper's in 1884, it was entitled *The Entailed Hat, or
Patty Cannon's Times;* and it bore on its title page an
engraving of the steep-roofed Teackle mansion which had
been Patty Cannon's den in the forest. The dual nature
of the book, which was really two novels in one, is a fault

of construction; some of the writing is in the inflated, romantic style of the period; but the narrative is absorbing and the descriptions of scenes and people are enchanting in their power to carry the reader into the long-forgotten past of the Peninsula.

The novel added enormously to Gath's reputation as a literary man. Before it was in print he had begun on another, a novel based on the John Wilkes Booth conspiracy. He had planned such a book long ago, as he stood in the White House looking down on the dead face of Abraham Lincoln. Now, nineteen years later, he went down into southern Maryland and followed Booth's footsteps on his flight into Virginia; he talked with men who had aided Booth and with men who were present at his capture. He went to Harper's Ferry to get material on John Brown's raid, with which the book begins, visiting on the way the hilly country of western Maryland where much of the story is laid. In his preface to the novel, which was called *Katy of Catoctin, or The Chain Breakers,* and was published by Appleton in 1886, Townsend said that the theme appealed to him, as a descendant of Marylanders. But the Maryland of this novel was not the Maryland of the peninsula, where he had found his best and truest inspiration; and, bound by his own recollections of the scenes he portrayed, he could not unleash his imagination and escape, as he did in *The Entailed Hat,* from journalism into literature.

Indirectly, however, the Maryland novel contributed more to the legend of Gath than the Delaware novel did. It was responsible for Gapland, a cluster of buildings on a mountaintop that remained an object of wonder and speculation long after Gath was dead and his books were forgotten. He first saw the site when he was returning from Harper's Ferry in a buggy on an October day in 1884: a hundred acres of wooded land at Crampton's Gap that commanded a fine view of the fertile valley of Middletown. With characteristic impulsiveness he bought the land at once and began to build a country house that

he designed himself and called "Askelon," a name coupled
in the Bible with "Gath."

It was here that he finished *Katy of Catoctin*. He had
dreamed all his life of having a quiet place in which he
would write poetry and novels that would live. It was
still a reasonable dream, for he was only forty-five; but it
was not to be realized. In the time that he could spare
at Gapland from the pressure of newspaper work in
Washington, he wrote page after page, novels and short
stories and verse, but except for a story or two in *Lippin-
cott's Magazine*, he wrote nothing of popular appeal. Perhaps he had written himself out, or it may be that he had
transplanted himself too far from tidewater.

He turned his tremendous energy to Gapland. He had
always like to draw, and he now began to design and to
build fantastic structures that covered the top of the little
mountain and gave it the look of a summer resort. In 1890
he built "The Hall," which had eleven rooms; five years
later there was the "Den and Library," which had fifteen;
there were added, for guests, "Mount Gath" of five rooms,
and the "Lodge" with four. With stables and barns and
summer-houses, there were nine buildings in all. They
were constructed for the most part of stone, ornamented
with terra cotta busts and medallions; there were rambling
wooden verandahs, stained-glass windows, mansard roofs,
and turrets. In such a setting it is easy to imagine carriages
driving out from Washington on a summer evening,
groups gathered on the verandahs or in the big rooms
blazing with lamps; and the sociable host, who could talk
so informatively on such a wide variety of topics or en-
tertain everybody with his favorite recitation, "Little
Grisette."

The Den and Library was his; Mrs. Townsend lived in
the Hall, and their married daughter Genevieve stayed,
with her children, in Askelon. Gapland was permanent,
Gapland was to be the place where the itinerant preacher's
son would put his roots down in Maryland soil. At a short
distance from the main buildings a brick tomb was built,
with room for all the family; over the entrance there was

placed a marble slab on which was carved in the handwriting familiar to so many people, "Good Night Gath."

The tomb remained empty. In 1903 Mrs. Townsend died, and Gapland was never the same. Gath seemed to age very rapidly and became more or less an invalid, spending most of his time at his house in Washington. On a visit to his daughter in New York in the spring of 1914 he became ill and died there on April 15, 1914, at the age of seventy-three. His daughter sold Gapland. For a long time the buildings stood empty; the rafters fell, the underbrush grew up over the windows, and vandals carried away the marble slab over the tomb.

Yet there is a memorial at Gapland—not to Gath, but to the George Alfred Townsend who reported the Civil War. On the summit of the mountain there rises fifty feet in the air a stone monument commemorating all the correspondents of the war. In shape it is like the gateway to a castle: on a Moorish arch are superimposed three Roman arches and a turret. Flanking the main arch are marble tablets containing the names of one hundred and fifty-seven Civil War correspondents and artists; around the smaller arches are terra cotta horses' heads, niches containing statues representing Mercury, Electricity, and Poetry, and tablets inscribed with the words "Speed" and "Heed" and with quotations on war reporting taken from many sources, including the Old Testament.

There is not much doubt that Gath, architect of Gapland, had a hand in the design. He had conceived the idea for the memorial and raised the money, five thousand dollars, from such men as J. Pierpont Morgan, Levi P. Morton, George M. Pullman, Joseph Pulitzer, Chauncey M. Depew, John Wanamaker, and Thomas A. Edison. His name, under that of the Governor of Maryland, headed the list of directors, which included the names of other famous Civil War correspondents—John Hay, Whitelaw Reid, Edmund C. Stedman, and Joseph B. McCullaugh, who had covered the war for the North, and Henry Watterson, who had covered it for the South.

They dedicated the memorial on October 16, 1896. The

autumn foliage burned brightly and through the great stone arch the spectators could look down on the peaceful corn-shocked fields of a Maryland valley. Thirty-five years before, on the spot where the memorial was built, there had been violence and death: forty men had died on this ground in the battle of Crampton's Gap. The man who stood there in the autumn of his life felt close to those soldiers. Poignant recollections of the tragedy and the glory of his time came upon him and it seemed that he could hear, far off, cannon on a battlefield in Virginia.

Rustics in Rebellion

CHAPTER I

The War Correspondent's First Day

———————

Looking back over the four years of the war, and noting how indurated I have at last become, both in body and in emotion, I recall with a sigh that first morning of my correspondentship when I set out so light-hearted and yet so anxious. It was in 1861. I was accompanied to the War Department by an attaché of the United States Senate. The new Secretary, Mr. Edwin M. Stanton, referred me to a Mr. Sanford, "Military Supervisor of Army Intelligence," and after a brief delay I was requested to sign a parole and duplicate specifying my loyalty to the Federal Government and my promise to publish nothing detrimental to its interests. I was then given a circular, which stated explicitly the kind of news termed contraband, and also a printed pass, filled in with my name, age, residence, and newspaper connection. The latter enjoined upon all guards to pass me in and out of camps and authorized persons in Government employ to furnish me with information.

Our Washington superintendent sent me a beast, and in compliment to what the animal might have been, called the same a horse. I wish to protest, in this record, against any such misnomer. The creature possessed no single equine element. Experience has satisfied me that horses stand on four legs; the horse in question stood upon three. Horses may either pace, trot, run, rack, or gallop; but mine made all the five movements at once. I think I may call his gait an eccentric stumble. That he had endurance I admit; for he survived perpetual beating; and his beauty might have been apparent to an anatomist, but would be scouted by the world at large. I asked, ruefully, if I was expected to go into battle so mounted; but was peremptorily forbidden, as a valuable property might be endangered thereby. I was assigned to the Pennsylvania Reserve Corps in the anticipated advance, and my friend the attaché, whom I shall call "S.," accompanied me to its rendezvous at Hunter's Mill. We started at two o'clock, and occupied an hour in passing the city limits. I calculated that, advancing at the same ratio, we should arrive in camp at noon next day. We presented ludicrous figures to the grim sabremen that sat erect at street corners, and ladies at the windows of the dwellings smothered with suppressed laughter as we floundered along. My friend had the better horse; but I was the better rider; and if at any time I grew wrathful at my sorry plight, I had but to look at his and be happy again. He appeared to be riding on the neck of his beast, and when he attempted to deceive me with a smile, his face became horribly contorted. Directly his breeches worked above his boots, and his bare calves were objects of hopeless solicitude. Caricatures rather than men, we toiled bruisedly through Georgetown, and falling in the wake of supply teams on the Leesburg turnpike, rode between the Potomac on one side and the dry bed of the canal on the other, till we came at last to Chain Bridge.

There was a grand view from the point of Little Falls above, where a line of foamy cataracts ridged the river, and the rocks towered gloomily on either hand; and of the city below, with its buildings of pure marble, and the yellow earthworks that crested Arlington Heights. The clouds over the Potomac were gorgeous in hue, but forests of melancholy pine clothed the sides of the hills, and the roar of the river made such beautiful monotone that I almost thought it could be translated into words. Our passes were now demanded by a fat, bareheaded officer, and while he panted through their content, two privates crossed their bayonets before us.

"News?" he said, in the shortest remark of which he was capable. When assured that we had nothing to reveal, he seemed immeasurably relieved, and added, "Great labor, reading!" At this his face grew so dreadfully purple that I begged him to sit down and tax himself with no further exertion. He wiped his forehead, in reply, gasping like a triton and muttering the expressive direction, "right!" disappeared into a guard-box. The two privates winked as they removed their muskets, and we both laughed immoderately when out of hearing. Our backs were now turned to the Maryland shore, and jutting grimly from the hill before us the black guns of Fort Ethan Allen pointed down the bridge. A double line of sharp abatis protected it from assault, and sentries walked lazily up and down the parapet. The colors hung against the mast in the dead calm, and the smoke curled straight upward from some log huts within the fort. The wildness of the surrounding landscape was most remarkable. Within sight of the Capital of the Republic, the fox yet kept the covert, and the farms were few and far apart. It seemed to me that little had been done to clear the country of its primeval timber, and the war had accomplished more to give evidence of man and industry than two centuries of occupation. A military road had been cut through the solid rocks here; and the original turnpike, which had been little more than a cart track, was now graded and macadamized. I passed multitudes of teams, struggling up the slopes, and the carcasses of mules littered every rod of the way. The profanity of the teamsters was painfully apparent. I came unobserved upon one who was berating his beasts with a refinement of cruelty. He cursed each of them separately, swinging his long-lashed whip the while, and then damned the six in mass. He would have made a dutiful overseer. The soldiers had shown quite as little consideration for the residences along the way. I came to one dwelling where some pertinacious vandal had even pried out the window-frames and imperilled his neck to tear out the roof-beams; a dead vulture was pinned over the door by pieces of broken bayonets.

"Langley's"—a few plank houses, clustering around a tavern and a church—is one of those settlements whose sounding names beguile the reader into an idea of their importance. A lonesome haunt in time of peace, it had lately been the winter quarters of fifteen thousand soldiers, and a multitude of log huts had grown up around it. I tied my horse to the window-shutter of a dwelling, and picked my way over a slimy sidewalk to the rickety tavern-porch. Four or five privates lay here fast asleep, and the bar-room was occupied by a bevy of young officers, who were emptying the contents of sundry pocket-flasks. Behind the bar sat a person with strongly-marked Hebrew features, and a watchmaker was plying his avocation in a corner. Two great dogs crouched under a bench, and some highly-colored portraits were nailed to the wall. The floor was bare, and some clothing and miscellaneous articles hung from beams in the ceiling.

"Is this your house?" I said to the Hebrew.

"I keepsh it now."

"By right or by conquest?"

"By ze right of conquest," he said, laughing; and at once proposed to sell me a bootjack and an India-rubber overcoat. I compromised upon a haversack, which he filled with sandwiches and sardines, and which I am bound to say fell apart in the course of the afternoon. The watch-maker was an enterprising young fellow, who had resigned his place in a large Broadway establishment to speculate in cheap jewelry and do itinerant repairing. He said that he followed the "Army paymasters, and sold numbers of watches, at good premiums, when the troops had money." Soldiers, he informed me, were reckless spendthrifts; and the prey of sutlers and sharpers. When there was nothing at hand to purchase, they gambled away their wages, and most of them left the service penniless and in debt. He thought it perfectly legitimate to secure some silver while "going," but complained that the value of his stock rendered him liable to theft and murder. "There are men in every regiment," said he, "who would blow out my brains in any lonely place to plunder me of these watches."

At this point, a young officer, in a fit of bacchanal laughter, staggered rather roughly against me.

"Begurpardon," he said, with an unsteady bow, "never ran against person in life before."

I smiled assuringly, but he appeared to think the offence unpardonable.

"Do asshu a, on honor of gentlemand officer, not in custom of behaving offensively. Azo! leave it to my friends. Entirely due to injuries received at battle Dranesville."

As the other gentlemen laughed loudly here, I took it for granted that my apologist had some personal hallucination relative to that engagement.

"What giggling for, Bob?" he said; "honor concerned in this matter, Will! Do asshu a, fell under Colonel's horse, and Company A walked over small of my back." The other officers were only less inebriated and most of them spoke boastfully of their personal prowess at Dranesville. This was the only engagement in which the Pennsylvania Reserves had yet participated, and few officers that I met did not ascribe the victory entirely to their own individual gallantry. I inquired of these gentlemen the route to the new encampments of the Reserves. They lay five miles south of the turnpike, close to the Loudoun and Hampshire railroad, and along both sides of an unfrequented lane. They formed in this position the right wing of the Army of the Potomac, and had been ordered to hold themselves in hourly readiness for an advance.

By this time my friend S. came up, and leaving him to restore his mortified body, I crossed the road to the churchyard and peered through the open door into the edifice. The seats of painted pine had been covered with planks, and a sick man lay above every pew. At the ringing of my spurs in the threshold, some of the sufferers looked up through the red eyes of fever, and the faces of others were spectrally white. A few groaned as they turned with difficulty, and some shrank in pain from the glare of the light. Medicines were kept in the altar-place, and a doctor's clerk was writing requisitions in the pulpit. The sickening smell of the hospital forbade me to enter, and walking across the trampled yard, I crept through a rent in the paling, and examined the huts in which the Reserves

had passed the winter. They were built of logs, plastered
with mud, and the roofs of some were thatched with straw.
Each cabin was pierced for two or more windows; the
beds were simply shelves or berths; a rough fireplace of
stones and clay communicated with the wooden chimney;
and the floors were in most cases damp and bare. Streets,
fancifully designated, divided the settlement irregularly;
but the tenements were now all deserted save one, where
I found a whole family of "contrabands," or fugitive slaves.
These wretched beings, seven in number, had escaped
from a plantation in Albemarle County, and travelling
stealthily by night, over two hundred miles of precipitous
country, reached the Federal lines on the thirteenth day.
The husband said that his name was "Jeems," and that his
wife was called "Kitty"; that his youngest boy had passed
the mature age of eight months, and that the "big girl,
Rosy," was "twelve years Christmas comin'." While the
troops remained at Langley's, the man was employed at
seventy-five cents a week to attend to an officer's horse.
Kitty and Rose cooked and washed for soldiers, and the
boys ran errands to Washington and return—twenty-five
miles! The eldest boy, Jefferson, had been given the use
of a crippled team-horse, and traded in newspapers, but
having confused ideas of the relative value of coins, his
profits were only moderate. The nag died before the troops
removed, and a sutler, under pretence of securing their
passage to the North, disappeared with the little they had
saved. They were quite destitute now, but looked to the
future with no foreboding, and, huddled together in the
straw, made a picture of domestic felicity that impressed
me greatly with the docility, contentment, and unfailing
good humor of their dusky tribe. The eyes of the children
were large and lustrous, and they revealed the clear pearls
beneath their lips as they clung bashfully to their mother's
lap. The old lady was smoking a clay pipe, the man running over some castaway jackets and boots. I remarked
particularly the broad shoulders and athletic arms of the
woman, whose many childbirths had left no traces upon

her comeliness. She asked me, wistfully: "Massar, how fur to de nawf?"

"A long way," said I, "perhaps two hundred miles."

"Lawd!" she said, buoyantly—"is dat all? Why, Jeems, couldn't we foot it, honey?"

"You a most guv out before, ole 'oman," he replied; "got a good ruff over de head now. Guess de white massar won't let um starve."

I tossed some coppers to the children and gave each a sandwich.

"You get up dar, John Thomas!" called the man vigorously; "you tank de gentleman, Jefferson, boy! I wonda wha your manners is. Tank you, massar! know'd you was a gentleman, sar! Massar, is your family from ole Virginny?"

It was five o'clock when I rejoined S., and the greater part of our journey had yet to be made. I went at his creeping pace until courtesy yielded to impatience, when spurring my Pegasus vigorously he fell into a bouncing amble and left the attaché far behind. My pass was again demanded above Langley's by a man who ate apples as he examined it, and who was disposed to hold a long parley. I entered a region of scrub timber farther on, and met with nothing human for four miles, at the end of which distance I reached Difficult Creek, flowing through a rocky ravine, and crossed by a military bridge of logs. Through the thick woods to the right, I heard the roar of the Potomac, and a finger-board indicated that I was opposite Great Falls. Three or four dead horses lay at the roadside beyond the stream, and I recalled the place as the scene of a recent cavalry encounter. A cartridge-box and a torn felt hat lay close to the carcasses: I knew that some soul had gone hence to its account.

The road now kept to the left obliquely, and much of my ride was made musical by the stream. Darkness closed solemnly about me, with seven miles of the journey yet to accomplish, and as, at eight o'clock, I turned from the turnpike into a lonesome by-road, full of ruts, pools, and quicksands, a feeling of delicious uneasiness for the first time possessed me. Some owls hooted in the depth of the woods, and wild pigs, darting across the road, went crashing into the bushes. The phosphorescent bark of a blasted tree glimmered on a neighboring knoll, and as I halted at a rivulet to water my beast, I saw a solitary star floating down the ripples. Directly I came upon a clearing where the moonlight shone through the rents of a crumbling dwelling, and from the far distance broke the faint howl of farm dogs. A sense of insecurity that I would not for worlds have resigned, now tingled, now chilled my blood. At last, climbing a stony hill, the skies lay beneath me reddening with the flame of camps and flaring and falling alternately, like the beautiful Northern lights. I heard the ring of hoofs as I looked entranced, and in a twinkling, a body of horsemen dashed past me and disappeared. A little beyond, the road grew so thick that I could see nothing of my way; but trusting doubtfully to my horse, a deep challenge came directly from the thicket, and I saw the flash of a sabre, as I stammered a reply. Led to a cabin close at hand, my pass was examined by candle-light, and I learned that the nearest camp of the Reserves was only a mile farther on, and the regiment of which I was in quest about two miles distant. After another half hour, I reached Ord's brigade, whose tents were pitched in a fine grove of oaks; the men talking, singing, and shouting, around open air fires; and a battery of brass Napoleons unlimbered in front, pointing significantly to the West and South. For a mile and a half I rode by the light of continuous camps, reaching at last the quarters of the ——th, commanded by a former newspaper associate of mine, with whom I had gone itemizing, scores of times. His regiment had arrived only the same afternoon, and their tents were not yet pitched. Their muskets were stacked along the roadside, and the men lay here and there wrapped in their blankets, and dozing around the fagots. The Colonel was asleep in a wagon, but roused up at the summons of his adjutant, and greeting me warmly, directed the cook to prepare a supper of coffee and fried pork. Too hungry to feel the chafing of my sores and bruises, I fell to the oleaginous repast with my teeth and fingers, and eating ravenously, asked at last to be shown to my apartments. These consisted of a covered wagon, already occupied by four teamsters, and a blanket which had evidently been in close proximity to the hide of a horse. A man named "Coggle," being nudged by the Colonel, and requested to take other quarters, asked dolorously if it was time to turn out, and roared "woa," as if he had some consciousness of being kicked. When I asked for a pillow, the Colonel laughed, and I had an intuition that the man Coggle was looking at me in the darkness with intense disgust. The Colonel said that he had once put a man on double duty for placing his head on a snowball, and warned me satirically that such luxuries were preposterous in the field. He recommended me not to catch cold if I could help it, but said that people in camp commonly caught several colds at once, and added grimly that if I wished to be shaved in the morning, there was a man close by who had ground a sabre down to the nice edge of a razor, and who could be made to accommodate me. There were cracks in the bottom of the wagon, through which the cold came like knives, and I was allotted a space four feet in length, by three feet in width.

Being six feet in height, my relation to these Procrustean quarters was most embarrassing; but I doubled up, chatteringly, and lay my head on my arm. In a short time I experienced a sensation akin to that of being guillotined, and sitting bolt upright, found the teamsters in the soundest of Lethean conditions. As the man next to me snored very loudly, I adopted the brilliant idea of making a pillow of his thigh; which answered my best expectations. I was aroused after a while by what I thought to be the violent hands of this person, but which, to my great chagrin, proved to be S., intent upon dividing my place wih me. Resistance was useless. I submitted to martyrdom with due resignation, but half resolved to go home in the morning and shun, for the future, the horrible romance of camps.

CHAPTER II

A General under the Microscope

WHEN I awoke at Colonel Taggert's tent the morning afterward, I had verified the common experience of camps by "catching several colds at once," and felt a general sensation of being cut off at the knees. Poor S., who joined me at the fire, stated that he believed himself to be tied in knots, and that he should return afoot to Washington. Our horses looked no worse, for that would have been manifestly impossible. We were made the butts of much jesting at breakfast; and S. said, in a spirit of atrocity, that camp wit was quite as bad as camp "wittles." I bade him adieu at five o'clock A. M., when he had secured passage to the city in a sutler's wagon. Remounting my own fiery courser, I bade the Colonel a temporary farewell, and proceeded in the direction of Meade's and Reynolds' brigades. The drum and fife were now beating reveille, and volunteers in various stages of undress were limping to roll-call. Some wore one shoe, and others appeared shivering in their linen. They stood ludicrously in rank, and a succession of short, dry coughs ran up and down the line, as if to indicate those who should escape the bullet for the lingering agonies of the hospital. The ground was damp, and fog was rising from the hollows and fens. Some signal corps officers were practicing with flags in a ploughed field, and Negro stewards were stirring about the cook fires. A few supply wagons that I passed the previous day were just creaking into camp, having travelled most of the night. I saw that the country was rude, but the farms were close, and the dwellings in many cases inhabited. The vicinity had previously been unoccupied by either army, and rapine had as yet appropriated only the fields for camps and the fences for fuel. I was directed to the headquarters of Major-General George A. McCall—a cluster of wall tents in the far corner of a grain-field, concealed from public view by a projecting point of woods. A Sibley tent stood close at hand, where a soldier in blue overcoat was reading signals through a telescope. I mistook the tent for the General's, and riding up to the soldier was requested to stand out of the way. I moved to his rear, but he said curtly that I was obstructing the light. I then dismounted, and led my horse to a clump of trees a rod distant.

"Don't hitch there," said the soldier; "you block up the view."

A little ruffled at this manifest discourtesy, I asked the man to denote some point within a radius of a mile where I would *not* interfere with his operations. He said in reply, that it was not his business to denote hitching-stalls for anybody. I thought, in that case, that I should stay where I was, and he politely informed me that I might stay and be——jammed. I found afterward that this individual was troubled with a kind of insanity peculiar to all headquarters, arising out of an exaggerated idea of his own importance. I had the pleasure a few minutes afterward of hearing him ordered to feed my horse. A thick-set, gray-haired man sat near by, undergoing the process of being shaved by a very nervous Negro. The thick-set man was also exercising the privileges of his rank; but the more he berated his attendant's awkwardness, the more nervous the other became. I addressed myself mutually to master and man, in an inquiry as to the precise quarters of the General in command. The latter pointed to a wall tent contiguous, and was cursed by the thick-set man for not minding his business. The thick-set man remarked substantially, that he didn't know anything about it, and was at that moment cut by the Negro, to my infinite delight. Before the wall tent in question stood a tall, broad-shouldered gentleman in shirt-sleeves and slippers, warming his back and hands at a fire. He was watching, through an aperture in the tent, the movements of a private who was cleaning his boots. I noticed that he wore a seal ring, and that he opened and shut his eyes very rapidly. He was, otherwise, a very respectable and dignified gentleman.

"Is this General McCall?" said I, a little discomposed. The gentleman looked abstractedly into my eyes, opening and shutting his own several times, as if doubtful of his personality, and at last decided that he *was* General McCall.

"What is it?" he said gravely, but without the slightest curiosity.

"I have a letter for you, sir, I believe."

He put the letter behind his back, and went on warming his hands. Having winked several times again, apparently forgetting all about the matter, I ventured to add that the letter was merely introductory. He looked at it, mechanically.

"Who opened it?" he said.

"Letters of introduction are not commonly sealed, General."

"Who are you?" he asked, indifferently.

I told him that the contents of the letter would explain my errand; but he had, meantime, relapsed into abstractedness, and winked, and warmed his hands, for at least five minutes. At the end of that time, he read the letter very deliberately, and said that he was glad to see me in camp. He intimated that if I was not already located I could be provided with bed and meals at headquarters. He stated, in relation to my correspondence, that all letters sent from the Reserve Corps must, without any reservations, be submitted to him in person. I was obliged to promise compliance, but had gloomy forebodings that the General would occupy a fortnight in the examination of each letter. He invited me to breakfast, proposed to make me acquainted with his staff, and was, in all respects, a very grave, prudent, and affable soldier. I may say, incidentally, that I adopted the device of penning a couple of gossipy epistles, the length and folly of which so irritated General McCall that he released me from the penalty of submitting my compositions for the future.

I took up my permanent abode with Quartermaster Kingwalt, a very prince of old soldiers, who had devoted much of a sturdy life to promoting the militia interests of the populous county of Chester. When the war-fever swept down his beautiful valley, and the drum called the young men from villages and farms, this ancient yeoman and miller—for he was both—took a musket at the sprightly age of sixty-five and joined a Volunteer company. Neither ridicule nor entreaty could bend his purpose; but the Secretary of War, hearing of the case, conferred a brigade quartermastership upon him. He threw off the infirmities of age, stepped as proudly as any youngster, and became, emphatically, the best quartermaster in the Division. He never delayed an advance with tardy teams, nor kept the General tentless, nor penned irregular requisitions, nor wasted the property of Government. The ague seized him occasionally, and shook his gray hairs fearfully; but he always recovered to ride his black stallion on long forages, and his great strength and bulk were the envy of all the young officers.

After grasping my hand so heartily that I positively howled, he commanded a tall sergeant, rejoicing in the name of Clover, to take away my horse and split him up for kindling wood.

"We must give him the blue roan that Fogg rides," said the Quartermaster, to the great dejection of Fogg, a short, stout youth, who was posting accounts. I was glad to see, however, that Fogg was not disposed to be angry, and when informed that a certain iron-gray nag was at his disposal, he was in a perfect glow of good humor. The other attachés were a German, whose name, as I caught it, seemed to be Skyhiski; and a pleasant lad called Owen, whose disposition was so mild that I wondered how he had adopted the bloody profession of arms. A black boy belonged to the establishment, remarkable chiefly for getting close to the heels of the black stallion and being frequently kicked. He was employed to feed and brush the said stallion, and the antipathy between them was intense.

The above curious military combination slept under a great tarpaulin canopy, originally used for covering commissary stores from the rain. Our meals were taken in the open air, and prepared by Skyhiski; but there was a second tent, provided with desk and secretary, where Mr. Fogg performed his clerk duties, daily. When I had relieved my Pegasus of his saddle, and penned some paragraphs for a future letter, I strolled down the road with the old gentleman, who insisted upon showing me Hunter's Mill, a storm-beaten structure, that looked like a great barn. The millrace had been drained by some soldiers for the purpose of securing the fish contained in it, and the mill-wheel was quite dry and motionless. Difficult Creek ran impetuously across the road below, as if anxious to be put to some use again; and the miller's house, adjoining, was now used as a hospital for Lieutenant-Colonel Kane and some inferior officers. It was a favorite design of the Quartermaster's to scrape the mill-stone, repair the race, and put the great breast-wheel to work. One could see that the soldier had not entirely obliterated the miller, and as he related, with a glowing face, the plans that he had proposed to recuperate the tottering structure and make it serviceable to the army, I felt a regret that such peaceful ambitions should have ever been overruled by the call to arms.

While we stood at the mill window watching the long stretches of white tents and speculating upon the results of war, we saw several men running across the road toward a hill-top cottage, where General George G. Meade made his quarters. A small group was collected at the cottage reconnoitring something through their telescopes. As I hastened in that direction, I heard confused voices, thus: "No, it isn't!" "It is!" "Can you make out his shoulder-bar?" "What is the color of his coat?" "Gray!" "No, it's butternut!" "Has he a musket?" "Yes, he is levelling it!" At this the group scattered in every direction. "Pshaw!" said one, "we are out of range; besides, it is a telescope that he has. By——, it is a Rebel, reconnoitring our camp!" There was a manifest sensation here, and one man wondered how he had passed the picket. Another suggested that he might be accompanied by a troop, and a third convulsed the circle by declaring that there were six other Rebels visible in a woods to the left. Mr. Fogg had meantime come up and proffered me a fieldglass, through which I certainly made out a person in gray, standing in the middle of the road just at the ridge of a hill. When I dropped my glass I saw him distinctly with the naked eye. He was probably a mile distant, and his gray vesture was little relieved by the blue haze of the forest.

"He is going," exclaimed a private, excitedly; "where's the man that was to try a lead on him?" Several started impulsively for their pieces, and some officers called for their horses. "There go his knees!" "His body is behind the hill!" "Now his head——"

"Crack! crack! crack!" spluttered musketry from the edge of the mill, and like as many rockets darted a score of horsemen through the creek and up the steep. Directly a faint hurrah pealed from the camp nearest the mill. It passed to the next camp and the next; for all were now earnestly watching; and finally a medley of cheers shook the air and the ear. Thousands of brave men were shouting the requiem of one paltry life. The rash fool had bought with his temerity a bullet in the brain. When I saw him—dusty and still bleeding—he was beset by a full regiment of idlers, to whom death had neither awe nor respect. They talked of the delicate shot, as connoisseurs in the art of murder, and two men dug him a grave on the green before the mill, wherein he was tossed like a dog or a vulture, to be lulled, let us hope, by the music of the grinding, when grain shall ripen once more.

I had an opportunity after dinner to inspect the camp of the "Bucktails," a regiment of Pennsylvania backwoodsmen, whose efficiency as skirmishers has been adverted to by all chroniclers of the Civil War. They wore the common blue blouse and breeches, but were distinguished by squirrel tails fastened to their caps. They were reputed to be the best marksmen in the service, and were generally allowed, in action, to take their own positions and fire at will. Crawling through thick woods, or trailing serpent-like through the tangled grass, these mountaineers were for a time the terror of the Confederates; but when their mode of fighting had been understood, their adversaries improved upon it to such a degree that at the date of this writing there is scarcely a corporal's guard of the original Bucktail regiment remaining. Slaughtered on the field, perishing in prison, disabled or paroled, they have lost both their prestige and their strength. I remarked among these worthies a partiality for fisticuffs, and a dislike for the manual of arms. They drilled badly, and were reported to be adepts at thieving and unlicensed foraging.

The second night in camp was pleasantly passed. Some sociable officers—favorites with Captain Kingwalt—congregated under the tarpaulin, after supper-hour, and when a long-necked bottle had been emptied and replenished, there were many quaint stories related and curious individualities revealed. I dropped asleep while the hilarity was at its height, and Fogg covered me with a thick blanket as I lay. The enemy might have come upon us in the darkness; but if death were half so sound as my slumber afield, I should have bid it welcome.

CHAPTER III

A Foraging Adventure

THERE was a newsboy named Charley who slept at Captain Kingwalt's every second night, and who returned my beast to his owner in Washington. The aphorism that a Yankee can do anything was exemplified by this lad; for he worked my snail into a gallop. He was born in Chelsea, Massachusetts, and appeared to have taken to speculation at the age when most children are learning A B C. He was now in his fourteenth year, owned two horses, and employed another boy to sell papers for him likewise. His profits upon daily sales of four hundred journals were about thirty-two dollars. He had five hundred dollars in the bank, and was debating with Captain Kingwalt the propriety of founding an army express and general agency. Such a self-reliant, swaggering, far-sighted, and impertinent boy I never knew. He was a favorite with the Captain's black boy, and upon thorough terms of equality with the Commanding General. His papers cost him in Washington a cent and a half each, and he sold them in camp for ten cents each. I have not the slightest doubt that I shall hear of him again as the proprietor of an overland mail, or the patron and capitalist of Greenland emigration.

I passed the second and third days quietly in camp, writing a couple of letters, studying somewhat of fortification, and making flying visits to various officers. There was but one other reporter with this division of the army. He represented a New York journal, and I could not but contrast his fine steed and equipments with the scanty accommodations that my provincial establishment had provided for me. His saddle was a cushioned McClellan, with spangled breast strap and plump saddle-bags, and his bridle was adorned with a bright curb bit and twilled reins. He wore a fieldglass belted about his body, and was plentifully provided with money to purchase items of news, if they were at any time difficult to obtain. I resolved inwardly to seize the first opportunity of changing establishments, so that I might be placed upon as good a footing. My relations with camp, otherwise, were of the happiest character; for the troops were State-people of mine, and, as reporters had not yet abused the privileges accorded them, my profession was held in some repute. I made the round of various "messes," and soon adopted the current dissipations of the field—late hours, long stories, incessant smoking, and raw spirits. There were some restless minds about me, whose funds of anecdote and jest were apparently inexhaustible. I do not know that so many eccentric, adventurous, and fluent people are to be found among any other nationality of soldiers, not excepting the Irish.

The blue roan of which friend Fogg had been deprived, exhibited occasional evidences of a desire to break my neck. I was obliged to dispense with the spur in riding him, but he nevertheless dashed off at times, and put me into an agony of fear. On those occasions I managed to retain my seat, and gained thereby the reputation of being a very fine equestrian. As there were few civilians in camp, and as I wore a gray suit, and appeared to be in request at headquarters, a rumor was developed and gained currency that I was attached to the Division in the capacity of a scout. When my horse became unmanageable, therefore, his speed was generally accelerated by the cheers of soldiers, and I became an object of curiosity in every quarter, to my infinite mortification and dread.

The Quartermaster was to set off on the fourth day to purchase or seize some hay and grain that were stacked at neighboring farms. We prepared to go at eight o'clock, but were detained somewhat by reason of Shyhiski being inebriated the night before, and thereby delaying the breakfast, and afterward the fact that the black stallion had laid open the black boy's leg. However, at a quarter past nine, the Quartermaster, Sergeant Clover, Fogg, Owen, and myself, with six four-horse wagons, filed down the railroad track until we came to a bridge that some laborers were repairing, where we turned to the left through some soggy fields, and forded Difficult Creek. As there was no road to follow, we kept straight through a wood of young maples and chestnut trees. Occasionally a trunk or projecting branch stopped the wagons, when the teamsters opened the way with their axes. After two hours of slow advance, we came to the end of the wood and climbed a succession of hilly fields. From the summit of the last of these, a splendid sweep of farm country was revealed, dotted with quaint Virginia dwellings, stackyards, and Negro cabins, and divided by miles of tortuous wormfence. The eyes of the Quartermaster brightened at the prospect, though I am afraid that he thought only of the abundant forage; but my own grew hazy as I spoke of the peaceful people and the neglected fields. The plough had furrowed none of these acres, and some crows that screamed gutturally from a neighboring ash tree seemed lean and pinched for lack of their plunder of corn.

Many of the dwellings were guarded by soldiers; but of the resident citizens only the women and the old men remained. I did not need to ask where the young men were exiled. The residue that prayed with their faces toward Richmond told me the story with their eyes. There was, nevertheless, no melodramatic exhibition of feeling among the bereaved. I did not see any defiant postures, nor hear any melting apostrophes. Marius was not mouthing by the ruins of Carthage, nor even Rachel weeping for her Hebrew children. But there were on every hand manifestations of adherence to the Southern cause, except among a few males who feared unutterable things and were disposed to cringe and prevaricate. The women were not generally handsome; their faces were indolent, their dress slovenly, and their manner embarrassed. They lopped off the beginnings and the ends of their sentences, generally commencing with a verb, as thus: "Told soldiers not to carr' off the rye; declared they would; said they bound do jest what they pleased. Let 'em go!"

The Quartermaster stopped at a spruce residence, approached by a long lane, and on knocking at the porch with his ponderous fist, a woman came timidly to the kitchen window.

"Who's thar?" she said, after a moment.

"Come out, young woman," said the Quartermaster, soothingly; "we don't intend to murder or rob you, ma'am!"

There dropped from the doorsill into the yard, not one, but three young women, followed by a very deaf old man, who appeared to think that the Quartermaster's visit bore some reference to the hencoop.

"I wish to buy for the use of the United States Government," said the Quartermaster, "some stacks of hay and corn fodder, that lie in one of your fields."

"The last hen was toted off this morning before breakfast," said the old man; "they took the turkeys yesterday, and I was obliged to kill the ducks or I shouldn't have had anything to eat."

Here Fogg so misdemeaned himself as to laugh through his nose, and the man Clover appeared to be suddenly interested in something that lay in a mulberry tree opposite.

"I am provided with money to pay liberally for your produce, and you cannot do better than to let me take the stacks, leaving you, of course, enough for your own horses and cattle."

Here the old man pricked up his ears and said that he hadn't heard of any recent battle; for his part, he had never been a politician; but thought that both parties were a little wrong; and wished that peace would return, for he was a very old man, and was sorry that folks couldn't let quiet folks' property alone. How far his garrulity might have betrayed him could be conjectured only by one of the girls taking his hand and leading him submissively into the house.

The eldest daughter said that the Quartermaster might take the stacks at his own valuation, but trusted to his honor as a soldier and, as he seemed, a gentleman, to deal

justly by them. There could be no crop harvested for a
twelvemonth, and beggary looked them in the face. I
have never beheld anything more chivalrously gallant than
the sturdy old Quartermaster's attitude. He blended in
tone and face the politeness of a diplomat and the gentleness of a father. They asked him to return to the house,
with his *officers*, when he had loaded the wagons; for dinner was being prepared, and they hoped that Virginians
could be hospitable, even to their enemies. As to the hay
and fodder, none need be left; for the Confederates had
seized their horses some months before, and driven off
their cows when they retired from the neighborhood.

I so admired the queer gables and great brick ovens of
the house that I resolved to tie my horse and rest under
the crooked porch. The eldest young lady had taken me
to be a prisoner and was greatly astonished that the
Quartermaster permitted me to go at large. She asked me
to have a chair in the parlor, but when I made my appearance there, the two younger sisters fled precipitately. The
old man was shaking his head sadly by the fireplace. Some
logs burned on the andirons with a red flame. The furniture consisted of a mahogany sideboard, table, and chairs
—ponderous in pattern; and a series of family portraits, in
a sprawling style of art, smirked and postured on the wall.
The floor was bare, but shone by reason of repeated scrub-
bing, and the black mantel-piece was a fine specimen of
colonial carving in the staunchest of walnut-wood.

Directly the two younger girls—though the youngest
must have been twenty years of age—came back with
averted eyes and the silliest of giggles. They sat a little
distance apart, and occasionally nodded or signalled like
school children.

"Wish you *would* stop, Bell!" said one, a dark miss with
roguish eyes and fat, plump figure, and curls that shook
ever so merrily about her shoulders.

"See if I don't tell on you," said the other of these misses,
whose flaxen hair was plastered across her eyebrows, and
who was very tall and slender.

"Declar' I never said so, if he asks me; declar' I will."

"Tell on you—you see! Won't he be jealous? How he will car' on!"

I made out that these young ladies were intent upon publishing their obligations to certain sweethearts of theirs, who, as it afterward seemed, were in the army at Manassas Junction. I said to the curly-haired miss that she was endangering the life of her enamored; for it would become an object with all the anxious troops in the vicinity to shorten his days. The old man roused up here, and remarked that his health certainly was declining; but he hoped to survive a while longer for the sake of his children; that he was no politician, and always said that the Negroes were very ungrateful people. He caught his daughter's eye finally, and cowered stupidly, nodding at the fire.

I remarked to the eldest young woman—called Prissy (Priscilla) by her sister—that the country hereabout was pleasantly wooded. She said, in substance, that every part of Virginia was beautiful, and that she did not wish to survive the disgrace of the old commonwealth.

"Become right down hateful since Yankees invaded it!" exclaimed Miss Bell.

"*Some* Yankee's handsome, sister," said Miss Bessie, the proprietor of the curls, "think some Yankees puffick gentlemen!"

"Oh, you traitor!" said the other—"wish *Henry* heard you say that!"

Miss Bell intimated that she should take the first opportunity of telling him the same, and I eulogized her good judgment. Priscilla now begged to be excused for a moment, as, since the flight of the Negro property, the care of the table had devolved mainly upon her. A single aged servant, too feeble or too faithful to decamp, still attended to the menial functions, and two mulatto children remained to relieve them of light labor. Priscilla was a dignified, matronly young lady, and, as one of the sisters informed me, plighted to a major in the Confederate service. The others chattered flippantly for an hour, and said that the old place was dreadfully lonesome of late. Miss

Bell was *sure* she should die if another winter, similar to the last, occurred. She loved company, and had always found it *so* lively in Loudoun before; whereas she had positively been but twice to a neighbor's for a twelve-month, and had quite forgotten the road to the mill. She said, finally, that, rather than undergo another such isolation, she would become a *Vivandiere* in the Yankee army. The slender sister was altogether wedded to the idea of her lovers. "*Wouldn't* she tell Henry? and *shouldn't* she write to Jeems? and oh, Bessie, you would not *dare* to repeat that before *him.*" In short, I was at first amused, and afterwards annoyed, by this young lady, whereas the roguish-eyed miss improved greatly upon acquaintance.

After a while, Captain Kingwalt came in, trailing his spurs over the floor, and leaving sunshine in his wake. There was something galvanic in his gentleness and infectious in his merriment. He told them at dinner of his own daughters on the Brandywine, and invented stories of Fogg's courtships, till that young gentleman first blushed, and afterward dropped his plate. Our meal was a frugal one, consisting mainly of the ducks referred to, some vegetables, corn-bread, and coffee made of wasted rye. There was neither sugar, spices, nor tea on the premises, and the salt before us was the last in the dwelling. The Quartermaster promised to send them both coffee and salt, and Fogg volunteered to bring the same to the house, whereat the Quartermaster teased him till he left the table.

At this time, a little boy, who was ostensibly a waiter, cried: "Miss Prissy, soldiers is climbin' in de hog-pen."

"I knew we should lose the last living thing on the property," said this young lady, much distressed.

The Quartermaster went to the door, and found three strolling Bucktails looking covetously at the swine. They were a little discomposed at his appearance, and edged off suspiciously.

"Halt!" said the old man in his great voice, "where are you men going?"

"Just makin' reconnoissance," said one of the freebooters; "s'pose a feller has a right to walk around, hain't he?"

"Not unless he has a pass," said the Quartermaster; "have you written permission to leave camp?"

"Left'nant s'posed we might. Don't know as it's your business. Never see *you* in the regiment."

"It is my business, as an officer of the United States, to see that no soldier strays from camp unauthorizedly, or depredates upon private property. I will take your names, and report you, first for straggling, secondly for insolence!"

"Put to it, Bill!" said the speaker of the foragers; "run, Bob! go it hearties!" And they took to their heels, cleared a pair of fences, and were lost behind some outbuildings. The Quartermaster could be harsh as well as generous, and was about mounting his horse impulsively, to overtake and punish the fugitives, when Priscilla begged him to refrain, as an enforcement of discipline on his part might bring insult upon her helpless household. I availed myself of a pause in the Quartermaster's wrath to ask Miss Priscilla if she would allow me to lodge in the dwelling. Five nights' experience in camp had somewhat reduced my enthusiasm, and I already wearied of the damp beds, the hard fare, and the coarse conversation of the bivouac. The young lady assented willingly, as she stated that the presence of a young man would both amuse and protect the family. For several nights she had not slept, and had imagined footsteps on the porch and the drawing of window-bolts. There was a bed, formerly occupied by her brother, that I might take, but must depend upon rather laggard attendance. I had the satisfaction, therefore, of seeing the Quartermaster and retinue mount their horses and wave me a temporary good-bye. Poor Fogg looked back so often and so seriously that I expected to see him fall from the saddle. The young ladies were much impressed with the Quartermaster's manliness, and Miss Bell wondered *how* such a *puffick* gentleman could *reconcile* himself to the Yankee cause. She had felt a desire to speak to him upon that point as she was *sure* he was of fine stock, and entirely averse to the invasion of such territory as that of *dear* old Virginia. There was something in his manner that *so* reminded her of some one who should be *nameless* for the present; but the "nameless" was, *of course,* young, *handsome,* and *so* brave. I ruthlessly dissipated her theory of the Quartermaster's origin, by stating that he was of humble German descent, so far as I knew, and had probably never beheld Virginia till preceded by the bayonets of his neighbors.

After tea Miss Bessie produced a pitcher of rare cider that came from a certain mysterious quarter of the cellar. A chessboard was forthcoming at a later hour, when we amused ourselves with a couple of games, facetiously dubbing our chessmen Federals and Confederates. Miss Bell, meanwhile, betook herself to a diary, wherein she minutely related the incidents and sentiments of successive days. The quantity of words underscored in the same autobiography would have speedily exhausted the case of italics, if the printer had obtained it. I was so beguiled by these patriarchal people, that I several times asked myself if the circumstances were real. Was I in a hostile country, surrounded by thousands of armed men? Were the incidents of this evening portions of an historic era, and the ground about me to be commemorated by bloodshed? Was this, in fact, revolution, and were these simple country girls and their lovers revolutionists? The logs burned cheerily upon the hearth, and the ancestral portraits glowered contemplatively from the walls. Miss Prissy looked dreamily into the fire, and the old man snored wheezily in a corner. A gray cat purred in Miss Bell's lap, and Miss Bessie was writing some nonsense in my note-book.

A sharp knock fell upon the door, and something that sounded like the butt of a musket shook the porch without. The girls turned pale, and I think that Miss Bessie seized my arm and clung to it. I think also, that Miss Bell attempted to take the other arm, to which I demurred.

"Those brutal soldiers again!" said Priscilla, faintly.

"I think one of the andirons has fallen down, darter!" said the old man, rousing up.

"Tremble for my life," said Miss Bell; "*sure* shall die if it's *a man.*"

I opened the door after a little pause, when a couple of rough privates in uniform confronted me.

"We're two guards that General Meade sent to protect the house and property," said the tallest of these men; "might a feller come in and warm his feet!"

I understood at once that the Quartermaster had obtained these persons; and the other man coming forward, said—

"I fetched some coffee over, and a bag o' salt, with Corporal Fogg's compliments."

They deposited their muskets in a corner, and balanced their boots on the fender. Nothing was said for a time.

"Did you lose yer poultry?" said the tall man, at length.

"All," said Miss Priscilla.

"Fellers loves poultry!" said the man, smacking his lips.

"Did you lose yer sheep?" said the same man, after a little silence.

"The Bucktails cut their throats the first day that they encamped at the mill," said Miss Priscilla.

"Them Bucktails great fellers," said the tall man; "them Bucktails awful on sheep: they loves 'em so!"

He relapsed again for a few minutes, when he continued:

"You don't like fellers to bag yer poultry and sheep, do you?"

Miss Priscilla replied that it was both dishonest and cruel. Miss Bell intimated that none but Yankees would do it.

"P'raps not," said the tall soldier, dryly; "did you ever grub on fat pork, Miss? No? Did you ever gnaw yer hard tack after a spell o' sickness, and a ten-hour march? No? P'raps you might like a streak o' mutton arterwards! P'raps you might take a notion for a couple o' chickens or so! No? How's that, Ike? What do you think, pardner? (to me) I ain't over and above cruel, mum. I don't think the Bucktails is over and above dishonest to home, mum. But, gosh hang it, I think I *would* bag a chicken any day! I say that above board. Hey, Ike?"

When the tall man and his inferior satellite had warmed

their boots till they smoked, they rose, recovered their muskets, and bowed themselves into the yard. Soon afterward I bade the young ladies good night, and repaired to my room. The tall man and his associate were pacing up and down the grass-plot, and they looked very cold and comfortless, I thought. I should have liked to obtain for them a draught of cider, but prudently abstained; for every man in the army would thereby become cognizant of its existence. So I placed my head once more upon a soft pillow, and pitied the chilled soldiers who slept upon the turf. I thought of Miss Bessie with her roguish eyes, and wondered what themes were now engrossing her. I asked myself if this was the romance of war, and if it would bear relating to one's children when he grew as old and as deaf as the wheezy gentleman downstairs. In fine, I was a little sentimental, somewhat reflective, and very drowsy. So, after a while, processions of freebooting soldiers, foraging quartermasters, deaf gentlemen, Fogg's regiment, and multitudes of ghosts from Manassas, drifted by in my dreams. And, in the end, Miss Bessie's long curls brushed into my eyes, and I found the morning, ruddy as her cheeks, blushing at the window.

CHAPTER IV

What a March Is

———

I FOUND at breakfast that Miss Bessie had been placed beside me, and I so far forgot myself as to forget all other persons at the table. Miss Priscilla asked to be helped to the corn-bread, and I deposited a quantity of the same upon Miss Bessie's plate. Miss Bell asked if I did not love *dear* old Virginia, and I replied to Miss Bessie that it had lately become very attractive, and that, in fact, I was decidedly rebellious in my sympathy with the distressed Virginians. I *did* except, however, the man darkly mooted as "Henry," and hoped that he would be disfigured—not killed—at the earliest engagement. The deaf old gentleman bristled up here and asked *who* had been killed at the recent engagement. There was a man named Jeems Lee—a distant connection of the Lightfoots—not the Hampshire Lightfoots, but the Fauquier Lightfoots—who had distinctly appeared to the old gentleman for several nights, robed in black and carrying a coffin under his arm. Since I had mentioned his name, he recalled the circumstance and hoped that Jeems Lightfoot had not disgraced his ancestry. Nevertheless, the deaf gentleman was not to be understood as expressing any opinion upon the merits of the war. For *his* part he thought both sides a little wrong, and the crops were really in a dreadful state. The Negroes were very ungrateful people and property should be held sacred by all belligerents.

At this point he caught Miss Priscilla's eye, and was transfixed with conscious guilt.

I had, meantime, been infringing upon Miss Bessie's feet

28

—very pretty feet they were!—which expressive but not very refined method of correspondence caused her to blush to the eyes. Miss Bell, noticing the same, was determined to tell *Henry* at once, and I hoped in my heart that she would set out for Manassas to further that purpose.

The door opened here, and the rubicund visage of Mr. Fogg appeared like the head of the Medusa. He said that "Captain" had ordered the blue roan to be saddled and brought over to me, but I knew that this was a cunning device on his part to revisit the dwelling. Miss Bell somehow caught the idea that Fogg was enamored of her, and the poor fellow was subjected to a volley of tender innuendoes and languishing glances that by turn mortified and enraged him.

I bade the good people adieu at eight o'clock, promising to return for dinner at five; and Miss Bessie accompanied me to the lane, where I took leave of her with a secret whisper and a warm grasp of the hand. One of her rings had somehow adhered to my finger, which Fogg remarked with a bilious expression of countenance. I had no sooner got astride of the blue roan than he darted off like the wind and subjected me to great terror, alternating to chagrin, when I turned back and beheld all the young ladies waving their handkerchiefs. They evidently thought me an unrivalled equestrian.

I rode to a picket-post two miles from the mill, passing over the spot where the Confederate soldier had fallen. The picket consisted of two companies or one hundred and sixty men. Half of them were sitting around a fire concealed in the woods, and the rest were scattered along the edges of a piece of close timber. I climbed a lookout tree by means of cross-strips nailed to the trunk, and beheld from the summit a long succession of hazy hills, valleys, and forests, with the Blue Ridge Mountains bounding the distance, like some mighty monster, enclosing the world in its coils. This was the country of the enemy, and a lieutenant obligingly pointed out to me the curling smoke of their pickets, a few miles away. The cleft of Manassas was plainly visible, and I traced the line of the Gap Railway to its junction with the Orange and Alexandria road, below Bull Run. For aught that I knew, some concealed observer might now be watching me from the pine-tops on the nearest knoll. Some rifleman might be running his practiced eye down the deadly groove, to topple me from my perch, and send me crashing through the boughs. The uncertainty, the hazard, the novelty of my position had at this time an indescribable charm; but subsequent exposures dissipated the romance and taught me the folly of such adventures.

The afternoon went dryly by, for a drizzling rain fell at noon; but at four o'clock I saddled the blue roan and went to ride with Fogg. We retraced the road to Colonel T——s, and crossing a boggy brook, turned up the hills and passed toward the Potomac. Fogg had been a schoolmaster, and many of his narrations indicated keen perception and clever comprehension. He so amused me on this particular occasion that I quite forgot my engagement for dinner, and unwittingly strolled beyond the farthest brigade.

Suddenly, we heard a bugle-call from the picket-post before us, and, at the same moment, the drums beat from the camp behind. Our horses pricked up their ears and Fogg stared inquiringly. As we turned back we heard approaching hoofs and the blue roan exhibited intentions of running away. I pulled his rein in vain. He would neither be soothed nor commanded. A whole company of cavalry closed up with him at length, and the sabres clattered in their scabbards as they galloped toward camp at the top of their speed. With a spring that almost shook me from the saddle and drove the stirrups flying from my feet, the blue roan dashed the dust into the eyes of Fogg and led the race.

Not the wild yager on his gait to perdition rode so fearfully. Trees, bogs, huts, bushes, went by like lightning. The hot breath of the nag rose to my nostrils and at every leap I seemed vaulting among the spheres.

I speak thus flippantly now of what was then the agony of death. I grasped the pommel of my saddle, mechanically winding the lines about my wrist, and clung with the tenacity of sin clutching the world. Some soldiers looked wonderingly from the wayside, but did not heed my shriek of "stop him, for God's sake!" A ditch crossed the lane— deep and wide—and I felt that my moment had come: with a spring that seemed to break thew and sinew, the blue roan cleared it, pitching upon his knees, but recovered directly and darted onward again. I knew that I should fall headlong now, to be trampled by the fierce horsemen behind, but retained my grasp though my heart was choking me. The camps were in confusion as I swept past them. A sharp clearness of sense and thought enabled me to note distinctly the minutest occurrences. I marked long lines of men cloaked and carrying knapsacks; drummer-boys beating music that I had whistled in many a ramble; field-officers shouting orders from their saddles; and cannon limbered up as if ready to move; tents taken down and teams waiting to be loaded—all the evidences of an advance, that I alas should never witness, lying bruised and mangled by the roadside. A cheer saluted me as I passed some of Meade's regiments. "It is the scout that fetched the orders for an advance!" said several, and one man remarked that that feller was the most reckless rider he had ever beheld. The crisis came at length: a wagon had stopped the way; my horse in turning it, stepped upon a stake, and slipping rolled heavily upon his side, tossing me like an acrobat, over his head, but without further injury than a terrible nervous shock and a rent in my pantaloons.

I employed a small boy to lead the blue roan to Captain Kingwalt's quarters, and as I limped wearily after, some regiments came toward me through the fields. General McCall responded to my salute; he rode in the advance. The Quartermaster's party was loading the tents and utensils. The rain fell smartly as dusk deepened into night, and the brush tents, now deserted by the soldiers, were set on fire. Being composed of dry combustible material, they burned rapidly and with an intense flame. The fields in every direction were revealed, swarming with men, horses, batteries, and wagons. Some of the regiments began the march in silence; others sang familiar ballads as they moved in column. A few, riotously disposed, shrieked, whistled, and cheered. The standards were folded; the drums did not mark time; the orders were few and short. The cannoneers sat moodily upon the caissons, and the cavalry-men walked their horses sedately. Although fifteen thousand men comprised the whole corps, each of its three brigades would have seemed as numerous to a novice. The teams of each brigade closed up the rear, and a quarter-master's guard was detailed from each regiment to march beside its own wagons. When the troops were fairly under way, and the brush burning along for continuous miles of road, the effect was grand beyond all that I had witnessed. The country people gathered in fright at the cottage doors, and the farm-dogs bayed dismally at the unwonted scene. I refused to ride the blue roan again, but transferred my saddle to a team horse that appeared to be given to a sort of equine somnambulism, and once or twice attempted to lie down by the roadside. At nine o'clock I set out with Fogg, who slipped a flask of spirits into my haversack. Following the tardy movement of the teams, we turned our faces toward Washington. I was soon wet to the skin, and my saddle cushion was soaking with water. The streams crossing the road were swollen with rain, and the great team wheels clogged on the slimy banks. We were sometimes delayed a half hour by a single wagon, the storm beating pitilessly in our faces the while. During the stoppages, the quartermaster's guards burned all the fence rails in the vicinity, and some of the more indurated sat round the fagots and gamed with cards.

Cold, taciturn, miserable, I thought of the quiet farm-house, the ruddy hearth-place, and the smoking supper. I wondered if the roguish eyes were not a little sad, and the trim feet a little restless, the chessmen somewhat stupid, and the good old house a trifle lonesome. Alas! the intimacy so pleasantly commenced, was never to be renewed. With the thousand and one airy palaces that youth builds and time annihilates, my first romance of war towered to the stars in a day, and crumbled to earth in a night.

At two o'clock in the morning we halted at Metropolitan Mills, on the Alexandria and Leesburg turnpike. A bridge had been destroyed below, and the creek was so swollen that neither artillery nor cavalry could ford it. The meadows were submerged and the rain still descended in torrents. The chilled troops made bonfires of some new panel fence, and stormed all the henroosts in the vicinity. Some pigs, that betrayed their whereabouts by inopportune whines and grunts, were speedily confiscated, slaughtered, and spitted. We erected our tarpaulin in a ploughed field, and Fogg laid some sharp rails upon the ground to make us a dry bed. Skyhiski fried a quantity of fresh beef, and boiled some coffee; but while we ate heartily, theorizing as to the destination of the corps, the poor Quartermaster was terribly shaken by his ague.

I woke in the morning with inflamed throat, rheumatic limbs, and every indication of chills and fever. Fogg whispered to me at breakfast that two men of Reynolds' brigade had died during the night, from fatigue and exposure. He advised me to push forward to Washington and await the arrival of the division, as, unused to the hardships of a march, I might, after another day's experience, become dangerously ill. I set out at five o'clock, resolving to ford the creek, resume the turnpike, and reach Long Bridge at noon. Passing over some dozen fields in which my horse at every step sank to the fetlocks, I travelled along the brink of the stream till I finally reached a place that seemed to be shallow. Bracing myself firmly in the saddle, I urged my unwilling horse into the waters, and emerged half drowned on the other side. It happened, however, that I had crossed only a branch of the creek and gained an island. The main channel was yet to be attempted, and I saw that it was deep, broad, and violent. I followed the margin despairingly for a half-mile, when I came to a log footbridge, where I dismounted and swam my horse through the turbulent waters. I had now so far diverged from the turnpike that I was at a loss to recover it, but straying forlornly through the woods, struck a wagon track at last, and pursued it hopefully, until, to my confusion, it resolved itself to two tracks, that went in contrary directions. My horse preferred taking to the left, but after riding a full hour, I came to some felled trees, beyond which the traces did not go. Returning, weak and bewildered, I adopted the discarded route, which led me to a worm-fence at the edge of the woods. A house lay some distance off, but a wheat field intervened, and I might bring the vengeance of the proprietor upon me by invading his domain. There was no choice, however; so I removed the rails, and rode directly across the wheat to some Negro quarters, a little removed from the mansion. They were deserted, all save one, where a black boy was singing some Negro hymns in an uproarious manner. The words, as I made them out, were these:

> Stephen came a runnin',
>   His Marster fur to see;
> But Gabriel says he is not yar';
>   He gone to Calvary!
>   O,—O,—Stephen, Stephen,
>   Fur to see;
>   Stephen, Stephen, get along up Calvary!

I learned from this person two mortifying facts—that I was farther from Washington than at the beginning of my journey, and that the morrow was Sunday. War, alas! knows no Sabbaths, and the Negro said, apologetically—

"I was a seyin' some ole hymns, young Mars'r. Sence dis yer war we don't have no more meetin's, and a body mos' forgits his pra'rs. Dere hain't been no church in all Fairfax, sah, fur nigh six months."

Washington was nineteen miles distant, and another creek was to be forded before gaining the turnpike. The Negro sauntered down the lane, and opened the gate for me. "You jes keep from de creek, take de mill road, and enqua' as ye get furder up," said he; "it's mighty easy, sah, an' you can't miss de way."

I missed the way at once, however, by confounding the
mill road with the mill lane, and a shaggy dog that lay in a
wagon shed pursued me about a mile. The road was full
of mire; no dwellings adjoined it, and nothing human was
to be seen in any direction. I came to a crumbling Negro
cabin after two plodding hours, and, seeing a figure flit by
the window, called aloud for information. Nobody replied,
and when, dismounting, I looked into the den, it was, to
my confusion, vacant.

The soil hereabout was of a sterile red clay, spotted
with scrub cedars. Country more bleak and desolate I have
never known, and when at noon the rain ceased, a keen
wind blew dismally across the barriers. I reached a turnpike at length, and, turning, as I thought, toward Alexandria, goaded my horse into a canter. An hour's ride brought
me to a wretched hamlet, whose designation I inquired of
a cadaverous old woman—

"Dranesville," said she.

"Then I am not upon the Alexandria turnpike?"

"No. You're sot for Leesburg. This is the Georgetown
and Chain Bridge road."

With a heavy heart, I retraced my steps, crossed Chain
Bridge at five o'clock, and halted at Kirkwood's at seven.
After dinner, falling in with the manager of the Washington Sunday morning *Chronicle,* I penned, at his request, a
few lines relative to the movements of the Reserves; and,
learning in the morning that they had arrived at Alexandria, set out on horseback for that city.

Many hamlets and towns have been destroyed during
the war. But, of all that in some form survive, Alexandria
has most suffered. It has been in the uninterrupted possession of the Federals for twenty-two months, and has become essentially a military city. Its streets, its docks, its
warehouses, its dwellings, and its suburbs have been absorbed to the thousand uses of war.

I was challenged thrice on the Long Bridge, and five
times on the road, before reaching the city. I rode under
the shadows of five earthworks, and saw lines of white
tents sweeping to the horizon. Gayly caparisoned officers

passed me, to spend their Sabbath in Washington, and
trains laden with troops, ambulances, and batteries sped
along the line of railway, toward the rendezvous at Alexandria. A wagoner, looking forlornly at his splintered
wheels; a slovenly guard, watching some bales of hay; a
sombre Negro, dozing upon his mule; a slatternly Irish
woman gossiping with a sergeant at her cottage door; a
sutler in his "dear-born," running his keen eye down the
limbs of my beast; a spruce civilian riding for curiosity; a
gray-haired gentleman, in a threadbare suit, going to
camp on foot to say good-bye to his boy—these were some
of the personages that I remarked, and each was a study,
a sermon, and a story. The Potomac, below me, was dotted
with steamers and shipping. The bluffs above were trodden bare, and a line of dismal marsh bordered some stag-
nant pools that blistered at their bases. At points along the
river-shore, troops were embarking on board steamers;
transports were taking in tons of baggage and subsistence.
There was a schooner, laden to the water-line with locomotive engines and burden carriages; there, a brig, shipping artillery horses by a steam derrick, that lifted them
bodily from the shore and deposited them in the hold of
the vessel. Steamers, from whose spacious saloons the
tourist and the bride have watched the picturesque margin
of the Hudson, were now black with clusters of rollicking
volunteers, who climbed into the yards, and pitched headlong from the wheel-houses. The "grand movement," for
which the people had waited so long, and which General
George B. McClellan had promised so often, was at length
to be made. The Army of the Potomac was to be transferred to Fortress Monroe, at the foot of the Chesapeake,
and to advance by the peninsula of the James and the
York, upon the city of Richmond.

I rode through Washington Street, the seat of some ancient residences, and found it lined with freshly arrived
troops. The grave-slabs in a fine old churchyard were
strewn with weary cavalry-men, and they lay in some side
yards, soundly sleeping. Some artillery-men chatted at
doorsteps, with idle house-girls; some courtesans flaunted

in furs and ostrich feathers, through a group of coarse engineers; some sergeants of artillery, in red trimmings, and
caps gilded with cannon, were reining their horses to leer
at some ladies, who were taking the air in their gardens;
and at a wide place in the street, a provost-major was
manœuvring some companies, to the sound of the drum
and fife. There was much drunkenness, among both soldiers and civilians; and the people of Alexandria were, in
many cases, crushed and demoralized by reason of their
troubles. One man of this sort led me to a sawmill, now
run by Government, and pointed to the implements.

"I bought 'em and earned 'em," he said. "My labor and
enterprise set 'em there; and while my mill and machinery
are ruined to fill the pockets o' Federal sharpers, I go
drunk, ragged, and poor about the streets o' my native
town. My daughter starves in Richmond; God knows I
can't get to her. I wish to h—l I was dead."

Further inquiry developed the facts that my acquaintance had been a thriving builder, who had dotted all
northeastern Virginia with evidences of his handicraft. At
the commencement of the war, he took certain contracts
from the Confederate government, for the construction of
barracks at Richmond and Manassas Junction; returning
inopportunely to Alexandria, he was arrested, and kept
some time in Capitol-Hill prison; he had not taken the
oath of allegiance, and consequently he could obtain no
recompense for the loss of his mill property. Domestic misfortunes, happening at the same time, so embittered his
days that he resorted to dissipation. Alexandria is filled
with like ruined people; they walk as strangers through
their ancient streets, and their property is no longer theirs
to possess, but has passed into the hands of the dominant
nationalists. My informant pointed out the residences of
many leading citizens: some were now hospitals, others
armories and arsenals, others offices for inspectors, super-
intendents, and civil officials. The few people that remained upon their properties obtained partial immunity
by courting the acquaintance of Federal officers, and, in
many cases, extending the hospitalities of their homes to

the invaders. I do not know that any Federal functionary was accused of tyranny, or wantonness, but these things ensued, as the natural results of civil war; and one's sympathies were everywhere enlisted for the poor, the exiled, and the bereaved.

My dinner at the City Hotel was scant and badly prepared. I gave a Negro lad who waited upon me a few cents, but a burly Negro carver, who seemed to be his father, boxed the boy's ears and put the coppers into his pocket. The proprietor of the place had voluntarily taken the oath of allegiance, and had made more money since the date of Federal occupation than during his whole life previously. He said to me, curtly, that if by any chance the Confederates should reoccupy Alexandria, he could very well afford to relinquish his property. He employed a smart barkeeper, who led guests by a retired way to the drinking-rooms. Here, with the gas burning at a taper point, cobblers, cocktails, and juleps were mixed stealthily and swallowed in the darkness. The bar was like a mint to the proprietor; he only feared discovery and prohibition. It would not accord with the chaste pages of this narrative to tell how some of the noblest residences in Alexandria had been desecrated to licentious purposes; nor how, by night, the parlors of cosy homes flamed with riot and orgy. I stayed but a little time, having written an indiscreet paragraph in the Washington *Chronicle*, for which I was pursued by the War Department, and the management of my paper, lacking heart, I went home in a pet.

CHAPTER V

Down the Chesapeake

DISAPPOINTED in the unlucky termination of my adventures afield, I now looked ambitiously toward New York. As London stands to the provinces, so stands the empire city to America. Its journals circulate by hundreds of thousands; its means are only rivalled by its enterprise; it is the end of every young American's aspiration, and the New Bohemia for the restless, the brilliant, and the industrious. It seemed a great way off when I first beheld it, but I did not therefore despair. Small matters of news that I gathered in my modest city, obtained space in the columns of the great metropolitan journal, the ———. After a time I was delegated to travel in search of special incidents, and finally, when the noted Tennessee Unionist, "Parson" Brownlow, journeyed eastward, I joined his suite, and accompanied him to New York. The dream of many months now came to be realized. A correspondent on the ———'s staff had been derelict, and I was appointed to his division. His horse, saddle, field-glasses, blankets, and pistols were to be transferred, and I was to proceed without delay to Fortress Monroe, to keep with the advancing columns of General George B. McClellan.

At six in the morning I embarked; at eleven I was whirled through my own city, without a glimpse of my friends; at three o'clock I dismounted at Baltimore, and at five was gliding down the Patapsco, under the shadows of Fort Federal Hill, and the white walls of Fort McHenry. The latter defence is renowned for its gallant resistance to a British fleet in 1814, and the American national anthem,

"The Star-Spangled Banner," was written to commemorate
that bombardment. Fort Carroll, a massive structure of
hewn stone, with arched bomb-proof and three tiers of
mounted ordnance, its smooth walls washed by the waves,
and its unfinished floors still ringing with the trowel and
the adze, lies some miles below, at a narrow passage in the
stream. Below, the shores diverge, and at dusk we were
fairly in the Chesapeake, under steam and sail, speeding
due southward.

The *Adelaide* was one of a series of boats making daily
trips between Baltimore and Old Point. Fourteen hours
were required to accomplish the passage, and we were
not to arrive till seven o'clock next morning. I was so fortunate as to obtain a state-room, but many passengers
were obliged to sleep upon sofas or the cabin floor. These
boats monopolized the civil traffic between the North and
the army, although they were reputed to be owned and
managed by Secessionists. None were allowed to embark
unless provided with Federal passes; but there were, nevertheless, three or four hundred people on board. About
one fourth of these were officers and soldiers; one half sutlers, traders, contractors, newsmen, and idle civilians, anxious to witness a battle, or stroll over the fields of Big
Bethel, Lee's Mills, Yorktown, Gloucester, Williamsburg, or West Point; the rest were females on missions
of mercy, on visits to sons, brothers, and husbands, and
on the way to their homes at Norfolk, Suffolk, or Hampton.
Some of these were citizens of Richmond, who believed
that the Federals would occupy the city in a few days,
and enable them to resume their professions and homes.
The lower decks were occupied by Negroes. The boat
was heavily freighted, and among the parcels that littered the hold and steerage, I noticed scores of box coffins
for the removal of corpses from the field to the North.
There were quantities of spirits, consigned mainly to quartermasters, but evidently the property of certain Shylocks,
who watched the barrels greedily. An embalmer was also
on board, with his ghostly implements. He was a sallow
man, shabbily attired, and appeared to look at all the pas-

sengers as so many subjects for the development of his art. He was called "Doctor" by his admirers, and conversed in the blandest manner of the triumphs of his system.

"There are certain pretenders," he said, "who are at this moment imposing upon the Government. I regret that it is necessary to repeat it, but the fact exists that the Government is the prey of harpies. And in the art of which I am an humble disciple—that of injecting, commonly called embalming—the frauds are most deplorable. There was Major Montague—a splendid subject, I assure you—a subject that any *Professor* would have beautifully preserved— a subject that one esteems it a favor to obtain—a subject that I in particular would have been proud to receive! But what were the circumstances? I do assure you that a person named Wigwart—who I have since ascertained to be a veterinary butcher; in plain language, a doctor of horses and asses—imposed upon the relatives of the deceased, obtained the body, and absolutely ruined it!—absolutely *mangled* it! I may say, shamefully disfigured it! He was a man, sir, six feet two—about your height, I think! (to a bystander). About your weight, also! Indeed quite like you! And allow me to say that, if you should fall into my hands, I would leave your friends no cause for offence! (Here the bystander trembled perceptibly, and I thought that the doctor was about to take his life.) Well! *I* should have operated thus:—"

Then followed a description of the process, narrated with horrible circumstantiality. A fluid holding in solution pounded glass and certain chemicals, was, by the doctor's "system," injected into the blood vessels, and the subject at the same time bled at the neck. The body thus became hard and stony, and would retain its form for years. He had, by his account, experimented for a lifetime, and said that little "Willie," the son of President Lincoln, had been so preserved that his fond parents must have enjoyed his decease.

It seemed to me that the late lamented practitioners, Messrs. Burke and Hare, were likely to fade into insignificance, beside this new light of science.

I went upon deck for some moments, and marked the beating of the waves; the glitter of sea-lights pulsing on the ripples; the sweep of belated gulls through the creaking rigging; the dark hull of a passing vessel with a grinning topmast lantern; the vigilant pilot, whose eyes glared like a fiend's upon the waste of blackness; the foam that the panting screw threw against the cabin windows; the flap of fishes caught in the threads of moonlight; the depths over which one bent, peering half wistfully, half abstractedly, almost crazily, till he longed to drop into their coolness, and let the volumes of billow roll musically above him.

A woman approached me, as I stood against the great anchor, thus absorbed. She had a pale, thin face, and was scantily clothed, and spoke with a distrustful, timorous voice:—

"You don't know the name of the surgeon-general, do you, sir!"

"At Washington, ma'am?"

"No, sir; at Old Point."

I offered to inquire of the Captain; but she stopped me, agitatedly. "It's of no consequence," she said—"that is, it is of great consequence to me; but perhaps it would be best to wait." I answered, as obligingly as I could, that any service on my part would be cheerfully rendered.

"The fact is, sir," she said, after a pause, "I am going to Williamsburg, to—find—the—the body—of my—boy."

Here her speech was broken, and she put a thin, white hand tremulously to her eyes. I thought that any person in the Federal service would willingly assist her, and said so.

"He was not a Federal soldier, sir. He was a Confederate!"

This considerably altered the chances of success, and I was obliged to undeceive her somewhat. "I am sure it was not my fault," she continued, "that he joined the Rebellion. You don't think they'll refuse to let me take his bones to Baltimore, do you, sir? He was my oldest boy, and his brother, my second son, was killed at Ball's Bluff: *He* was

in the Federal service. I hardly think they will refuse me
the poor favor of laying them in the same grave."

I spoke of the difficulty of recognition, of the remoteness
of the field, and of the expense attending the recovery of
any remains, particularly those of the enemy, that, left
hastily behind in retreat, were commonly buried in
trenches without headboard or record. She said, sadly, that
she had very little money, and that she could barely afford the journey to the Fortress and return. But she esteemed her means well invested if her object could be
attained.

"They were both brave boys, sir; but I could never get
them to agree politically. William was a Northerner by
education, and took up with the New England views, and
James was in business at Richmond when the war commenced. So he joined the Southern army. It's a sad thing
to know that one's children died enemies, isn't it? And
what troubles me more than all, sir, is that James was at
Ball's Bluff where his brother fell. It makes me shudder
to think, sometimes, that *his* might have been the ball that
killed him."

The tremor of the poor creature here was painful to
behold. I spoke soothingly and encouragingly, but with a
presentiment that she must be disappointed. While I was
speaking the supper-bell rang, and I proposed to get her a
seat at the table.

"No, thank you," she replied, "I shall take no meals on
the vessel; I must travel economically, and have prepared
some lunch that will serve me. Good-bye, sir!"

Poor mothers looking for dead sons! God help them! I
have met them often since; but the figure of that pale, frail
creature flitting about the open deck—alone, hungry, very
poor—troubles me still, as I write. I found, afterward, that
she had denied herself a state-room, and intended to sleep
in a saloon chair. I persuaded her to accept my berth, but
a German, who occupied the same apartment, was unwilling to relinquish his bed, and I had the power only to give
her my pillow.

Supper was spread in the forecabin, and at the signal to

assemble the men rushed to the tables like as many beasts
of prey. A captain opposite me bolted a whole mackerel in
a twinkling, and spread the half-pound of butter that was
to serve the entire vicinity upon a single slice of bread. A
sutler beside me reached his fork across my neck, and
plucked a young chicken bodily, which he ate, to the great
disgust of some others who were eyeing it. The waiter advanced with some steak, but before he reached the table, a
couple of Zouaves dragged it from the tray, and laughed
brutally at their success. The motion of the vessel caused
a general unsteadiness, and it was absolutely dangerous to
move one's coffee to his lips. The inveterate hate with
which corporations are regarded in America was here evidenced by a general desire to empty the ship's larder.

"Eat all you can," said a soldier ferociously—"fare's
amazin' high. Must make it out in grub."

"I always gorges," said another, "on a railroad or a
steamboat. Cause why? You must eat out your passage,
you know!"

Among the passengers were a young officer and his
bride. They had been married only a few days, and she
had obtained permission to accompany him to Old Point.
Very pretty, she seemed, in her travelling hat and flowing
robes; and he wore a handsome new uniform with prodigious shoulder-bars. There was a piano in the saloon,
where another young lady of the party performed during
the evening, and the bride and groom accompanied her
with a song. It was the popular Federal parody of "Gay
and Happy":

> Then let the South fling aloft what it will,—
> We are for the Union still!
>   For the Union! For the Union!
> We are for the Union still!

The bride and groom sang alternate stanzas, and the con-
course of soldiers, civilians, and females swelled the
chorus. The reserve being thus broken, the young officer
sang the "Star-Spangled Banner," and the refrain must

have called up the mermaids. Dancing ensued, and a soldier volunteered a hornpipe. A young man with an astonishing compass of lungs repeated something from Shakespeare, and the night passed by gleefully and reputably. One could hardly realize, in the cheerful eyes and active figures of the dance, the sad uncertainties of the time. Youth trips lightest, somehow, on the brink of the grave.

The hilarities of the evening so influenced the German quartered with me, that he sang snatches of foreign ballads during most of the night, and obliged me, at last, to call the steward and insist upon his good behavior.

In the gray of the morning I ventured on deck, and, following the silvery line of beach, made out the shipping at anchor in Hampton Roads. The *Minnesota* flagship lay across the horizon, and after a time I remarked the low walls and black derricks of the Rip Raps. The white tents at Hampton were then revealed, and finally I distinguished Fortress Monroe, the key of the Chesapeake, bristling with guns, and floating the Federal flag. As we rounded to off the quay, I studied with intense interest the scene of so many historic events. Sewall's Point lay to the south, a stretch of woody beach, around whose western tip the dreaded *Merrimac* had so often moved slowly to the encounter. The spars of the *Congress* and the *Cumberland* still floated along the strand, but, like them, the invulnerable monster had become the prey of the waves. The guns of the Rip Raps and the terrible broadsides of the Federal gunboats had swept the Confederates from Sewall's Point—their flag and battery were gone—and farther seaward, at Willoughby Spit, some figures upon the beach marked the route of the victorious Federals to the city of Norfolk.

The mouth of the James and the York were visible from the deck, and long lines of shipping stretched from each to the Fortress. The quay itself was like the pool in the Thames, a mass of spars, smoke-stacks, ensigns, and swelling hills. The low deck and quaint cupola of the famous *Monitor* appeared close into shore, and near at hand rose the thick body of the *Galena*. Long boats and flat boats went hither and thither across the blue waves: the grim ports of the men of war were open and the guns frowned darkly from their coverts; the seamen were gathering for muster on the flagship, and drums beat from the barracks on shore; the Lincoln gun, a fearful piece of ordnance, rose like the Sphinx from the Fortress sands, and the sodded parapet, the winding stone walls, the tops of the brick quarters within the Fort, were some of the features of a strangely animated scene, that has yet to be perpetuated upon canvas, and made historic.

At eight o'clock the passengers were allowed to land, and a provost guard marched them to the Hygeia House— of old a watering-place hotel—where, by groups, they were ushered into a small room, and the oath of allegiance administered to them. The young officer who officiated repeated the words of the oath with a broad grin upon his face, and the passengers were required to assent by word and by gesture. Among those who took the oath in this way, was a very old sailor, who had been in the Federal service for the better part of his life, and whose five sons were now in the army. He called "Amen" very loudly and fervently, and there was some perceptible disposition on the part of other ardent patriots to celebrate the occasion with three cheers. The quartermaster stationed at the Fortress gave me a pass to go by steamer up the York to White House, and as there were three hours to elapse before departure, I strolled about the place with our agent. In times of peace, Old Point was simply a stone fortification, and one of the strongest of its kind in the world. Many years and many millions of dollars were required to build it, but it was, in general, feebly garrisoned, and was, altogether, a stupid, tedious locality, except in the bathing months, when the beauty and fashion of Virginia resorted to its hotel. A few cottages had grown up around it, tenanted only in "the season"; and a little way off, on the mainland, stood the pretty village of Hampton.

By a strange oversight, the South failed to seize Fortress Monroe at the beginning of the Rebellion; the Federals soon made it the basis for their armies and a leading naval station. The battle of Big Bethel was one of the first occurrences in the vicinity. Then the dwellings of Hampton were burned and its people exiled. In rapid succession followed the naval battles in the Roads, the siege and surrender of Yorktown, the flight of the Confederates up the Peninsula to Richmond, and finally the battles of Williamsburg and West Point, and the capture of Norfolk. These things had already transpired; it was now the month of May; and the victorious army, following up its vantages, had pursued the fugitives by land and water to White House, at the head of navigation on the Pamunkey River. Thither it was my lot to go, and witness the turning-point of their fortunes, and their subsequent calamity and repulse.

I found Old Point a weary place of resort, even in the busy era of civil war. The bar at the Hygeia House was beset with thirsty and idle people, who swore instinctively, and drank raw spirits passionately. The quantity of shell, ball, ordnance, camp equipage, and war munitions of every description piled around the fort was marvellously great. It seemed to me that Xerxes, the first Napoleon, or the greediest of conquerors, ancient or modern, would have beheld with amazement the gigantic preparations at command of the Federal Government. Energy and enterprise displayed their implements of death on every hand. One was startled at the prodigal outlay of means, and the reckless summoning of men. I looked at the starred and striped ensign that flaunted above the Fort, and thought of Madame Roland's appeal to the statue by the guillotine.

The settlers were numbered by regiments here. Their places of business were mainly structures or "shanties" of rough plank, and most of them were the owners of sloops, or schooners, for the transportation of freight from New York, Philadelphia, or Baltimore, to their depots at Old Point. Some possessed a dozen wagons that plied regularly between these stores and camps. The traffic was not confined to men; for women and children kept pace with the army, trading in every possible article of necessity or luxury. For these—disciples of the dime and the dollar— war had no terrors. They took their muck-rakes, like the man in Bunyan, and gathered the almighty coppers, from the pestilential camp and the reeking battle-field.

CHAPTER VI

On to Richmond

—————

YORKTOWN lies twenty-one miles northwestward from Old Point, and thither I turned my face at noon, resolving to delay my journey to White House till the next morning. Crossing an estuary of the bay upon a narrow causeway, I passed Hampton—half burned, half desolate—and at three o'clock came to Big Bethel, the scene of the battle of June 10, 1861. A small earthwork marks the site of Magruder's field-pieces, and hard by the slain were buried. The spot was noteworthy to me, since Lieutenant Greble, a fellow alumnus, had perished here, and likewise, Theodore Winthrop, the gifted author of *Cecil Dreeme* and *John Brent*. The latter did not live to know his exaltation. That morning never came whereon he "woke, and found himself famous."

The road ran parallel with the deserted defences of the Confederates for some distance. The country was flat and full of swamps, but marked at intervals by relics of camps. The farm-houses were untenanted, the fences laid flat or destroyed, the fields strewn with discarded clothing, arms, and utensils. By and by, we entered the outer line of Federal parallels, and wound among lunettes, crémaillères, redoubts, and rifle-pits. Marks of shell and ball were frequent, in furrows and holes, where the clay had been upheaved. Every foot of ground, for fifteen miles henceforward, had been touched by the shovel and the pick. My companion suggested that as much digging, concentred upon one point, would have taken the Federals to China. The sappers and miners had made their stealthy trenches,

rod by rod, each morning appearing closer to their adversaries, and finally completed their work at less than a hundred yards from the Confederate defences. Three minutes
would have sufficed from the final position to hurl columns
upon the opposing outworks, and sweep them with the
bayonet. Then days only had elapsed since the evacuation
(May 4, 1862), and the siege guns still remained in some
of the batteries. McClellan worshipped great ordnance,
and some of his Columbiads that were mounted in the
water battery yawned cavernously through their embrasures, and might have furnished sleeping accommodations
to the gunners. A few mortars stood in position by the river
side, and there were Parrott, Griffin, and Dahlgren pieces
in the shore batteries.

However numerous and powerful were the Federal fortifications, they bore no comparison, in either respect, to
those relinquished by the revolutionists. Miniature mountain ranges they seemed, deeply ditched, and revetted
with sods, fascines, hurdles, gabions or sand bags. Along
the York riverside there were water batteries of surpassing
beauty, that seemed, at a little distance, successions of
gentle terraces. Their pieces were likewise of enormous
calibre, and their number almost incredible. The advanced
line of fortifications stretched from the mouth of Warwick
Creek on the South, to a point fifteen miles distant on the
York: one hundred and forty guns were planted along
this chain of defences; but there were two other concen-
tric lines, mounting, each, one hundred and twenty, and
two hundred and forty guns. The remote series consisted
of six forts of massive size and height, fronted by swamps
and flooded meadows, with frequent creeks and ravines
interposing; sharp fraise and abatis planted against scarp
and slope, pointed cruelly eastward. There were two water
batteries, of six and four thirty-two Columbiads respectively, and the town itself, which stands upon a red clay
bluff, was encircled by a series of immense rifled and
smooth-bore pieces, including a powerful pivot-gun, that
one of McClellan's shells struck during the first day's bombardment, and split it into fragments. At Gloucester Point,

across the York River, the great guns of the *Merrimac*
were planted, it is said, and a fleet of firerafts and torpedo-
ships were moored in the stream. By all accounts, there
could have been no less than five hundred guns behind
the Confederate entrenchments, the greater portion, of
course, field-pieces, and, as the defending army was composed of one hundred thousand men, we must add that
number of small arms to the list of ordnance. If we compute the Federals at so high a figure—and they could
scarcely have had less than a hundred thousand men afield
—we must increase the enormous amount of their field,
siege, and small ordnance, by the naval guns of the fleet
that stood anchored in the bay. It is probable that a thousand cannon and two hundred thousand muskets were assembled in and around Yorktown during this memorable
siege. The mind shudders to see the terrible deductions of
these statistics. The monster, who wished that the world
had but one neck, that he might sever it, would have
gloated at such realization! How many days or hours
would have here sufficed to annihilate all the races of men?
Happily, the world was spared the spectacle of these
deadly mouths at once aflame. Beautiful but awful must
have been the scene, and the earth must have staggered
with the shock. One might almost have imagined that
man, in his ambition, had shut his God in heaven, and
besieged him there.

While the fortifications defending it amazed me, the village of Yorktown disappointed me. I marvelled that so
paltry a settlement should have been twice made historic.
Here, in the year 1781, Lord Cornwallis surrendered his
starving command to the American colonists and their
French allies. But the entrenchments of that earlier day
had been almost obliterated by these recent labors. The
field where the Earl delivered up his sword was trodden
bare, and dotted with ditches and ramparts; while a small
monument that marked the event had been hacked to
fragments by the Southerners, and carried away piecemeal. Yet strange to say, relics of the first bombardment

had just been discovered, and, among them, a gold-hilted sword.

I visited, in the evening, the late quarters of General Hill, a small white house with green shutters, and also the famous "Nelson House," a roomy mansion where, of old, Cornwallis slept, and where, a few days past, Jefferson Davis and General Lee had held with John B. Magruder, and his associates, a council of war. It had been also used for hospital purposes, but some Negroes were now the only occupants.

The Confederates left behind them seventy spiked and shattered cannon, some powder, and a few splintered wagons; but in all material respects, their evacuation was thorough and creditable. Some deserters took the first tidings of the retreat to the astonished Federals, and they raised the national flag within the fortifications, in the gray of the morning of the 4th of May. Many Negroes also escaped the vigilance of their taskmasters, and remained to welcome the victors. The fine works of Yorktown are monuments to Negro labor, for *they* were the hewers and the diggers. Every slave-owner in eastern Virginia was obliged to send one half of his male servants between the ages of sixteen and fifty to the Confederate camps, and they were organized into gangs and set to work. In some cases they were put to military service and made excellent sharpshooters. The last gun discharged from the town was said to have been fired by a Negro.

I slept on board a barge at the wharf that evening, and my dreams ran upon a thousand themes. To every American this was hallowed ground. It had been celebrated by the pencil of Trumbull, the pen of Franklin, and the eloquence of Jefferson. Scarce eighty years had elapsed since those great minds established a fraternal government; but the site of their crowning glory was now the scene of their children's shame. Discord had stolen upon their councils and blood had profaned their shrine.

I visited next day a bomb-proof postern, or subterranean passage, connecting the citadel with the outworks, and loitered about the fortifications till noon, when I took pas-

sage on the mail steamer, which left the Fortress at eleven
o'clock, and reached White House at dusk the same evening. The whole river as I ascended was filled with mer-
chant and naval craft. They made a continuous line from
Old Point to the mouth of York River, and the masts and
spars environing Yorktown and Gloucester, reminded one
of a scene on the Mersey or the Clyde. At West Point, there
was an array of shipping scarcely less formidable, and the
windings of the interminably crooked Pamunkey were
marked for leagues by sails, smoke-stacks, and masts. The
landings and wharves were besieged by flat-boats and
sloops, and Zouaves were hoisting forage and commissary
stores up the red bluffs at every turn of our vessel.

The Pamunkey was a beautiful stream, densely wooded,
and occasional vistas opened up along its borders of
wheatfields and meadows, with Virginia farm-houses and
Negro quarters on the hilltops. Some of the houses on the
river banks appeared to be tenanted by white people, but
the majority had a haunted, desolate appearance, the only
signs of life being strolling soldiers, who thrust their legs
through the second-story windows, or contemplated the
river from the chimney-tops, and groups of Negroes who
sunned themselves on the piazza, or rushed to the margin
to gaze and grin at the passing steamers. There were occasional residences not unworthy of old manorial and
baronial times, and these were attended at a little distance
by Negro quarters of logs, arranged in rows, and provided
with mud chimneys built against their gables. Few of the
Northern navigable rivers were so picturesque and varied.

We passed two Confederate gunboats, that had been
half completed, and burned on the stocks. Their charred
elbows and ribs stared out, like the remains of some ex-
tinct monsters; a little delay might have found each of
them armed and manned, and carrying havoc upon the
rivers and the seas. West Point was simply a tongue, or
spit of land, dividing the Mattapony from the Pamunkey
River at their junction; a few houses were built upon the
shallow, and some wharves, half demolished, marked the
terminus of the York and Richmond railroad. A paltry

water-battery was the sole defence. Below Cumberland (a collection of huts and a wharf), a number of schooners had been sunk across the river, and, with the aid of an island in the middle, these constituted a rather rigid blockade. The steamboat passed through, steering carefully, but some sailing vessels that followed required to be towed between the narrow apertures. The tops only of the sunken masts could be discerned above the surface, and much time and labor must have been required to place the boats in line and sink them. Vessels were counted by scores above and below this blockade, and at Cumberland the masts were like a forest; clusters of pontoons were here anchored in the river, and a short distance below we found three of the light-draught Federal gunboats moored in the stream. It was growing dark as we rounded to at White House; the camp fires of the grand army lit up the sky, and edged the tree-boughs on the margin with ribands of silver. Some drums beat in the distance; sentries paced the strand; the hum of men, and the lowing of commissary cattle, were borne towards us confusedly; soldiers were bathing in the river; team-horses were drinking at the brink; a throng of motley people were crowding about the landing to receive the papers and mails. I had at last arrived at the seat of war, and my ambition to chronicle battles and bloodshed was about to be gratified.

At first, I was troubled to make my way; the tents had just been pitched; no one knew the location of divisions other than their own, and it was now so dark that I did not care to venture far. After a vain attempt to find some flat-boats where there were lodgings and meals to be had, I struck out for general headquarters, and, undergoing repeated snubbings from pert members of staff, fell in at length with a very tall, spare, and angular young officer, who spoke broken English, and who heard my inquiries courteously; he stepped into General Randolph B. Marcy's tent, but the Chief of Staff did not know the direction of Smith's division; he then repaired to General Van Vliet, the chief Quartermaster, but with ill success. A party of

officers were smoking under a "fly," and some of these
called to him, thus—

"Captain! Duke! De Chartres! What do you wish?"

It was, then, the Orleans Prince who had befriended me,
and I had the good fortune to hear that the division of
which I was in search lay a half mile up the river. I never
spoke to the Bourbon afterward, but saw him often; and
that he was as chivalrous as he was kind, all testimony
proved.

A private escorted me to a Captain Mott's tent, and this
officer introduced me to General Winfield Scott Hancock.
I was at once invited to mess with the General's staff, and
in the course of an hour felt perfectly at home. Hancock
was one of the handsomest officers in the army; he had
served in the Mexican War, and was subsequently a Captain in the Quartermaster's department. But the Rebellion
placed stars in many shoulder-bars, and few were more
worthily designated than this young Pennsylvanian. His
first laurels were gained at Williamsburg; but the story
of a celebrated charge that won him the day's applause,
and McClellan's encomium of the "Superb Hancock,"
was altogether fictitious. The musket, not the bayonet,
gave him the victory. I may doubt, in this place, that any
extensive bayonet charge has been known during the war.
Some have gone so far as to deny that the bayonet has
ever been used at all.

Hancock's regiments were the 5th Wisconsin, 49th
Pennsylvania, 43d New York, and 6th Maine. They represented widely different characteristics, and I esteemed
myself fortunate to obtain a position where I could so
eligibly study men, habits, and warfare. During the evening I fell in with the Colonel of each of these regiments,
and from the conversation that ensued, I gleaned a fair
idea of them all.

The Wisconsin regiment was from a new and ambitious
State of the Northwest. The men were rough-mannered,
great-hearted farmers, wood-choppers, and tradesmen.
They had all the impulsiveness of the Yankee, with less
selfishness, and quite as much bravery. The Colonel was

named Cobb, and he had held some leading offices in Wisconsin. A part of his life had been adventurously spent, and he had participated in the Mexican War. He was an ardent Republican in politics, and had been Speaker of a branch of the State Legislature. He was an attorney in a small country town when the war commenced, and his name had been broached for the Governorship. In person he was small, lithe, and capable of enduring great fatigue. His hair was a little gray, and he had no beard. He did not respect appearances, and his sword, as I saw, was antique and quite different in shape from the regulation weapon. He had penetrating gray eyes, and his manners were generally reserved. One had not to regard him twice to see that he was both cautious and resolute. He was too ambitious to be frank, and too passionate not to be brave. In the formula of learning he was not always correct; but few were of quicker perception or more practical and philosophic. He might not, in an emergency, be nicely scrupulous as to means, but he never wavered in respect to objects. His will was the written law to his regiment, and I believed his executive abilities superior to those of any officer in the brigade, not excepting the General's.

The New York regiment was commanded by a young officer named Francis Vinton. He was not more than thirty-five years of age, and was a graduate of the United States Military Academy. Passionately devoted to engineering, he withdrew from the army, and passed five years in Paris at the study of his art. Returning homeward by way of the West Indies, he visited Honduras, and projected a filibustering expedition to its shores from the States. While perfecting the design, the Rebellion commenced, and his old patron, General Scott, secured him the colonelcy of a volunteer regiment. He still cherished his scheme of "colonization," and half of his men were promised to accompany him. Personally, Colonel Vinton was straight, dark, and handsome. He was courteous, affable, and brave—but wedded to his peculiar views, and, as I thought, a thorough "Young American."

The Maine regiment was fathered by Colonel Burnham,

a staunch old yeoman and soldier, who has since been made a general. His probity and good-nature were adjuncts of his valor, and his men were of the better class of New Englanders. The fourth regiment fell into the hands of a lawyer from Lewistown, Pennsylvania. He had been also in the Mexican War, and was remarkable mainly for strictness with regard to the sanitary regulations of his camps. He had wells dug at every stoppage, and his tents were generally fenced and canopied with cedar arbors. General Hancock's staff was composed of a number of young men, most of whom had been called from civil life. His brigade constituted one of three commanded by General W. F. Smith. Four batteries were annexed to the division so formed; the entire number of muskets was perhaps eight thousand. The Chief of Artillery was Captain Romeyn Beck Ayres, whose battery saved the three months' army at Bull Run. It so happened that he came into the General's during the evening, and recited the particulars of a gunboat excursion, thirty miles up the Pamunkey, wherein he had landed his men, and burned a quantity of grain, some warehouses, and shipping. I pencilled the facts at once, made up my letter, and mailed it early in the morning.

CHAPTER VII

Rustics in Rebellion

———————————

At White House, I met some of the mixed Indians and Negroes from Indiantown Island, which lies among the osiers in the stream. One of these ferried me over, and the people received me obsequiously, touching their straw hats, and saying, "Sar, at your service!" They were all anxious to hear something of the war, and asked, solicitously, if they were to be protected. Some of them had been to Richmond the previous day, and gave me some unimportant items happening in the city. I found that they had Richmond papers of that date, and purchased them for a few cents. They knew little or nothing of their own history, and had preserved no traditions of their tribe. There was, however, I understood, a very old woman extant, named "Mag," of great repute at medicines, powwows, and divination. I expressed a desire to speak with her, and was conducted to a log-house, more rickety and ruined than any of the others. About fifty half-breeds followed me in respectful curiosity, and they formed a semicircle around the cabin. The old woman sat in the threshold, barefooted, and smoking a stump of clay pipe.

"Yaw's one o' dem Nawden soldiers, Aunt Mag!" said my conductor. "He wants to talk wid ye."

"Sot down, honey," said the old woman, producing a wooden stool; "is you a Yankee, honey? Does you want yo fauchun told by de ole 'oman?"

I perceived that the daughter of the Delawares smelt strongly of fire-water, and the fumes of her calumet were most unwholesome. She was greatly disappointed that I did not require her prophetic services, and said, appealingly—

"Why, sar, all de gen'elmen an' ladies from Richmond has dere fauchuns told. I tells 'em true. All my fauchuns comes out true. Ain't dat so, chillen?"

A low murmur of assent ran round the group, and I was obviously losing caste in the settlement.

"Here is a dime," said I, "that I will give you, to tell me the result of the war. Shall the North be victorious in the next battle? Will Richmond surrender within a week? Shall I take my cigar at the Spotswood on Sunday fortnight?"

"I'se been a lookin' into dat," she said, cunningly; "I'se had dreams on dat ar'. Le'um see how de armies stand!"

She brought from the house a cup of painted earthenware containing sediments of coffee. I saw her crafty white eyes look up to mine as she muttered some jargon, and pretended to read the arrangement of the grains.

"Honey," she said, "gi' me de money, and let de ole 'oman dream on it once mo'! It ain't quite clar' yit, young massar. Tank you, honey! Tank you! Let de old 'oman dream! Let de ole 'oman dream!"

She disappeared into the house, chuckling and chattering, and the sons of the forest, loitering awhile, dispersed in various directions. As I followed my conductor to the riverside, and he parted the close bushes and boughs to give us exit, the glare of the camp-fires broke all at once upon us. The ship-lights quivered on the water; the figures of men moved to and fro before the fagots; the stars peeped timorously from the vault; the woods and steep banks were blackly shadowed in the river. Here was I, among the aborigines; and as my dusky acquaintance sent his canoe skimming across the ripples, I thought how inexplicable were the decrees of Time and the justice of God. Two races united in these people, and both of them we had wronged. From the one we had taken lands; from the other liberties. Two centuries had now elapsed. But the little remnant of the African and the American were to

look from their Island Home upon the clash of our armies
and the murder of our braves.

By the 19th of May the skirts of the grand army had
been gathered up, and on the 20th the march to Richmond
was resumed. The troops moved along two main roads, of
which the right led to New Mechanicsville and Meadow
Bridges, and the left to the railroad and Bottom's Bridge.
My division formed the right centre, and although the
Chickahominy fords were but eighteen miles distant, we
did not reach them for three days. On the first night we
encamped at Tunstall's, a railroad-station on Black Creek;
on the second at New Cold Harbor, a little country tavern,
kept by a cripple; and on the night of the third day at
Hogan's farm, on the north hills of the Chickahominy. The
railroad was opened to Despatch Station at the same time,
but the right and centre were still compelled to "team"
their supplies from White House. In the new position, the
army extended ten miles along the Chickahominy hills;
and while the engineers were driving pile, trestle, pontoon,
and corduroy bridges, the cavalry was scouring the country, on both flanks, far and wide.

The advance was full of incident, and I learned to keep
as far in front as possible, that I might communicate with
scouts, contrabands, and citizens. Many odd personages
were revealed to me at the farm-houses on the way, and I
studied, with curious interest, the native Virginian character. They appeared to be compounds of the cavalier and
the boor. There was no old gentleman who owned a thousand barren acres, spotted with scrub timber; who lived in
a weather-beaten barn, with a multiplicity of porch and a
quantity of chimney; whose means bore no proportion to
his pride, and neither to his indolence—that did not talk
of his ancestry, proffer his hospitality, and defy me to an
argument. I was a civilian—they had no hostility to me—
but the blue-coats of the soldiers seared their eyeballs.
In some cases their daughters remained upon the property;
but the sons and the Negroes always fled—though in contrary directions. The old men used to peep through the
windows at the passing columns; and as their gates were

wrenched from the hinges, their rails used to pry wagons
out of the mud, their pump-handles shaken till the buckets
splintered in the shaft, and their barns invaded by greasy
agrarians, they walked to and fro, half-weakly, half-wrath-
fully, but with a pluck, fortitude, and devotion that wrung
my respect. Some aged Negro women commonly remained, but these were rather incumbrances than aids,
and they used the family meal to cook bread for the
troops. An old, toothless, grinning African stood at every
lane and gate, selling buttermilk and corn-cakes. Poor
mortal, sinful old women! They had worked for nothing
through their three-score and ten, but avarice glared from
their shrivelled pupils, and their last but greatest delight
lay in the coppers and the dimes. One would have thought
that they had outlived the greed of gold; but wages deferred make the dying miserly.

The lords of the manors were troubled to know the
number of our troops. For several days the columns passed
with their interminable teams, batteries, and adjuncts, and
the old gentlemen were loth to compute us at less than
several millions.

"Why, look yonder," said one, pointing to a brigade;
"I declar' to gracious, there ain't no less than ten thousand
in *them!*"

"Tousands an' tousands!" said a wondering Negro at
his elbow. "I wonda if dey'll take Richmond dis yer day?"

Many of them hung white flags at their gate-posts, im-
plying neutrality; but nobody displayed the Federal colors.
If there were any covert sympathizers with the purposes
of the army, they remembered the vengeance of the neighbors and made no demonstrations. There was a prodigious
number of stragglers from the Federal lines, and these
were the bane of the country people. They sauntered along
by twos and threes, rambling into all the fields and green-
apple orchards, intruding their noses into old cabins, pry-
ing into smokehouses, and cellars, looking at the stock in
the stables, and peeping on tiptoe into the windows of
dwellings. These stragglers were true exponents of Yankee
character—always wanting to know—averse to discipline,

eccentric in their orbits, entertaining profound contempt for everything that was not up to the measure of "to hum."

"Look here, Bill, I say!" said one, with a great grin on his face; "did you ever, neow! I swan! they call that a plough down in these parts."

"Devilishest people I ever see!" said Bill, "stick their meetin'-houses square in the woods! Build their chimneys first and move the houses up to 'em! All the houses breakin' out in perspiration of porch! All their machinery with Noah in the ark! Pump the soil dry! Go to sleep a milkin' a keow! Depend entirely on Providence and the nigger!"

There was a mill on the New Bridge road, ten miles from White House, with a tidy farm-house, stacks, and cabins adjoining. The road crossed the mill-race by a log bridge, and a spreading pond or dam lay to the left—the water black as ink, the shore sandy, and the stream disappearing in a grove of straight pines. A youngish woman, with several small children, occupied the dwelling, and there remained, besides, her fat sister-in-law and four or five faithful Negroes. I begged the favor of a meal and bed in the place one night, and shall not forget the hospitable table with its steaming biscuit; the chubby baby, perched upon his high stool; the talkative elderly woman, who took snuff at the fireplace; the contented black girl, who played the Hebe; and above all, the trim, plump, pretty hostess, with her brown eyes and hair, her dignity and her fondness, sitting at the head of the board. When she poured the bright coffee into the capacious bowl, she revealed the neatest of hands and arms, and her dialect was softer and more musical than that of most Southerners. In short, I fell almost in love with her; though she might have been a younger playmate of my mother's, and though she was the wife of a quartermaster in a Virginia regiment. For, somehow, a woman seems very handsome when one is afield; and the contact of rough soldiers gives one a partiality for females. It must have required some courage to remain upon the farm; but she hoped thereby to save the property from spoliation. I played a game of whist

with the sister-in-law, arguing all the while; and at nine
o'clock the servant produced some hard cider, shellbarks,
and apples. We drank a cheery toast: "an early peace and
old fellowship!"—to which the wife added a sentiment
of "always welcome," and the baby laughed at her knee.
How brightly glowed the fire! I wanted to linger for a
week, a month, a year—as I do now, thinking it all over—
and when I strolled to the porch—hearing the pigeons
cooing at the barn; the water streaming down the dam;
the melancholy monotony of the pine boughs—there only
lacked the humming mill-wheel, and the strong grip of
the miller's hand, to fill the void corner of one's happy
heart.

But this was a time of war, when dreams are rudely
broken, and mine could not last. The next day some great
wheels beat down the bridge, and the teams clogged the
road for miles; the waiting teamsters saw the miller's
sheep, and the geese, chickens, and pigs rashly exposed
themselves in the barnyard; these were killed and eaten,
the mill stripped of flour and meal, and the garden
despoiled of its vegetables. A quartermaster's horse foun-
dered, and he demanded the miller's, giving therefor a
receipt, but specifying upon the same the owner's relation
to the Rebellion; and, to crown all, a group of stragglers
butchered the cows, and heaped the beef in their wagons
to feed their regimental friends. When I presented myself,
late in the afternoon, the yard and porches were filled
with soldiers; the wife sat within, her head thrown upon
the window, her bright hair unbound, and her eyes red
with weeping. The baby had cried itself to sleep, the sister-
in-law took snuff fiercely, at the fire; the black girl cowered in a corner.

"There is not bread in the house for my children," she
said; "but I did not think they could make me shed a tear."

If there were Spartan women, as the story-books say, I
wonder if their blood died with them! I hardly think so.

If I learned anything from my quiet study of this and
subsequent campaigns, it was the heartlessness of war.
War brutalizes! The most pitiful become pitiless afield,

and those who are not callous, must do cruel duties. If the quartermaster had not seized the horses, he would have been accountable for his conduct; had he failed to state the miller's disloyalty in the receipt, he would have been punished. The men were thieves and brutes, to take the meal and meat; but they were perhaps hungry and weary, and sick of camp food; on the whole, I became a devotee of the George Fox faith, and hated warfare, though I knew nothing to substitute for it, in *crises*.

Besides, the optimist might have seen much to admire. Individual merits were developed around me; I saw shop-keepers and mechanics in the ranks, and they looked to be better men. Here were triumphs of engineering; there perfections of applied ingenuity. I saw how the weakest natures girt themselves for great resolves, and how forti-tude outstripped itself. It is a noble thing to put by the fear of death. It was a grand spectacle, this civil soldiery of both sections, supporting their principles, ambitions, or whatever instigated them, with their bodies; and their bones, lie where they will, must be severed, when the ploughshare some day heaves them to the ploughman.

One morning a friend asked me to go upon a scout.

"Where are your companies?" said I.

"There are four behind, and we shall be joined by six at Old Cold Harbor."

I saw, in the rear, filing through a belt of woods, the tall figures of the horsemen, approaching at a canter.

"Do you command?" said I again.

"No! the Major has charge of the scout, and his orders are secret."

I wheeled beside him, as the cavalry closed up, waved my hand to Plumley, and the girls, and went forward to the rendezvous, about six miles distant. The remaining companies of the regiment were here drawn up, watering their nags. The Major was a thick, sunburnt man, with grizzled beard, and as he saw us rounding a corner of hilly road, his voice rang out—

"Attention! Prepare to mount!"

Every rider sprang to his nag; every nag walked instinctively to his place; every horseman made fast his girths, strapped his blankets tightly, and laid his hands upon bridle-rein and pommel.

"Attention! Mount!"

The riders sprang to their seats; the bugles blew a lively strain; the horses pricked up their ears; and the long array moved briskly forward, with the Captain, the Major, and myself at the head. We were joined in a moment by two pieces of flying artillery, and five fresh companies of cavalry. In a moment more we were underway again, galloping due northward, and, as I surmised, toward Hanover Court House.

If any branch of the military service is feverish, adventurous, and exciting, it is that of the cavalry. One's heart beats as fast as the hoof-falls; there is no music like the winding of the bugle, and no monotone so full of meaning as the clink of sabres rising and falling with the dashing pace. Horse and rider become one—a new race of centaurs—and the charge, the stroke, the crack of carbines, are so quick, vehement, and dramatic, that we seem to be watching the joust of tournaments or following fierce Saladins and Crusaders again.

We had ridden two hours at a fair canter, when we came to a small stream that crossed the road obliquely, and gurgled away through a sandy valley into the deepnesses of the woods. A cart-track, half obliterated, here diverged, running parallel with the creek, and the Major held up his sword as a signal to halt; at the same moment the bugle blew a quick, shrill note.

"There are hoof-marks here!" grunted the Major—"five of 'em. The Dutchman has gone into the thicket. Hulloo!" he added, precipitately—"there go the carbines!"

I heard, clearly, two explosions in rapid succession; then a general discharge, as of several persons firing at once, and at last, five continuous reports, fainter, but more regular, and like the several emptyings of a revolver. I had scarcely time to note these things, and the effect produced upon the troop, when strange noises came from the woods to the right: the floundering of steeds, the cries and curses

of men, and the ringing of steel striking steel. Directly
the boughs crackled, the leaves quivered, and a horse and
rider plunged into the road, not five rods from my feet.
The man was bareheaded, and his face and clothing were
torn with briars and branches. He was at first riding fairly
upon our troops, when he beheld the uniform and standards, and with a sharp oath flung up his sword and hands.

"I surrender!" he said; "I give in! Don't shoot!"

The scores of carbines that were levelled upon him at
once dropped to their rests at the saddles; but some unseen
avenger had not heeded the shriek; a ball whistled from
the woods, and the man fell from his cushion like a stone.
In another instant, the German sergeant bounded through
the gap, holding his sabre aloft in his right hand; but the
left hung stiff and shattered at his side, and his face was
deathly white. He glared an instant at the dead man by
the roadside, leered grimly, and called aloud—

"Come on, Major! Dis vay! Dere are a squad of dem
ahead!"

The bugle at once sounded a charge, the Major rose in
the stirrups, and thundered "Forward!" I reined aside,
intuitively, and the column dashed hotly past me. With a
glance at the heap of mortality littering the way, I spurred
my nag sharply, and followed hard behind. The riderless
horse seemed to catch the fever of the moment, and closed
up with me, leaving his master the solitary tenant of the
dell. For perhaps three miles we galloped like the wind,
and my brave little traveller overtook the hindmost of the
troop, and retained the position. Thrice there were discharges ahead; I caught glimpses of the Major, the Captain, and the wolfish sergeant, far in the advance; and once
saw, through the cloud of dust that beset them, the pursued and their individual pursuers, turning the top of a
hill. But for the most part, I saw nothing; I *felt* all the
intense, consuming, burning ardor of the time and the
event. I thought that my hand clutched a sabre, and despised myself that one was not there. I stood in the
stirrups, and held some invisible enemy by the throat. In
a word, the bloodiness of the chase was upon me. I real-

ized the fierce infatuation of matching life with life, and
standing arbiter upon my fellow's body and soul. It
seemed but a moment, when we halted, red and panting,
in the paltry Court House village of Hanover; the field-
pieces hurled a few shells at the escaping Confederates,
and the men were ordered to dismount.

It seemed that a Confederate picket had been occupy-
ing the village, and the creek memorized by the skirmish
was an outpost merely. Two of the man Otto's party had
been slain in the woods, where also lay as many Southerners.

Hanover Court House is renowned as the birthplace of
Patrick Henry, the colonial orator, called by Byron the
"forest-born Demosthenes." In a little tavern, opposite
the old Court House building, he began his humble career
as a measurer of gills to convivials, and *in* the Court House
—a small brick edifice, plainly but quaintly constructed—
he gave the first exhibitions of his matchless eloquence.
Not far away, on a by-road, the more modern but not less
famous orator, Henry Clay, was born. The region adjacent
to his father's was called the "Slashes of Hanover," and
thence came his appellation of the "Mill Boy of the
Slashes." I had often longed to visit these shrines; but
never dreamed that the booming of cannon would an-
nounce me. The soldiers broke into both the tavern and
courthouse, and splintered some chairs in the former to
obtain relics of Henry. I secured Richmond newspapers
of the same morning, and also some items of intelligence.
With these I decided to repair at once to White House,
and formed the rash determination of taking the direct
or Pamunkey road, which I had never travelled, and which
might be beset by Confederates. The distance to White
House, by this course, was only twenty miles; whereas it
was nearly as far to headquarters; and I believed that my
horse had still the persistence to carry me. It was past four
o'clock; but I thought to ride six miles an hour while daylight lasted, and, by good luck, get to the depot at nine.
The Major said that it was foolhardiness; the Captain bantered me to go. I turned my back upon both, and bade
them good-bye.

CHAPTER VIII

Under Arrest

WHILE daylight remained, I had little reason to repent my wayward resolve. The Pamunkey lay to my left, and the residences between it and the road were of a better order than others that I had seen. This part of the country had not been overrun, and the wheat and young corn were waving in the river-breeze. I saw few Negroes, but the porches were frequently occupied by women and white men, who looked wonderingly toward me. There were some hoof-marks in the clay, and traces of a broad tire that I thought belonged to a gun-carriage. The hills of King William County were but a little way off, and through the wood that darkened them, sunny glimpses of vari-colored fields and dwellings now and then appeared. I came to a shabby settlement called New Castle, at six o'clock, where an evil-looking man walked out from a frame house, and inquired the meaning of the firing at Hanover.

I explained hurriedly, as some of his neighbors meantime gathered around me. They asked if I was not a soldier in the Yankee army, and as I rode away, followed me suspiciously with their eyes and wagged their heads. To end the matter I spurred my pony and soon galloped out of sight. Henceforward I met only stern surprised glances, and seemed to read "murder" in the faces of the inhabitants. A wide creek crossed the road about five miles further on, where I stopped to water my horse. The shades of night were gathering now; there was no moon; and for the first time I realized the loneliness of my position. Hitherto, adventure had laughed down fear; hereafter my mind was to be darkened like the gloaming, and peopled with ghastly shadows.

I was yet young in the experience of death, and the toppled corpse of the slain cavalry-man on the scout, somehow haunted me. I heard his hoof-falls chiming with my own, and imagined, with a cold thrill, that his steed was still following me; then, his white rigid face and uplifted arms menaced my way; and, at last, the ruffianly form of his slayer pursued him along the wood. They glided like shadows over the foliage, and flashed across the surfaces of pools and rivulets. I heard their steel ringing in the underbrush, and they flitted around me, pursuing and retreating, till my brain began to whirl with the motion. Suddenly my horse stumbled, and I reined him to a halt.

The cold drops were standing on my forehead. I found my knees a-quiver and my breathing convulsive. With an expletive upon my unmanliness, I touched the nag with my heel, and whistled encouragingly. Poor pony! Fifty miles of almost uninterrupted travel had broken his spirit. He leaped into his accustomed pace; but his legs were unsteady and he floundered at every bound. There were pools, ruts, and boughs across the way, with here and there stretches of slippery corduroy; but the thick blackness concealed these, and I expected momentarily to be thrown from the saddle. By and by he dropped from a canter into a rack; from a rack to an amble; then into a walk, and finally to a slow painful limp. I dismounted and took him perplexedly by the bit. A light shone from the window of a dwelling across some open fields to the left, and I thought of repairing thither; but some deep-mouthed dogs began to bay directly, and then the lamp went out. A tiny stream sang at the roadside, flowing toward some deeper tributary; lighting a cigar, I made out, by its fitful illuminings, to wash the limbs of the jaded nag. Then I led him for an hour, till my own limbs were weary, troubled all the time by weird imaginings, doubts, and regrets. When I resumed the saddle the horse had a firmer step and walked pleasantly. I ventured after a time to incite him to a trot, and was going nicely forward, when a deep voice, that almost took my breath, called from the gloom—

"Who comes there? Halt, or I fire! Guard, turn out!"

Directly the road was full of men, and a bull's-eye lantern flashed upon my face. A group of foot-soldiery, with drawn pistols and sabres, gathered around me, and I heard the neigh of steeds from some imperceptible vicinity. "Who is it, Sergeant?" said one. "Is there but one of 'em?" said another. "Cuss him!" said a third; "I was takin' a bully snooze." "Who are yeou?" said the Sergeant, sternly; "what are yeou deouin' aout at this hour o' the night? Are yeou a rebbil?"

"No!" I answered, greatly relieved; "I am a newspaper correspondent of Smith's division, and there's my pass!"

I was taken over to a place in the woods, where some fagots were smouldering, and, stirring them to a blaze, the Sergeant read the document and pronounced it right.

"Yeou hain't got no business, nevertheless, to be roamin' araound outside o' picket; but seein' as it's yeou, I reckon yeou may trot along!"

I offered to exchange my information for a biscuit and a drop of coffee, for I was well-nigh worn out; while one of the privates produced a canteen more wholesome than cleanly, another gave me a lump of fat pork and a piece of corn bread. They gathered sleepily about me, while I told of the scout, and the Sergeant said that my individual ride was "game enough, but nothin' but darn nonsense." Then they fed my horse with a trifle of oats, and after awhile I climbed, stiff and bruised, to the saddle again, and bade them good night.

I knew now that I was at "Putney's," a ford on the Pamunkey, and an hour later I came in sight of the ship-lights at White House, and heard the steaming of tugs and draught-boats, going and coming by night. I hitched my horse to a tree, pilfered some hay and fodder from two or three nags tied adjacent, and picked my way across a gangway, several barge-decks, and a floating landing, to the mail steamer that lay outside. Her deck and cabin were filled with people, stretched lengthwise and cross-

wise, tangled, grouped, and snoring, but all apparently fast
asleep. I coolly took a blanket from a man that looked as
though he did not need it, and wrapped myself cosily
under a bench in a corner. The cabin light flared dimly,
half irradiating the forms below, and the boat heaved a
little on the river-swells. The night was cold, the floor hard,
and I almost dead with fatigue. But what of that! I felt the
newspapers in my breast pocket, and knew that the mail
could not leave me in the morning. Blessed be the newsgatherer's sleep! I think he earned it.

It was very pleasant, at dawn, to receive the congratula-
tions of our agent, with whom I breakfasted, and to whom
I consigned a hastily written letter and all the Richmond
papers of the preceding day. He was a shrewd, sanguine,
middle-aged man, of large experience and good standing
in our establishment. He was sent through the South at
the beginning of the Rebellion, and introduced into all
public bodies and social circles, that he might fathom the
designs of Secession, and comprehend its spirit. Afterward
he accompanied the Hatteras and Port Royal expeditions,
and witnessed those celebrated bombardments. Such a
thorough individual abnegation I never knew. He was a
part of the establishment, body and soul. He agreed with
its politics, adhered to all its policies, defended it, upheld
it, revered it. The Federal Government was, to his eye,
merely an adjunct of the paper. Battles and sieges were
simply occurrences for its columns. Good men, brave men,
bad men, died to give it obituaries. The whole world was
to him a reporter's district, and all human mutations plain
matters of news. I hardly think that any city, other than
New York, contains such characters. The journals there are
full of fever, and the profession of journalism is a disease.

He cashed me a draft for a hundred dollars, and I filled
my saddle-bags with smoking-tobacco, spirits, a meer-
schaum pipe, packages of sardines, a box of cigars, and
some cheap publications. Then we adjourned to the quay,
where the steamer was taking in mails, freight, and passengers. The papers were in his side-pocket, and he was
about to commit them to a steward for transmission to

Fortress Monroe, when my name was called from the strand by a young mounted officer, connected with one of the staffs of my division. I thought that he wished to exchange salutations or make some inquiries, and tripped to his side.

"General McClellan wants those newspapers that you obtained at Hanover yesterday!"

A thunderbolt would not have more transfixed me. I could not speak for a moment. Finally, I stammered that they were out of my possession.

"Then, sir, I arrest you, by order of General McClellan. Get your horse!"

"Stop!" said I, agitatedly, "—it may not be too late. I can recover them yet. Here is our agent—I gave them to him."

I turned, at the word, to the landing where he stood a moment before. To my dismay, he had disappeared.

"This is some frivolous pretext to escape," said the Lieutenant; "you correspondents are slippery fellows, but I shall take care that you do not play any pranks with me. The General is irritated already, and if you prevaricate relative to those papers he may make a signal example of you."

I begged to be allowed to look for ——; but he answered cunningly, that I had better mount and ride on. An acquaintance of mine here interfered, and testified to the existency of the agent and his probable connection with the journals. Pale, flurried, excited, I started to discover him, the Lieutenant following me closely meantime. We entered every booth and tent, went from craft to craft, sought among the thick clusters of people, and even at the Commissary's and Quartermaster's pounds, that lay some distance up the railroad.

"I am sorry for you, old fellow," said the Lieutenant, "but your accomplice has probably escaped. It's very sneaking of him, as it makes it harder for you; but I have no authority to deal with him, though I shall take care to report his conduct at headquarters."

I found that the Lieutenant was greatly gratified with
the duty entrusted to him. He had been at the cavalry
quarters on the return of the scouting party, and had overheard the Major muttering something as to McClellan's
displeasure at receiving no Richmond journals. The Major
had added that one of the correspondents took them to
White House, and, mentioning me by name, this young
and aspiring satellite had blurted out that he knew me,
and could doubtless overtake me at the mail-boat in the
morning. The Commanding General authorized him to
arrest me *with the papers,* and report at headquarters.
This was then a journey to recommend him to authority,
and it involved no personal danger. I was not so intimi-
dated that I failed to see how the Lieutenant would lose
his gayest feather by failing to recover the journals, and
I dexterously insinuated that it would be well to recom-
mence the search. This time we were successful. The
shrewd, sanguine, middle-aged man was coolly contem-
plating the river from an outside barge, concealed from
the shore by piled boxes of ammunition. He was reading
a phonetic pamphlet, and appeared to take his apprehen-
sion as a pleasant morning call. I caught one meaning
glance, however, that satisfied me how clearly he understood the case.

"Ha! Townsend," said he, smilingly, "back already?
I thought we had lost you. One of your military friends?
Good-day, Lieutenant."

"I am under arrest, my boy," said I, "and you will much
aggravate General McClellan, if you do not consign those
Richmond journals to his deputy here."

"Under arrest? You surprise me! I am sorry, Lieutenant, that you have had so fatiguing a ride, but the fact is,
those papers have gone down the river. If the General is
not in a great hurry, he will see their columns reproduced
by us in a few days."

"How did they go?" said the Lieutenant, with an oath;
"if by the mail-boat I will have General Van Vliet despatch
a tug to overhaul her."

"I am very sorry again," said the bland civilian, smoothing his hands: "but they went by the *South America* at a much earlier hour."

I looked appealingly to him; the satellite stared down the river perplexedly, but suddenly his eye fell upon something that absorbed it; and he turned like a madman to ——.

"By —— sir, you are lying to me! There is the *South America* moored to a barge, and her steam is not up!"

"Those words are utterly uncalled for," said the agent—"but you cannot irritate me, my dear sir! I know that youth is hot—particularly military youth yet inexperienced; and therefore I pardon you. I made a mistake. It was not the *South America*, it was—it was—upon my word I cannot recall the name!"

"You do not mean to!" thundered the young Ajax, to whose vanity ——'s speech had been gall; "my powers are discretionary: I arrest you in the name of General McClellan."

"Indeed! Be sure you understand your orders! It isn't probable that such a fiery blade is allowed much discretionary margin. The General himself would not assume such airs. Why don't you shoot me? It might contribute to your promotion, and that is, no doubt, your object. I knew General McClellan very well. He is a personal friend of mine."

His manner was so self-possessed, his tone so cutting, that the young man of fustian—whose name was Kenty—fingered his sword hilt, and foamed at the lips.

"March on," said he—"I will report this insolence word for word."

He motioned us to the quay; we preceded him. The sanguine gentleman keeping up a running fire of malevolent sarcasm.

"Stop!" said he quietly, as we reached his tent—"I have not sent them at all. They are here. And you have made all this exhibition of yourself for nothing. I am the better soldier, you see. You are a drummer-boy, not an officer. Take off your shoulder-bars, and go to school again."

He disappeared a minute, returned with two journals, and looking at me, meaningly, turned to their titles.

"Let me see!" he said, smoothly—"Richmond *Examiner,* May 28, Richmond *Enquirer,* May 22. There! You have them! Go in peace! Give my respects to General Mc-Clellan! Townsend, old fellow, you have done your full duty. Don't let this young person frighten you. Good-bye."

He gave me his hand, with a sinister glance, and left something in my palm when his own was withdrawn. I examined it hastily when I girt up my saddle. It said: *"Your budget got off safe, old fellow."* He had given Kenty some old journals that were of no value to anybody. When we were mounted and about to start, the Lieutenant looked witheringly upon his persecutor—

"Allow me to say, sir," he exclaimed, "that you are the most unblushing liar I ever knew."

"Thank you, kindly," said ——, taking off his hat, "you do me honor!"

Our route was silent and weary enough. The young man at my side, unconscious of his wily antagonist's deception, boasted for some time that he had attained his purposes. As I could not undeceive him, I held my tongue; but feared that when this trick should be made manifest, the vengeance would fall on me alone. I heartily wished the unlucky papers at the bottom of the sea. To gratify an adventurous whim, and obtain a day's popularity at New York, I had exposed my life, crippled my nag, and was now to be disgraced and punished. What might or might not befall me, I gloomily debated. The least penalty would be expulsion from the army; but imprisonment till the close of the war was a favorite amusement with the War Office. How my newspaper connection would be embarrassed was a more grievous inquiry. It stung me to think that I had blundered twice on the very threshold of my career. Was I not acquiring a reputation for rashness that would hinder all future promotion and cast me from the courts of the press? Here the iron entered into my soul; for be it known, I loved Bohemia! This roving commission, these vagabond habits, this life in the open air among the armies, the white tents, the cannon, and the drums, they were my elysium, my heart! But to be driven away, as one who had broken his trust, forfeited favor and confidence, and that too on the eve of grand events, was something that would embitter my existence.

We passed the familiar objects that I had so often buoy-antly beheld—deserted encampments, cross-roads, rills, farm houses, fields, and at last came to Daker's. I called out to them, and explained my woeful circumstances with rueful conciseness.

It was growing dark when we came to general head-quarters, two miles beyond Gaines's Mill. The tents were scattered over the surface of a hill, and most of them were illumined by candles.

The Lieutenant gave our horses to an orderly, and led the way through two outer circles of wall-tents, between which and the inner circle, guards were pacing, to deny all vulgar ingress.

A staff officer took in our names, and directly returned with the reply of "Pass in!" We were now in the sacred enclosure, secured by flaming swords. Four tents stood in a row, allotted respectively to the Chief of Staff, the Adjutant-General, the telegraph operators, and the select staff officers. Just behind them, embowered by a covering of cedar boughs, stood the tent of General McClellan. Close by, from an open plot or area of ground, towered a pine trunk, floating the national flag. Lights burned in three of the tents; low voices, as of subdued conversation, were heard from the first.

A little flutter of my heart, a drawing aside of canvas, two steps, an uncovering, and a bow—I stood at my tribunal! A couple of candles were placed upon a table, whereat sat a fine specimen of man, with kindly features, dark, grayish, flowing hair, and slight marks of years upon his full, purplish face. He looked to be a well-to-do citizen, whose success had taught him sedentary convivialities. A fuming cigar lay before him; some empty champagne bot-tles sat upon a pine desk; tumblers and a decanter rested upon a camp-stool; a bucket, filled with water and a great block of ice, was visible under the table. Five other gentle-men, each with a star in his shoulder-bar, were dispersed upon chairs and along a camp bedside. The tall, angular, dignified gentleman with compressed lips and a "charac-ter" nose, was General William F. Barry, Chief of Artillery. The lithe, severe, gristly, sanguine person, whose eyes flashed even in repose, was General George Stoneman, Chief of Cavalry. The large, sleepy-eyed, lympathic, elderly man, clad in dark, civil gray, whose ears turned up habitually as from deafness, was Prince de Joinville, son of Louis Philippe, King of France. The little man with red hair and beard, who moved quickly and who spoke sharply, was Seth Williams, Adjutant-General. The stout person with florid face, large, blue eyes, and white, straight hair, was General Van Vliet, Quartermaster-General. And the man at the table was General Marcy, father-in-law to McClellan, and Executive Officer of the army.

Maps, papers, books, and luggage lay around the room; all the gentlemen were smoking and wine sparkled in most of the glasses. Some swords were lying upon the floor, a pair of spurs glistened by the bed, and three of the officers had their feet in the air.

"What is it you wish, Lieutenant?" said General Marcy, gravely.

The boor in uniform at my side related his errand and order, gave the particulars of my arrest, declaimed against our agent, and submitted the journals. He told his story stammeringly, and I heard one of the officers in the back-ground mutter contemptuously when he had finished.

"Were you aware of the order prohibiting correspond-ents from keeping with the advance?" said the General, looking up.

"I had not been notified from headquarters. I have been with the army only a week."

"You knew that you had no business upon scouts, for-ages, or reconnoissances; why did you go?"

"I went by invitation."

"Who invited you?"

"I would prefer not to state, since it would do him an injury."

Here the voices in the background muttered, as I thought, applaudingly. Gaining confidence as I proceeded, I spoke more boldly—

"I am sure I regret that I have disobeyed any order of General McClellan's; but there can nothing occur in the rear of an army. Obedience, in this case, would be indolence and incompetence; for only the reliable would stay behind and the reckless go ahead. If I am accredited here as a correspondent, I must keep up with the events. And the rivalries of our tribe, General, are so many, that the best of us sometimes forget what is right for what is expedient. I hope that General McClellan will pass by this offence."

He heard my rambling defence quietly, excused the Lieutenant, and whistled for an orderly.

"I don't think that you meant to offend General McClellan," he said, "but he wishes you to be detained. Give me your pass. Orderly, take this gentleman to General Porter, and tell him to treat him kindly. Good night."

When we got outside of the tent, I slipped a silver half-dollar into the orderly's hand, and asked him if he understood the General's final remark. He said, in reply, that I was directed to be treated with courtesy, kindness, and care, and asked me, in conclusion, if there were any adjectives that might intensify the recommendation. When we came to General Andrew Porter, the Povost-Marshal, however, he pooh-poohed the qualifications, and said that *his* business was merely to put me under surveillance. This unamiable man ordered me to be taken to Major Willard, the deputy Provost, whose tent we found after a long search. The Major was absent, but some young officers of his mess were taking supper at his table, and with these I at once engaged in conversation.

I knew that if I was to be spared an immersion in the common guardhouse, with drunkards, deserters, and prisoners of war, I must win the favor of these men. I gave them the story of my arrest, spoke lightly of the offence

and jestingly of the punishment, and, in fact, so improved
my cause that, when the Major appeared, and the Sergeant consigned me to his custody, one of the young officers took him aside, and, I am sure, said some good words
in my favor.

The Major was a bronzed, indurated gentleman, scrupu-
lously attired, and courteously stern. He looked at me
twice or thrice, to my confusion; for I was dusty, wan,
and running over with perspiration. His first remark had,
naturally, reference to the lavatory, and, so far as my face
and hair were concerned, I was soon rejuvenated. I found
on my return to the tent a clean plate and a cup of steaming coffee placed for me, and I ate with a full heart though
pleading covertly the while. When I had done, and the
tent became deserted by all save him and me, he said,
simply—

"What am I to do with you, Mr. Townsend?"

"Treat me as a gentleman, I hope, Major."

"We have but one place of confinement," said he, "the
guardhouse; but I am loth to send you there. Light your
pipe, and I will think the matter over."

He took a turn in front, consulted with some of his associates, and directly returning, said that I was to be quartered in his office-tent, adjoining. A horror being thus lifted
from my mind, I heard with sincere interest many revela-
tions of his military career. He had been a common soldier in the Mexican War, and had fought his way, step by
step, to repeated commissions. He had garrisoned Fort
Yuma, and other posts on the far plains, and at the beginning of the war was tendered a volunteer brigade, which
he modestly declined. His tastes were refined, and a warm
fancy, approaching poetry, enhanced his personal reminiscences. His face softened, his eyes grew milder, his large,
commanding mouth relaxed—he was young again, living
his adventures over. We talked thus till almost midnight,
when two regulars appeared in front—stiff, ramrodish figures, that came to a jerking "present," tapped their caps
with two fingers, and said, explosively: "Sergeant of
Guard, Number Five!"

The Major rose, gave me his hand, and said that I would find a candle in my tent, with waterproof and blankets on the ground. I was to give myself no concern about the nag, and might, if I chose, sit for an hour to write, but must, on no account, attempt to leave the canvas, for the guard would instantly shoot me down. The guard in question had a *doppel-ganger*—counterpart of himself in inflexibility—and both were appendages of their muskets. He was not probably a sentient being, certainly not a conversational one. He knew the length of a stride, and the manual of bayonet exercise, but was, during his natural life, a blind idolater of a deity called "Orders." The said Orders, for the present evening, were walking, not talking, and he was dumb to all conciliatory words. He took a position at one end of my tent, and his double at the other end. They carried their muskets at "support arms," and paced up and down, measuredly, like two cloaked and solemn ghosts. I wrapped myself in the damp blankets, and slept through the bangs of four or five court-martials and several executions. At three o'clock, they changed ramrods—the old doppel-gangers going away, and two new ones fulfilling their functions.

CHAPTER IX

After the Victory

THE TWO ramrods were still pacing to and fro, when I aroused in the gray of the morning; but they looked very misty and moist, as if they were impalpables that were shortly to evaporate. The Major poked his head between the flaps at eight o'clock, and said that breakfast was ready; but the ramrod nearest me kept vigilantly alongside, and I thought he had been invited also. The other ramrod guarded the empty tent, and I think that he believed me a doppelganger likewise.

I wondered what was to be done with me, as the hours slipped rapidly by. The guards were relieved again at ten o'clock, and quartermaster's men commenced to take down the tents. Camps were to be moved, and I inquired solicitously if I was to be moved also. The Major replied that prisoners were commonly made to walk along the road, escorted by horsemen, and I imagined, with dread, the companionship of Negroes, estrays, ragged Confederates, and such folk, while the whole army should witness my degradation. Finally, all the tents were lifted and packed in wagons, as well as the furniture. I adhered to a stool, at which the teamster looked wistfully, and the implacable sentinels walked to and fro. A rumor became current among the private soldiers, that I was the nephew of the Southern General Lee, whose wife had been meantime captured at Hanover Court House. Curious groups sauntered around me, and talked behind their hands. One man was overheard to say that I had fought desperately, and covered myself with glory, and another thought that I favored my uncle somewhat, and might succeed to his military virtues.

"I guess I'll take that cheer, if you ain't got no objection," said the teamster, and he slung it into the wagon. What to do now troubled me materially; but one of the soldiers brought a piece of rail, and I "squatted" lugubriously on the turf.

"If you ever get to Richmond," said I, "you shall be considerately treated." (Profound sensation.)

"Thankee!" replied the man, touching his cap; "but I'm werry well pleased *out* o' Richmond, Captain."

Here the Major was seen approaching, a humorous smile playing about his eyes.

"You are discharged," said he; "General Marcy will return your pass, and perhaps your papers."

I wrung his hand with indescribable relief, and he sent the "ramrod" on guard to saddle my horse. In a few minutes, I was mounted again, much to the surprise of the observers of young Lee, and directly I stood before the kindly Chief of Staff. At my request, he wrote a note to the division commander, specifying my good behavior, and restoring to me all privileges and immunities. He said nothing whatever as to the mistake in the papers, and told me that, on special occasions, I might keep with advances, by procuring an extraordinary pass at headquarters. In short, my arrest conduced greatly to my efficiency. I invariably carried my Richmond despatches to General Marcy, thereafter, and, if there was information of a legitimate description, he gave me the benefit of it.

My own brigade lay at Dr. Gaines's house, during this time, and we did not lack for excitement. Just behind the house lay several batteries of rifled guns, and these threw shells at hourly intervals, at certain Confederate batteries across the river. The distance was two miles or less; but the firing was generally wretched. Crowds of soldiers gathered around, to watch the practice, and they threw up their hats applaudingly at successful hits. Occasionally a great round shot would bound up the hill, and a boy, one day, seeing one of these spent balls rolling along the

ground, put out his foot to stop it, but shattered his leg so
dreadfully that it had to be amputated. Dr. Gaines was a
rich, aristocratic, and indolent old Virginian, whose
stables, summerhouses, orchards, and Negro quarters were
the finest in their district. The shooting so annoyed him
that he used to resort to the cellar; several shots passed
through his roof, and one of the chimneys was knocked
off. His family carriages were five in number, and as his
stables were turned into hospitals, these were all hauled
into his lawn, where their obsolete trimmings and queer
shape constantly amused the soldiers. About this time I
became acquainted with some officers of the 5th Maine
regiment, and by permission, accompanied them to
Mechanicsville. I was here, on the afternoon of Tuesday,
May 27, when the battle of Hanover Court House was
fought. We heard the rapid growl of guns, and continuous
volleys of musketry, though the place was fourteen miles
distant. At evening, a report was current that the Federals
had gained a great victory, and captured seven hundred
prisoners. The truth of this was established next morning;
for detachments of prisoners were from time to time
brought in, and the ambulances came to camp, laden with
the wounded. I took this opportunity of observing the
Confederate soldiers, as they lay at the provost quarters,
in a roped pen, perhaps one hundred rods square.

It was evening, as I hitched my horse to a stake near-by,
and pressed up to the receptacle for the unfortunates.
Sentries enclosed the pen, walking to-and-fro with loaded
muskets; a throng of officers and soldiers had assembled to
gratify their curiosity; and new detachments of captives
came in hourly, encircled by sabremen, the Southerners
being disarmed and on foot. The scene within the area was
ludicrously moving. It reminded me of the witch-scene
in *Macbeth*, or pictures of brigands or Bohemian gypsies
at rendezvous, not less than five hundred men, in motley,
ragged costumes, with long hair, and lean, wild, haggard
faces, were gathered in groups or in pairs, around some
fagot fires. In the growing darkness their expressions were
imperfectly visible; but I could see that most of them

were weary, and hungry, and all were depressed and ashamed. Some were wrapped in blankets of rag-carpet, and others wore shoes of rough, untanned hide. Others were without either shoes or jackets, and their heads were bound with red handkerchiefs. Some appeared in red shirts; some in stiff beaver hats; some were attired in shreds and patches of cloth; and a few wore the soiled garments of citizen gentlemen; but the mass adhered to homespun suits of gray, or "butternut," and the coarse blue kersey common to slaves. In places I caught glimpses of red Zouave breeches and leggings; blue Federal caps, Federal buttons, or Federal blouses; these were the spoils of anterior battles, and had been stripped from the slain. Most of the captives were of the appearances denominated "scraggy" or "knotty." They were brown, brawny, and wiry, and their countenances were intense, fierce, and animal. They came from North Carolina, the poorest and least enterprising Southern State, and ignorance, with its attendant virtues, were the common facial manifestations. Some lay on the bare ground, fast asleep; others chatted nervously as if doubtful of their future treatment; a few were boisterous, and anxious to beg tobacco or coffee from idle Federals; the rest—and they comprehended the greater number—were silent, sullen, and vindictive. They met curiosity with scorn, and spite with imprecations. A child—not more than four years of age, I think—sat sleeping in a corner upon an older comrade's lap. A gray-bearded pard was staunching a gash in his cheek with the tail of his coat. A fine-looking young fellow sat with his face in his hands, as if his heart were far off, and he wished to shut out this bitter scene. In a corner, lying morosely apart, were a major, three captains, and three lieutenants—young athletic fellows, dressed in rich gray cassimere, trimmed with black, and wearing soft black hats adorned with black ostrich-feathers. Their spurs were strapped upon elegantly fitting boots, and they looked as far above the needy, seedy privates, as lords above their vassals.

After a time, couples and squads of the prisoners were

marched off to cut and carry some firewood and water, for the use of their pen, and then each Confederate received coffee, pork, and crackers; they were obliged to prepare their own meals, but some were so hungry that they gnawed the raw pork, like beasts of prey. Those who were not provided with blankets, shivered through the night, though the rain was falling, and the succession of choking coughs that ran through the ranks, told how ill they could afford the exposure. Major Willard had charge of these men, and he sent a young officer to get me admittance to the pen, that I might speak with them.

"Good evening, Major," I said, to the ranking Confederate officer, and extended my hand. He shook it, embarrassedly, and ran me over with his eye, as if to learn my avocation. "Can I obtain any facts from you," I continued, "as to the battle of Hanover?"

"Fuh what puhpose?" he said, in his strong Southern dialect.

"For publication, sir."

He sat up at once, and said that he should be happy to tell me anything that would not be a violation of military honor. I asked him, therefore, the Confederate Commandant at Hanover, the number of brigades, regiments, and batteries engaged, the disposition of forces, the character of the battle, and the losses, so far as he knew, upon his own side. Much of this he revealed, but unguardedly let out other matters that direct inquiry could not have discovered. I took notes of the legitimate passages, trusting to memory for the rest; and think that I possessed his whole stock of information, in the course of an hour's manœuvring. It seemed that General Lawrence Branch, formerly a member of the Federal Congress, had been sent with some thousands of Carolina troops across the upper Chickahominy, to see if it would not be possible to turn the Federal right, and cut off one of its brigades; but a stronger Federal reconnoissance had gone northward the day before, and discovering Branch's camp-fires, sent, during the night, for reinforcements. In the end, the "North State" volunteers were routed, their cannon silenced or broken, and seven hundred of their number captured. The Federals lost a large number of men killed, and the wounded upon both sides were numerous.

The Confederate Major was of the class referred to in polite American parlance, as a "blatherskite." He boasted after the manner of his fellow-citizens from the county of "Bunkum," but nevertheless feared and trembled, to the manifest disgust of one of the young captains.

"Majuh!" said this young man, "what you doin' thah! That fellow's makin' notes of all your slack; keep your tongue! aftah awhile you'll tell the nombah of the foces! Don't you s'pose he'll prent it all?"

The Major had, in fact, been telling me how many regiments the "old Nawth State, suh," had furnished to the "suhvice," and I had the names of some thirty colonels, in order. The young Captain gave me a sketch of General Branch, and was anxious that I should publish something in extenuation of North Carolina valor.

"We have lost mo' men," said he, "than any otha' Commonwealth; but these Vuhginians, whose soil by ——! suh, we defend suh! Yes, suh! whose soil we defend; these Vuhginians, stigmatize us as cowads! *We*, suh! yes suh, *we*, that nevah wanted to leave the Union,—*we cowads!* Look at ou' blood, suh, ou' blood! That's it, by ——! look at that! shed on every field of the ole Dominion,—killed, muhdud, captued, crippled! We *cowads!* I want you prent that!"

I was able to give each of the officers a drop of whiskey from my flask, and I never saw men drink so thirstily. Their hands and lips trembled as they took it, and their eyes shone like lunacy, as the hot drops sank to the cold vitals, and pricked the frozen blood. Mingling with the privates, I stirred up some native specimens of patriotism, that appeared to be in great doubt as to the causes and ends of the war. They were very much in the political condition of a short, thick, sententious man, in blue drilling breeches, who said—

"Damn the country! What's to be done with *us?*"

One person said that he enlisted for the honor of his

family, that "fit in the American Revolution"; and another
came out to "hev a squint et the fightin'." Several were
Northern and foreign lads, that were working on Carolina
railroads, and could not leave the section, and some la-
bored under the impression that they were to have a
"slice" of land and a "nigger," in the event of Southern independence. A few comprehended the spirit of the contest,
and took up arms from principle; a few, also, declared
their enmity to "Yankee institutions," and had seized the
occasion to "polish them off," and "give them a ropein' in";
but many said it was "dull in our deestreeks, an' the niggers was runnin' away, so I thought I'ud jine the foces."
The great mass said that they never contemplated "this
box," or "this fix," or "these suckemstances," and all wanted
the war to close, that they might return to their families.
Indeed, my romantic ideas of rebellion were ruthlessly
profaned and dissipated. I knew that there was much selfishness, peculation, and "Hessianism" in the Federal lines,
but I had imagined a lofty patriotism, a dignified purpose,
and an inflexible love of personal liberty among the Confederates. Yet here were men who knew little of the principles for which they staked their lives; who enlisted from
the commonest motives of convenience, whim, pelf, adventure, and foray; and who repented, after their first
misfortune, with the salt rheum in their eyes. I think that
all "great uprisings" resolve to this complexion. With due
reverence for my own ancestry, I think that they sometimes stooped from greatness to littleness. I must confess
that certain admissions in my revolutionary textbook are
much clearer, now that I have followed a campaign. And
if, as I had proposed, I could have witnessed the further
fortunes of the illustrious Garibaldi, I think that some of
his compatriots would have been found equally inconsistent. Let no man believe that the noblest cause is fought
out alone by the unerring motives of duty and devotion.
The masses are never so constant. They cannot appreciate
an abstraction, however divine. Any of the gentlemen in
question would have preferred their biscuit and fat pork
before the political enfranchisement of the whole world!

I rode across the fields to the Hogan, Curtis, and Gaines mansions; for some of the wounded had meantime been deposited in each of them. All the cow-houses, wagon-sheds, hay-barracks, hen-coops, Negro cabins, and barns were turned into hospitals. The floors were littered with "corn-shucks" and fodder; and the maimed, gashed, and dying lay confusedly together. A few, slightly wounded, stood at windows, relating incidents of the battle; but at the doors sentries stood with crossed muskets, to keep out idlers and gossips. The mention of my vocation was an "open sesame," and I went unrestrained into all the largest hospitals. In the first of these an amputation was being performed, and at the door lay a little heap of human fingers, feet, legs and arms. I shall not soon forget the bare-armed surgeons, with bloody instruments, that leaned over the rigid and insensible figure, while the comrades of the subject looked horrifiedly at the scene. The grating of murderous saw drove me into the open air, but in the second hospital which I visited, a wounded man had just expired, and I encountered his body at the threshold. Within, the sickening smell of mortality was almost insupportable, but by degrees I became accustomed to it. The lanterns hanging around the room streamed fitfully upon the red eyes, and half-naked figures. All were looking up, and saying, in pleading monotone: "Is that you, doctor?" Men with their arms in slings went restlessly up and down, smarting with fever. Those who were wounded in the lower extremities, body, or head, lay upon their backs, tossing even in sleep. They listened peevishly to the wind whistling through the chinks of the barn. They followed one with their rolling eyes. They turned away from the lantern, for it seemed to sear them. Soldiers sat by the severely wounded, laving their sores with water. In many wounds the balls still remained, and the discolored flesh was swollen unnaturally. There were some who had been shot in the bowels, and now and then they were frightfully convulsed, breaking into shrieks and shouts. Some of them iterated a single word, as, "doctor," or "help," or "God," or "oh!" commencing with a loud spasmodic cry,

and continuing the same word till it died away in cadence.
The act of calling seemed to lull the pain. Many were unconscious and lethargic, moving their fingers and lips
mechanically, but never more to open their eyes upon
the light; they were already going through the valley of
the shadow. I think, still, with a shudder, of the faces of
those who were told mercifully that they could not live.
The unutterable agony; the plea for somebody on whom
to call; the longing eyes that poured out prayers; the looking on mortal as if its resources were infinite; the fearful
looking to the immortal as if it were so far off, so implacable, that the dying appeal would be in vain; the open
lips, through which one could almost look at the quaking
heart below; the ghastliness of brow and tangled hair; the
closing pangs; the awful *quietus*. I thought of Parrhasius,
in the poem, as I looked at these things:

> "Gods!
> Could I but paint a dying groan——."

And how the keen eye of West would have turned from
the reeking cockpit of the *Victory*, or the tomb of the Dead
Man Restored, to this old barn, peopled with horrors. I
rambled in and out, learning to look at death, studying
the manifestations of pain—quivering and sickening at
times, but plying my avocation, and jotting the names for
my column of mortalities.

At eleven o'clock there was music along the high-road,
and a general rushing from camps. The victorious regiments were returning from Hanover, under escort, and all
the bands were pealing national airs. As they turned down
the fields toward their old encampments, the several brigades stood under arms to welcome them, and the cheers
were many and vigorous. But the solemn ambulances still
followed after, and the red flag of the hospitals flaunted
bloodily in the blue midnight.

Both the prisoners and the wounded were removed between midnight and morning to White House, and as I
had despatches to forward by the mail-boat, I rode down
in an ambulance that contained six wounded men besides.

The wounded were to be consigned to hospital boats, and forwarded to hospitals in Northern cities, and the prisoners were to be placed in a transport, under guard, and conveyed to Fort Delaware, near Philadelphia.

Ambulances, it may be said, incidentally, are either two-wheeled or four-wheeled. Two-wheeled ambulances are commonly called "hop, step, and jumps." They are so constructed that the forepart is either very high or very low, and may be both at intervals. The wounded occupants may be compelled to ride for hours in these carriages, with their heels elevated above their heads, and may finally be shaken out, or have their bones broken by the terrible jolting. The four-wheeled ambulances are built in shelves, or compartments, but the wounded are in danger of being smothered in them. It was in one of these latter that I rode, sitting with the driver. We had four horses, but were thrice "swamped" on the road, and had to take out the wounded men once, till we could start the wheels. Two of these men were wounded in the face, one of them having his nose completely severed, and the other having a fragment of his jaw knocked out. A third had received a ball among the thews and muscles behind his knee, and his whole body appeared to be paralyzed. Two were wounded in the shoulders, and the sixth was shot in the breast, and was believed to be injured inwardly, as he spat blood, and suffered almost the pain of death. The ride with these men, over twenty miles of hilly, woody country, was like one of Dante's excursions into the Shades. In the awful stillness of the dark pines, their screams frightened the hooting owls, and the whirring insects in the leaves and tree-tops quieted their songs. They heard the gurgle of the rills, and called aloud for water to quench their insatiate thirst. One of them sang a shrill, fierce, fiendish ballad, in an interval of relief, but plunged, at a sudden relapse, into prayers and curses. We heard them groaning to themselves, as we sat in front, and one man, it seemed, was quite out of his mind. These were the outward manifestations; but what chords trembled and smarted within, we could only guess. What regrets for good resolves unfulfilled, and remorse for years misspent, made hideous these sore and panting hearts? The moonlight pierced through the thick foliage of the wood, and streamed into our faces, like invitations to a better life. But the crippled and bleeding could not see or feel it— buried in the shelves of the ambulance.

CHAPTER X

Balloon Battles

———————

THE aeronaut of the Army of the Potomac was Mr. S. T. C. Lowe; he had made seven thousand ascensions, and his army companion was invariably either an artist, a correspondent, or a telegrapher.

A minute insulated wire reached from the car to headquarters, and McClellan was thus informed of all that could be seen within the Confederate works. Sometimes they remained aloft for hours, making observations with powerful glasses, and once or twice the enemy tested their distance with shell.

On the 13th of April, the Confederates had sent up a balloon, the first they had employed, at which Lowe was infinitely amused. He said that it had neither shape nor buoyancy, and predicted that it would burst or fall apart after a week. It certainly occurred that, after a few fitful appearances, the stranger was seen no more, till, on the 28th of June, it floated, like a thing of omen, over the spires of Richmond. At that time the Federals were in full retreat, and all the acres were covered with their dead.

On the 11th of April, at five o'clock, an event at once amusing and thrilling had occurred at our quarters. The commander-in-chief had appointed his personal and confidential friend, General Fitz John Porter, to conduct the siege of Yorktown. Porter was a polite, soldierly gentleman, and a native of New Hampshire who had been in the regular army since early manhood. He fought gallantly in the Mexican War, being thrice promoted and once seriously wounded, and he was now forty years of age—hand-

some, enthusiastic, ambitious, and popular. He made frequent ascensions with Lowe, and learned to go aloft alone.
One day he ascended thrice, and finally seemed as cosily
at home in the firmament as upon the solid earth. It is
needless to say that he grew careless, and on this particular
morning leaped into the car and demanded the cables to
be let out with all speed. I saw with some surprise that the
flurried assistants were sending up the great straining canvas with a single rope attached. The enormous bag was
only partially inflated, and the loose folds opened and shut
with a crack like that of a musket. Noisily, fitfully, the
yellow mass rose into the sky, the basket rocking like a
feather in the zephyr; and just as I turned aside to speak
to a comrade, a sound came from overhead, like the explosion of a shell, and something striking me across the face
laid me flat upon the ground.

Half blind and stunned, I staggered to my feet, but the
air seemed full of cries and curses. Opening my eyes ruefully, I saw all faces turned upwards, and when I looked
above, the balloon was adrift.

The treacherous cable, rotted with vitriol, had snapped
in twain; one fragment had been the cause of my downfall,
and the other trailed, like a great entrail, from the reced-
ing car, where Fitz John Porter was bounding upward
upon a Pegasus that he could neither check nor direct.

The whole army was agitated by the unwonted occurrence. From battery No. 1, on the brink of the York, to
the mouth of Warwick River, every soldier and officer was
absorbed. Far within the Confederate lines the confusion
extended. We heard the enemy's alarm-guns, and directly
the signal flags were waving up and down our front.

The General appeared directly over the edge of the car.
He was tossing his hands frightenedly, and shouting something that we could not comprehend.

"O—pen—the—valve!" called Lowe, in his shrill tones;
"climb—to—the—netting—and—reach—the—valve—rope."

"The valve!—the valve!" repeated a multitude of
tongues, and all gazed with thrilling interest at the retreat-

ing hulk that still kept straight upward, swerving neither to the east nor the west.

It was a weird spectacle—that frail, fading oval, gliding against the sky, floating in the serene azure, the little vessel swinging silently beneath, and a hundred thousand martial men watching the loss of their brother in arms, but powerless to relieve or recover him. Had Fitz John Porter been drifting down the rapids of Niagara, he could not have been so far from human assistance. But we saw him directly, no bigger than a child's toy, clambering up the netting and reaching for the cord.

"He can't do it," muttered a man beside me; "the wind blows the valve-rope to and fro, and only a spry, cool-headed fellow can catch it."

We saw the General descend, and appearing again over the edge of the basket, he seemed to be motioning to the breathless hordes below the story of his failure. Then he dropped out of sight, and when we next saw him, he was reconnoitring the Confederate works through a long black spy-glass. A great laugh went up and down the lines as this cool procedure was observed, and then a cheer of applause ran from group to group. For a moment it was doubtful that the balloon would float in either direction; it seemed to falter, like an irresolute being, and moved reluctantly southeastward, towards Fortress Monroe. A huzza, half uttered, quivered on every lip. All eyes glistened, and some were dim with tears of joy. But the wayward canvas now turned due westward, and was blown rapidly toward the Confederate works. Its course was fitfully direct, and the wind seemed to veer often, as if contrary currents, conscious of the opportunity, were struggling for the possession of the daring navigator. The south wind held mastery for awhile, and the balloon passed the Federal front amid a howl of despair from the soldiery. It kept right on, over sharpshooters, rifle-pits, and outworks, and finally passed, as if to deliver up its freight, directly over the heights of Yorktown. The cool courage, either of heroism or despair, had seized upon Fitz John Porter. He turned his black glass upon the ramparts and masked cannon below, upon the remote camps, upon the beleaguered town, upon the guns of Gloucester Point, and upon distant Norfolk. Had he been reconnoitring from a secure perch at the tip of the moon, he could not have been more vigilant, and the Confederates probably thought this some Yankee device to peer into their sanctuary in despite of ball or shell. None of their great guns could be brought to bear upon the balloon; but there were some discharges of musketry that appeared to have no effect, and finally even these demonstrations ceased. Both armies in solemn silence were gazing aloft, while the imperturbable mariner continued to spy out the land.

The sun was now rising behind us, and roseate rays struggled up to the zenith, like the arcs made by showery bombs. They threw a hazy atmosphere upon the balloon, and the light shone through the network like the sun through the ribs of the skeleton ship in the *Ancient Mariner*. Then, as all looked agape, the air-craft "plunged, and tacked, and veered," and drifted rapidly toward the Federal lines again.

The allelujah that now went up shook the spheres, and when he had regained our camp limits, the General was seen clambering up again to clutch the valve-rope. This time he was successful, and the balloon fell like a stone, so that all hearts once more leaped up, and the cheers were hushed. Cavalry rode pell-mell from several directions, to reach the place of descent, and the General's personal staff galloped past me like the wind, to be the first at his debarkation. I followed the throng of soldiery with due haste, and came up to the horsemen in a few minutes. The balloon had struck a canvas tent with great violence, felling it as by a bolt, and the General, unharmed, had disentangled himself from innumerable folds of oiled canvas, and was now the cynosure of an immense group of people. While the officers shook his hands, the rabble bawled their satisfaction in hurrahs, and a band of music marching up directly, the throng on foot and horse gave him a vociferous escort to his quarters.

Five miles east of Richmond, in the middle of May, we

found the balloon already partially inflated, resting behind a ploughed hill that formed one of a ridge or chain of hills, bordering the Chickahominy. The stream was only a half-mile distant, but the balloon was sheltered from observation by reason of its position in the hollow.

Heretofore the ascensions had been made from remote places, for there was good reason to believe that batteries lined the opposite hills; but now, for the first time, Lowe intended to make an ascent whereby he could look into Richmond, count the forts encircling it, and note the number and position of the camps that intervened. The balloon was named the "Constitution," and looked like a semi-distended boa-constrictor, as it flapped with a jerking sound and shook its oiled and painted folds. It was anchored to the ground by stout ropes affixed to stakes, and also by sand-bags which hooked to its netting. The basket lay alongside; the generators were contained in blue wooden wagons, marked "U.S."; and the gas was fed to the balloon through rubber and metallic pipes. A tent or two, a quantity of vitriol in green and wicker carboys, some horses and transportation teams, and several men that assisted the inflation, were the only objects to be remarked. As some time was to transpire before the arrangements were completed, I resorted to one of the tents and took a comfortable nap. The "Professor" aroused me at three o'clock, when I found the canvas straining its bonds, and emitting a hollow sound, as of escaping gas. The basket was made fast directly; the telescopes tossed into place; the Professor climbed to the side, holding by the network; and I coiled up in a rope at the bottom.

"Stand by your cables," he said, and the bags of ballast were at once cut away. Twelve men took each a rope in hand, and played out slowly, letting us glide gently upward. The earth seemed to be falling away, and we poised motionless in the blue ether. The tree-tops sank downward, the hills dropped noiselessly through space, and directly the Chickahominy was visible beyond us, winding like a ribbon of silver through the ridgy landscape.

Far and wide stretched the Federal camps. We saw

faces turned upwards gazing at our ascent, and heard
clearly, as in a vacuum, the voices of soldiers. At every
second the prospect widened, the belt of horizon enlarged,
remote farmhouses came in view; the earth was like a perfectly flat surface, painted with blue woods, and streaked
with pictures of roads, fields, fences, and streams. As we
climbed higher, the river seemed directly beneath us, the
farms on the opposite bank were plainly discernible, and
Richmond lay only a little way off, enthroned on its many
hills, with the James stretching white and sinuous from its
feet to the horizon. We could see the streets, the suburbs,
the bridges, the outlying roads, nay, the moving masses
of people. The Capitol sat white and colossal on Shockoe
Hill, the dingy buildings of the Tredegar iron works blackened the river-side above, the hovels of Rockets clustered
at the hither limits, and one by one we made out familiar
hotels, public edifices, and vicinities. The fortifications
were revealed in part only, for they took the hue of the
soil, and blended with it; but many camps were plainly
discernible, and by means of the glasses we separated tent
from tent, and hut from hut. The Confederates were seen
running to the cover of the woods, that we might not discover their numbers, but we knew the location of their
camp-fires by the smoke that curled toward us.

A panorama so beautiful would have been rare at any
time, but this was thrice interesting from its past and coming associations. Across those plains the hordes at our feet
were either to advance victoriously, or be driven eastward
with dusty banners and dripping hands. Those white farm-
houses were to be receptacles for the groaning and the
mangled; thousands were to be received beneath the turf
of those pasture fields; and no rod of ground on any side,
should not, sooner or later, smoke with the blood of the
slain.

"Guess I got 'em now, jest where I want 'em," said
Lowe, with a gratified laugh; "jest keep still as you mind
to, and squint your eye through my glass, while I make a
sketch of the roads and the country. Hold hard there, and
anchor fast!" he screamed to the people below. Then he

fell imperturbably to work, sweeping the country with his hawk-eye, and escaping nothing that could contribute to the completeness of his jotting.

We had been but a few minutes thus poised, when close below, from the edge of a timber stretch, puffed a volume of white smoke. A second afterward, the air quivered with the peal of a cannon. A third, and we heard the splitting shriek of a shell, that passed a little to our left, but in exact range, and burst beyond us in the ploughed field, heaving up the clay as it exploded.

"Ha!" said Lowe, "they have got us foul! Haul in the cables—quick!" he shouted, in a fierce tone.

At the same instant, the puff, the report, and the shriek were repeated; but this time the shell burst to our right in mid-air, and scattered fragments around and below us.

"Another shot will do our business," said Lowe, between his teeth; "it isn't a mile, and they have got the range."

Again the puff and the whizzing shock. I closed my eyes, and held my breath hard. The explosion was so close that the pieces of shell seemed driven across my face, and my ears quivered with the sound. I looked at Lowe, to see if he was struck. He had sprung to his feet, and clutched the cordage frantically.

"Are you pulling in there, you men?" he bellowed, with a loud imprecation.

"Puff! bang! whiz-z-z-z! splutter!" broke a third shell, and my heart was wedged in my throat.

I saw at a glimpse the whole bright landscape again. I heard the voices of soldiers below, and saw them running across fields, fences, and ditches, to reach our anchorage. I saw some drummer-boys digging in the field beneath for one of the buried shells. I saw the waving of signal flags, the commotion through the camps—officers galloping their horses, teamsters whipping their mules, regiments turning out, drums beaten, and batteries limbered up. I remarked, last of all, the site of the battery that alarmed us, and, by a strange sharpness of sight and sense, believed that I saw the gunners swabbing, ramming, and aiming the pieces.

"Puff! bang! whiz-z-z-z! splutter! crash!"

"Puff! bang! whiz-z-z-z! splutter! crash!"

"My God!" said Lowe, hissing the words slowly and terribly, *"they have opened upon us from another battery!"*

The scene seemed to dissolve. A cold dew broke from my forehead. I grew blind and deaf. I had fainted.

"Pitch some water in his face," said somebody. "He ain't used to it. Hallo! there he comes to."

I staggered to my feet. There must have been a thousand men about us. They were looking curiously at the aeronaut and me. The balloon lay fuming and struggling on the clods.

"Three cheers for the Union bal-loon!" called a little fellow at my side.

"Hip, hip—hoorooar! hoorooar! hoorooar!"

"Tiger-r-r—yah! whoop!"

CHAPTER XI

Seven Pines and Fair Oaks

———————

RETURNING from White House on Thursday, May 29, I heard the cannon of Seven Pines. The roar of artillery came faintly upon the ear in the dells and woods, but in the open stretches of country, or from cleared hill-tops, I could hear also the volleys of musketry. It was the battle sound that assured me of bloody work; for the musket, as I had learned by experience, was the only certain signification of battle. It is seldom brought into requisition but at close quarters, when results are intended; whereas cannon may peal for a fortnight, and involve no other destruction than that of shell and powder. I do not think that any throb of my heart was unattended by some volley or discharge. Dull, hoarse, uninterrupted, the whole afternoon was shaken by the sound. It was with a shudder that I thought how every peal announced flesh and bone riven asunder. The country people, on the way, stood in their side yards, anxiously listening. Riders or teamsters coming from the field were beset with inquiries; but in the main they knew nothing. As I stopped at Daker's for dinner, the concussion of the battle rattled our plates, and the girls entirely lost their appetites, so that Glumley, who listened and speculated, observed that the baby face was losing all the lines of art, and was quite flat and faded in color. Resuming our way, we encountered a sallow, shabby person, driving a covered wagon, who recognized me at once. It was the "Doctor" who had lightened the journey down the Chesapeake by a discourse upon embalming.

He pointed toward the field with a long bony finger, and called aloud, with a smirk upon his face—

"I have the apparatus here, you see. They will need me out yonder, you know. There's opportunity there for the development of the 'system.'"

I did not reach my own camp at Gaines's farm, till late in the day. The firing had almost entirely ceased, but occasional discharges still broke the repose of evening, and at night signal rockets hissed and showered in every direction. Next day the contest recommenced; but although not farther in a direct line than seven miles from our encampment, I could not cross the Chickahominy, and was compelled to lie in my tent all day.

These two battles were offered by the Confederates, in the hope of capturing that portion of the Federal army that lay upon the Richmond side of the river. Some days previously, McClellan had ordered Keyes's corps, consisting of perhaps twelve thousand men, to cross Bottom's Bridge, eight miles down the Chickahominy, and occupy an advanced position on the York River railroad, six miles east of Richmond. Keyes's two divisions, commanded by Generals Couch and Casey, were thus encamped in a belt of woods remote from the body of the army, and little more than a mile from the enemy's line. Heintzelman's corps was lying at the Bridge, several miles in their rear, and the three finest corps in the army were separated from them by a broad, rapid river, which could be crossed at two places only. The troops of Keyes were mainly inexperienced, undisciplined volunteers from the Middle States. When their adversaries advanced, therefore, in force, on the twenty-ninth instant, they made a fitful, irregular resistance, and at evening retired in panic and disorder. The victorious enemy followed them so closely that many of the Federals were slain in their tents. During that night, the Chickahominy, swollen by rains, overflowed its banks, and swept away the bridges. The beaten and disorganized relic of the fight of Seven Pines, was thus completely isolated, and apparently to be annihilated at daybreak. But during the night, twenty thousand fresh men of

Sumner's corps forded the river, carrying across their artillery piece by piece, and at dawn they assumed the offensive, seconded by the encouraged columns of Keyes. The fight was one of desperation; at night the Federals reoccupied their old ground at Fair Oaks, and the Confederates retired, leaving their dead and wounded on the field. They lost, among their prisoners, General Pettigrew, of South Carolina, who was severely wounded, and with whom I talked as he lay in bed at Gaines's mansion. He appeared to be a chivalrous, gossipy old gentleman, and said that he was the last South Carolinian to stand by the Union.

On the succeeding day, Monday, June 2, I rode to Grapevine Bridge, and attempted to force my horse through the swamp and stream; but the drowned mules that momentarily floated down the current, admonished me of the folly of the hazard. The bridge itself was a swimming mass of poles and logs that yielded with every pressure; yet I saw many wounded men who waded through the water or stepped lightly from log to log, and so gained the shore, wet from head to foot. Long lines of supply teams and ambulances were wedged in the depth of the thick wood, bordering the river; but so narrow were the corduroy approaches to the bridge, and so fathomless the swamp on either hand, that they could neither go forward, nor return. The straggling troops brought the unwelcome intelligence that their comrades on the other side were starving, as they had crossed with a single ration of food, and had long ago eaten their last morsels. While I was standing close by the bridge, General McClellan and staff rode through the swamp, and attempted to make the passage. The "young Napoleon" urged his horse upon the floating timber, and at once sank over neck and saddle. His staff dashed after him, floundering in the same way; and when they had splashed and shouted till I believed them all drowned, they turned and came to shore, dripping and discomfited. There was another Napoleon, who, I am informed, slid down the Alps into Italy; the present descendant did not slide so far, and he shook himself, after the manner of a dog. I remarked with some surprise that he was growing obese; whereas the active labors of the campaign had reduced the dimensions of most of the generals.

I secured my horse, and placed a drummer-boy beside him, to prevent abduction or mistake; then stripping from top to toe, and holding my garments above my head, I essayed the difficult passage; as a commencement, I dropped my watch, but the guard-hook caught in a log and held it fast. Afterward, I slipped from the smooth butt of a tree, and thoroughly soused myself and clothing; a lumber-man from Maine beheld my ill luck, and kindly took my burden to the other side. An estuary of the Chickahominy again intervened, but a rough scow floated upon it, which the Captain of Engineers sent for me, with a soldier to man the oars. I neglected to "trim boat," I am sorry to add, although admonished to that effect repeatedly by the mariner; and we swamped in four feet of water. I resembled a being of one of the antediluvian eras, when I came to land, finally, and might have been taken for a slimy Iguanodon. I sacrificed some of my underclothing to the process of cleansing and drying, and so started with soaking boots, and a deficiency of dress, in the direction of Savage's. Passing the "bottom," or swampland, I ascended a hill, and following a lane, stopped after a half hour at a frame mansion, unpainted, with some barns and Negro-quarters contiguous, and a fine grove of young oaks shading the porch. An elderly gentleman sat on the porch, sipping a julep, with his feet upon the railing, and conversing with a stout, ruddy officer, of decidedly Milesian physiognomy. When I approached, the latter hurriedly placed a chair between himself and me, and said, with a stare—

"Bloodanowns! And where have ye been? Among the hogs, I think?" I assured him that I did not intend to come to close quarters, and that it would be no object on my part to contaminate him. The old gentleman called for "William," a tall, consumptive servant, whose walk reminded me of a stubborn convict's in the treadmill, and ordered him to scrape me, which was done, accordingly, with a caseknife. The young officer proposed to dip me in the well and wring me well out, but I demurred, mainly on the ground that some time would be so consumed, and that my horse was waiting on the other side. He at once said that he would send for it, and called "Pat," a civilian servant in military blue, who was nursing a Negro baby with an eye, it seemed, to obtain favor with the mother. The willingness of the man surprised me, but he said that it was a short cut of four miles to the railroad bridge, which had been repaired and floored, and that he could readily recover the animal and return at three o'clock. My benefactor, the officer, then mixed a julep, which brought a comfortable glow to my face, and said, without parley—

"You're a reporter, on the ——"

He said further, that he had been Coroner's Surgeon in New York for many years, and had learned to know the representatives of newspapers, one from the other, by generic manner and appearance. Three correspondents rode by at the time, neither of whom he knew personally, but designated them promptly, with their precise connections. In short, we became familiar directly, and he told me that his name was O'Ganlon, Quartermaster of Meagher's Irish brigade, Sumner's corps. He was established with the elderly gentleman—whose name was Michie—and had two horses in the stable, at hand. He proposed to send me to the field, with a note of introduction to the General, and another to Colonel Baker, of the New York 88th (Irish), who could show me the lines and relics of battle, and give me the lists of killed, wounded, and missing. I repaired to his room, and arrayed myself in a fatigue officer's suit, with clean underclothing, after which, descending, I climbed into his saddle, and dashed off, with a mettlesome, dapper pony.

The railroad track was about a mile from the house, and the whole country hereabout was sappy, dank, and almost barren. Scrub pines covered much of the soil, and the cleared fields were dotted with charred stumps. The houses were small and rude; the wild pigs ran like deer through the bushes and across my path; vultures sailed by hundreds between me and the sky; the lane was slippery and wound about slimy pools; the tree-tops, in many places, were splintered by ball and shell. I crossed the railroad, cut by a high bridge, and saw below the depot, at Savage's, now the headquarters of General Samuel P. H. Heintzelman. Above, in full view, were the commands at Peach Orchard and Fair Oaks, and to the south, a few furlongs distant, the Williamsburg and Richmond turnpike ran, parallel with the railway, toward the field of Seven Pines. The latter site was simply the junction of the turnpike with a roundabout way to Richmond, called the Nine Mile Road, and Fair Oaks was the junction of the diverging road with the railroad. Toward the latter I proceeded, and soon came to the Irish brigade, located on both sides of the way, at Peach Orchard. They occupied the site of the most desperate fighting.

A small farm hollowed in the swampy thicket and wood was here divided by the track, and a little farm-house, with a barn, granary, and a couple of cabins lay on the left side. In a hut to the right General Thomas Francis Meagher made his headquarters, and a little beyond, in the edges of the swamp timber, lay his four regiments, under arms.

A guard admonished me, in curt, lithe speech, that my horse must come no further; for the brigade held the advance post, and I was even now within easy musket range of the imperceptible enemy. An Irish boy volunteered to hold the rein, while I paid my respects to the Commander. I encountered him on the threshold of the hut, and he welcomed me in the richest and most musical of brogues. Large, corpulent, and powerful of body; plump and ruddy —or as some would say, bloated—of face; with resolute mouth and heavy animal jaws; expressive nose, and piercing blue eyes; brown hair, mustache, and eyebrows; a fair forehead, and short sinewy neck, a man of apparently thirty years of age, stood in the doorway, smoking a cigar, and trotting his sword fretfully in the scabbard. He wore the regulation blue cap, but trimmed plentifully with gold lace, and his sleeves were slashed in the same manner. A star glistened in his oblong shoulder-bar; a delicate gold cord seamed his breeches from his Hessian boots to his red tasselled sword-sash; a seal-ring shone from the hand with which he grasped his gauntlets, and his spurs were set upon small aristocratic feet.

A tolerable physiognomist would have resolved his temperament to an intense sanguine. He was fitfully impulsive, as all his movements attested, and liable to fluctuations of peevishness, melancholy, and enthusiasm. This was "Meagher of the Sword," the stripling who made issue with the renowned Daniel O'Connell, and divided his applauses; the "revolutionist," who had outlived exile to become the darling of the "Young Ireland" populace in his adopted country; the partisan, whose fierce, impassioned oratory had wheeled his factious element of the Democracy into the war cause; and the soldier, whose gallant bearing at Bull Run had won him a brigadiership. He was, to my mind, a realization of the Knight of Gwynne, or any of the rash, impolitic, poetic personages in Lever and Griffin. Ambitious without a name; an adventurer without a definite cause; an orator without policy; a General without caution or experience, he had led the Irish brigade through the hottest battles, and associated them with the most brilliant episodes of the war.

Every adjunct of the place was strictly Hibernian. The emerald green standard entwined with the red, white, and blue; the gilt eagles on the flag-poles held the shamrock sprig in their beaks; the soldiers lounging on guard had "69" or "88," the numbers of their regiments, stamped on a green hat-band; the brogue of every county from Down to Wexford fell upon the ear; one might have supposed that the "year '98" had been revived, and that these brawny Celts were again afield against their Saxon countrymen. The class of lads upon the staff of Meagher was an odd contrast to the mass of staff officers in the "Grand Army." Fox-hunters they all seemed to me, and there was one who wore a long, twisted, pomatumed moustache, who talked of steeple chases, all the while, and wanted to

have "a healthy dash" of some kind. A class of Irish ex-
quisites, they appeared to be—good for a fight, a card-
party, or a hurdle jumping—but entirely too Quixotic for
the sober requirements of Yankee warfare. When anything
absurd, forlorn, or desperate was to be attempted, the
Irish brigade was called upon. But, ordinarily, they were
regarded as a party of mad fellows, more ornamental than
useful, and entirely too clannish and factious to be entrusted with power. Meagher himself seemed to be less
erratic than his subordinates; for he had married a New
York lady, and had learned, by observation, the superiority
of the pelfish, plodding native before his own fitful, impracticable race. His address was infatuating; but there
was a certain airiness, indicative of vanity, that revealed
his great characteristic. He loved applause, and to obtain
it had frittered away his fine abilities upon petty, splendid,
momentary triumphs. He was generous to folly, and, I
have no doubt, maintained his whole staff.

When I requested to be shown the field and its relics,
Meagher said, in his musical brogue, that I need only look
around.

"From the edge of that wood," he said, "the Irish brigade charged across this field, and fell upon their faces
in the railway cutting below. A regiment of Alabamians
lay in the timber beyond, with other Southerners in their
rear, and on both flanks. They thought that we were
charging bayonets, and reserved their fire till we should
approach within butchering distance. On the contrary, I
ordered the boys to lie down, and load and fire at will. In
the end, sir, we cut them to pieces, and five hundred of
them were left along the swamp fence, that you see. There
isn't fifty killed and wounded in the whole Irish brigade."

A young staff officer took me over the field. We visited
first the cottage and barns across the road, and found the
house occupied by some thirty wounded Federals. They
lay in their blankets upon the floors—pale, helpless, hollow-
eyed, making low moans at every breath. Two or three
were feverishly sleeping, and, as the flies revelled upon
their gashes, they stirred uneasily and moved their hands

to and fro. By the flatness of the covering at the extremities, I could see that several had only stumps of legs. They had lost the sweet enjoyment of walking afield, and were but fragments of men, to limp forever through a painful life. Such wrecks of power I never beheld. Broad, brawny, buoyant, a few hours ago, the loss of blood, and the nervous shock, attendant upon amputation, had well-nigh drained them to the last drop. Their faces were as white as the tidy ceiling; they were whining like babies; and only their rolling eyes distinguished them from mutilated corpses. Some seemed quite broken in spirit, and one, who could speak, observing my pitiful glances toward his severed thigh, drew up his mouth and chin, and wept as if with the loss of comeliness all his ambitions were frustrated. A few attendants were brushing off the insects with boughs of cedar, laving the sores, or administering cooling draughts. The second story of the dwelling was likewise occupied by wounded, but in a corner clustered the terrified farmer and his family, vainly attempting to turn their eyes from the horrible spectacle. The farmer's wife had a baby at her breast, and its little blue eyes were straying over the room, half wonderingly, half delightedly. I thought, with a shudder, of babyhood thus surrounded, and how, in the long future, its first recollections of existence should be of booming guns and dying soldiers. The cow-shed contained seven corpses, scarcely yet cold, lying upon their backs, in a row, and fast losing all resemblance to man. The farthest removed, seemed to be a diminutive boy, and I thought if he had a mother, that she might sometime like to speak with me. When I took their names, I thought what terrible agencies I was fulfilling. Beyond my record, falsely spelled, perhaps, they would have no history. And people call such deaths glorious!

Upon a pile of lumber and some heaps of fence-rails, close by, sat some dozens of wounded men, mainly Federals, with bandaged arms and faces, and torn clothing. There was one, shot in the foot, who howled at every effort to remove his boot; the blood leaked from a rent in the side, and at last, the leather was cut, piecemeal from the flesh. These ate voraciously, though in pain and fear; for a little soup and meat was being doled out to them.

The most horrible of all these scenes—which I have described perhaps too circumstantially—was presented in the stable or barn, on the premises, where a bare dingy floor—the planks of which tilted and shook, as one made his way over them—was strewn with suffering people. Just at the entrance sat a boy, totally blind, both eyes having been torn out by a minnie-ball, and the entire bridge of the nose shot away. He crouched against the gable, in darkness and agony, tremulously fingering his knees. Near at hand, sat another, who had been shot through the middle of the forehead, but singular to relate, he still lived, though lunatic, and evidently beyond hope. Death had drawn blue and yellow circles beneath his eyes, and he muttered incomprehensibly, wagging his head. Two men, perfectly naked, lay in the middle of the place, wounded in bowels and loins; and at a niche in the weather-boarding, where some pale light peeped in, four mutilated wretches were gaming with cards. I was now led a little way down the railroad, to see the Confederates. The rain began to fall at this time, and the poor fellows shut their eyes to avoid the pelting of the drops. There was no shelter for them within a mile, and the mud absolutely reached half way up their bodies. Nearly one third had suffered amputation above the knee. There were about thirty at this spot, and I was told that they were being taken to Meadow Station on hand cars. As soon as the locomotive could pass the Chickahominy, they would be removed to White House, and comfortably quartered in the Sanitary and hospital boats. Some of them were fine, athletic, and youthful, and I was directed to one who had been married only three days before.

"Doctor," said one, feebly, "I feel very cold: do you think that this is death? It seems to be creeping to my heart. I have no feeling in my feet, and my thighs are numb."

A Federal soldier came along with a bucket of soup, and proceeded to fill the canteens and plates. He appeared to be a relative of Mark Tapley, and possessed much of that estimable person's jollity—

"Come, pardner," he said, "drink yer sup! now, old boy, this'ill warm ye; sock it down and ye'll see yer sweetheart soon. You dead, Ally-bammy? Go way, now. You'll live a hundred years, you will. That's wot you'll do. Won't he, lad? What? Not any? Get out! You'll be slap on your legs next week and hev another shot at me the week a'ter that. You know you will! Oh! you Rebil! You, with the butternut trousers! Say! Wake up and take some o' this. Hello! lad, pardner. Wake up!"

He stirred him gently with his foot; he bent down to touch his face. A grimness came over his merriment. The man was stiff and numb.

Colonel Baker, commanding the 88th New York, was a tall, martial Irishman, who opened his heart and bottle at the same welcome, and took me into the woods, where some of the slain still remained. He had slept not longer than an hour, continuously, for seventy hours, and during the past night had been called up by eight alarums. His men lay in the dark thickets, without fires or blankets, as they had crossed the Chickahominy in light marching order.

"Many a lad," said he, "will escape the bullet for a lingering consumption."

We had proceeded but a very little way, when we came to a trodden place beneath the pines, where a scalp lay in the leaves, and the imprint of a body was plainly visible. The bayonet scabbard lay at one side, the canteen at the other. We saw no corpses, however, as fatigue parties had been burying the slain, and the whole wood was dotted with heaps of clay, where the dead slept below in the oozy trenches. Quantities of cartridges were scattered here and there, dropped by the retreating Confederates. Some of the cartridge-pouches that I examined were completely filled, showing that their possessors had not fired a single round; others had but one cartridge missing. There were fragments of clothing, hair, blankets, murderous bowie and dirk knives, spurs, flasks, caps, and plumes, dropped

all the way through the thicket, and the trees on every
hand were riddled with balls. I came upon a squirrel, unwittingly shot during the fight. Not those alone who make
the war must feel the war! At one of the mounds the burying party had just completed their work, and the men were
throwing the last clods upon the remains. They had dug
pits of not more than two feet depth, and dragged the
bodies heedlessly to the edges, whence they were toppled
down and scantily covered. Much of the interring had
been done by night, and the flare of lanterns upon the discolored faces and dead eyes must have been hideously effective. The grave-diggers, however, were practical personages, and had probably little care for dramatic effects.
They leaned upon their spades, when the rites were finished, and a large, dry person, who appeared to be privi-
leged upon all occasions, said, grinningly—

"Colonel, your honor, them boys 'ill niver stand forninst
the Irish brigade again. If they'd ha' known it was us, sur,
begorra! they 'ud ha' brought coffins wid 'em."

"No, niver!" "They got their ticket for soup!" "We kiv-
ered them, fait', will inough!" shouted the other grave-
diggers.

"Do ye belave, Colonel," said the dry person, again,
"that thim ribals'll lave us a chance to catch them. Be me
sowl! I'm jist wishin to war-rum me hands wid rifle practice."

The others echoed loudly that they were anxious to be
ordered up, and some said that "Little Mac'll give 'em his
big whack now." The presence of death seemed to have
added no fear of death to these people. Having tasted
blood, they now thirsted for it, and I asked myself, fore-
bodingly, if a return to civil life would find them less fero-
cious.

I dined with Colonel Owen of the 69th Pennsylvania
(Irish) volunteers. He had been a Philadelphia lawyer,
and was, by all odds, the most consistent and intelligent
soldier in the brigade. He had been also a schoolmaster
for many years, but appeared to be in his element at the
head of a regiment, and was generally admitted to be an

efficient officer. He shared the prevailing antipathy to West Point graduates; for at this time the arrogance of the regular officers and the pride of the volunteers had embittered each against the other. His theory of military education was the establishment of State institutions and the reorganization of citizenship upon a strict militia basis. After dinner, I rode to Seven Pines, and examined some of the rifle pits used during the engagement. A portion of this ground only had been retaken, and I was warned to keep under cover; for sharpshooters lay close by, in the underbrush. A visit to the graves of some Federal soldiers completed the inspection. Some of the regiments had interred their dead in trenches; but the New Englanders were all buried separately, and smooth slabs were driven at the heads of the mounds, whereon were inscribed the names and ages of the deceased. Some of the graves were freshly sodded, and enclosed by rails and logs. They evidenced the orderly, religious habits of the sons of the Puritans; for, with all his hardness of manner and selfishness of purpose, I am inclined to think that the Yankee is the best manifestation of Northern character. He loves his home, at least, and he reveres his deceased comrades.

When I returned to Michie's, at six o'clock, the man Pat, with a glowing face, came out to the gate.

"That's a splendid baste of yours, sur," he said—"and sich a boi to gallop."

"My horse doesn't generally gallop," I returned, doubtfully.

When I passed to the barn in the rear, I found to my astonishment a sorrel stallion, magnificently accoutred. He thrust his foot at me savagely, as I stood behind him, and neighed till he frightened the spiders.

"Pat," said I, wrathfully, "you have stolen some colonel's nag, and I shall be hanged for the theft."

"Fait, sur," said Pat, "my ligs was gone intirely, wid long walkin', and I sazed the furst iligant baste I come to."

CHAPTER XII

Stuart's Raid

THE OLD Chickahominy bridges were soon repaired, and the whole of General William B. Franklin's corps passed to the south side. McClellan moved his headquarters to Dr. Trent's farm, a half-mile from Michie's, and the latter gentleman's fields and lawn were made white with tents. Among others, the Chief of Cavalry, George Stoneman, pitched his canopy under the young oaks, and the whole reserve artillery was parked in the woods, close to the house. The engineer brigade encamped in the adjacent peach orchard and corn field, and the wheat was trampled by battery and team-horses. Smith's division now occupied the hills on the south side of the Chickahominy, and the Federal line stretched southeastward, through Fair Oaks, to White Oak Swamp, seven miles away. Porter's corps still lay between Mechanicsville and New Bridge, on the north bank of the river, and my old acquaintances, the Pennsylvania Reserves, had joined the army, and now formed its extreme right wing. This odd arrangement of forces was a subject of frequent comment: for the right was thus four miles, and the left fourteen miles, from Richmond. The four corps at once commenced to entrench, and from Smith's redoubt on the river bluffs, to Casey's entrenched hill at White Oak, a continuous line of moderately strong earthworks extended. But Porter and the Reserves were not entrenched at all, and only a few horsemen were picketed across the long reach of country from Meadow Bridges to Hanover Court House. Both flanks, in fact, were open, and the left was a day's march from the right. We were, meantime, drawing our supplies from White House, twenty miles in the rear; there were no railroad guards along the entire line, and about five companies protected the grand depot. Two gunboats lay in the river, however, and as the teams still went to and fro, a second depot was established at a place called Putney's, or "Garlick's," five miles above White House. I went often, and at all hours of the day and night, over this exposed and lonely route. My horse had been, meantime, returned to the provost quarters, and the rightful owner had obtained his stallion in exchange. I rode the said stallion but once, when he proceeded to walk sideways, and several times rivalled the renowned Pegasus in his aerial flights. The man named Pat essayed to show his paces one day, but the stallion took him straight into Stoneman's wall-tent, and that officer shook the Irishman blind. My little bobtailed brownie was thrice endeared to me by our separation; but I warned the man Pat to keep clear of him thereafter. Pat was a very eccentric person, who slept on the porch at Michie's, and used to wake up the house in the small hours with the story that somebody was taking the chickens and the horses. He was the most impulsive person that I ever knew, and when I entrusted despatches to him once, he put them on the hospital boat by mistake, and they got to New York at the close of the campaign.

Michie's soon became a correspondents' rendezvous, and we have had at one time, at dinner, twelve representatives of five journals. The Hon. Henry J. Raymond, ex-Lieutenant Governor of New York, and proprietor of the *Times* newspaper, was one of our family for several weeks. He had been a New Hampshire lad, and, strolling to New York, took to journalism at the age of nineteen years. His industry and probity obtained him both means and credit, and, also, what few young journalists obtain, social position. He was the founder of *Harper's Magazine,* one of the most successful serials in America, and many English authors are indebted to him for a trans-Atlantic recognition of their works. He edited an American edition of *Jane Eyre* before it had attracted attention in England, and conducted the *Courier and Enquirer* with great success for many years. The *Times* is now the most reputable of the great New York dailies, and Mr. Raymond has made it influential both at home and abroad. He has retained, amidst his social and political successes, a predilection for "Bohemia," and became an indefatigable correspondent. I rode out with him sometimes, and heard, with interest, his accounts of the Italian war, whither he also went in furtherance of journalism. Among our quill cavalry-men was a fat gentleman from Philadelphia, who had great fear of death, and who used to "tear" to White House, if the man Pat shot a duck in the garden. He was a hearty, humorous person, however, and an adept at searching for news.

O'Ganlon rode with me several times to White House, and we have crossed the railroad bridge together, a hundred feet in the air, when the planks were slippery, the sides sloping, and the way so narrow that two horses could not pass abreast. He was a true Irishman, and leaped barricades and ditches without regard to his neck. He had, also, a partiality for by-roads that led through swamps and close timber. He discovered one day a cow-path between Daker's and an old mill at Grapevine Bridge. The long arms of oaks and beech trees reached across it, and young Absalom might have been ensnared by the locks at every rod therein. Through this devious and dangerous way, O'Ganlon used to dash, whooping, guiding his horse with marvellous dexterity, and bantering me to follow. I so far forgot myself generally, as to behave quite as irrationally, and once returned to Michie's with a bump above my right eye that rivalled my head in size. At other times I rode alone, and my favorite route was an unfrequented lane called the "Quaker Road," that extended from Despatch Station, on the line of rail, to Daker's, on the New Bridge Road. Much of this way was shut in by thick woods and dreary pine barrens; but the road was hard and light, and a few quiet farms lay by the roadside. There was a mill, also, three miles from Daker's, where a turbulent creek crossed the route, and at an oak-wood near by I used to frighten the squirrels so that they started up by pairs and families; I have chased them in this way a full mile, and they seemed to know me after a time. We used to be on the best of terms, and they would, at length, stand their ground saucily, and chatter, the one with the other, flourishing their bushy appendages, like so many straggling "Bucktails." When I turned from the beaten road, where the ruts were like a ditch and parapet, and dead horses blackened the fields; where teams went creaking day and night, and squads of sabremen drove pale, barefooted prisoners to and fro like swine or cattle, the silence and solitude of this bylane were beautiful as sleep. Many of the old people living in this direction had not seen even a soldier or a sutler, save some mounted scouts that vanished in clouds of dust; but they had listened with awe to the music of cannon, though they did not know either the place or the result of the fighting. If fate has ordained me to survive the Rebellion, I shall some day revisit these localities; they are stamped legibly upon my mind, and I know almost every old couple in New Kent or Hanover counties. I have lunched at all the little springs on the road, and eaten corn-bread and bacon at most of the cabins. I have swam the Pamunkey at dozens of places, and when my finances were low, and my nag hungry, have organized myself into a company of foragers, and broken into the good people's granaries. I do not know any position that admitted of as much adventure and variety. There was always enough danger to make my journeys precariously pleasant, and, when wearied of the saddle, my friends at Daker's and Michie's had a savory julep and a comfortable bed always prepared. I had more liberty than General McClellan, and a great deal more comfort.

Mrs. Michie was a warm-hearted, impulsive Virginia lady, with almost New England industry, and from very scanty materials she contrived to spread a bountiful table. Her coffee was bubbling with rich cream, and her "yellow pone" was overrunning with butter. A cleanly black girl shook a fly-brush over our shoulders as we ate, and the curious custom was maintained of sending a julep to our bedrooms before we rose in the mornings. Our hostess was too hospitable to be a bitter partisan, and during five weeks of tenure at her residence, we never held an hour's controversy. She had troubles, but she endured them patiently. She saw, one by one, articles of property sacrificed or stolen; she heard the servants speaking impudently; and her daughters and son were in a remote part of the State. The young man was a Confederate surgeon at Lynchburg, and the young ladies had taken refuge in Rockbridge County. The latter were, from all accounts, pretty and intelligent, and one day, as I examined some parcels of books in the parlors, I found a volume of amateur poems that some laboring bard had dedicated to the youngest of them. Mr. Michie was a fine old Virginia gentleman, who remembered Thomas Jefferson well, as he had been reared in that great statesman's village, Charlottesville. He told me many anecdotes of Patrick Henry, John Randolph, and other distinguished patriots.

I wrote in one of the absent daughter's albums the following lines:

Alas! for the pleasant peace we knew,
  In the happy summers of long ago,
When the rivers were bright, and the skies were blue,
  By the homes of Henrico:

We dreamed of wars that were far away,
  And read, as in fable, of blood that ran,
Where the James and Chickahominy stray,
  Through the groves of Powhattan.

'Tis a dream come true; for the afternoons
  Blow bugles of war, by our fields of grain,
And the sabres clink, as the dark dragoons
  Come galloping up the lane;
The pigeons have flown from the eves and tiles,
  The oat-blades have grown to blades of steel,
And the Huns swarm down the leafy aisles
  Of the grand old Commonweal.

They have torn the Indian fisher's nets,
   Where flows Pamunkey toward the sea,
And blood runs red in the rivulets,
   That babbled and brawled in glee;
The corpses are strewn in Fairoak glades,
   The hoarse guns thunder from Drury's Ridge,
The fishes that played in the cove, deep shades,
   Are frightened from Bottom Bridge.

I would that the year were blotted away,
   And the strawberry grew in the hedge again;
That the scythe might swing in the tangled hay,
   And the squirrel romp in the glen;
The walnut sprinkle the clover slopes,
   Where graze the sheep and the spotted steer;
And the winter restore the golden hopes,
   That were trampled in a year.

On Friday, June 13, I made one of my customary trips
to White House, in the company of O'Ganlon. The latter
individual, in the course of a "healthy dash" that he made
down the railroad ties—whereby two shoes shied from his
mare's hoofs—reined into a quicksand that threatened to
swallow his steed. He afterward left his sword at Summit
Station, and I, obligingly, rode back three miles to recover
it. We dined at Daker's, where Glumley sat beside the
baby-face, pursuant to his art-duties, and the plump, red-
cheeked miss sat beside me. O'Ganlon was entertained by
the talkative daughter, who drove him quite mad; so that,
when we resumed our horses, he insisted upon a second
"healthy dash," and disappeared through a strip of woods.
I followed, rationally, and had come to a blacksmith's
shop, at the corner of a diverging road, when I was made
aware of some startling occurrence in my rear. A mounted
officer dashed past me, shouting some unintelligible tidings, and he was followed in quick succession by a dozen
cavalry-men, who rode as if the foul fiend was at their
heels. Then came a teamster, bare-backed, whose rent
harness trailed in the road, and directly some wagons that

were halted before the blacksmith's, wheeled smartly, and
rattled off towards White House.

"What is the matter, my man?" I said to one of these
lunatics, hurriedly.

"The Rebels are behind!" he screamed, with white lips,
and vanished.

I thought that it might be as well to take some other
road, and so struck off, at a dapper pace, in the direction
of the new landing at Putney's or "Garlick's." At the same
instant I heard the crack of carbines behind, and they
had a magical influence upon my speed. I rode along a
stretch of chestnut and oak wood, attached to the famous
Webb estate, and when I came to a rill that passed by a
little bridge, under the way, turned up its sandy bed and
buried myself in the under-brush. A few breathless
moments only had intervened, when the roadway seemed
shaken by a hundred hoofs. The imperceptible horsemen
yelled like a war-party of Comanches, and when they had
passed, the carbines rang ahead, as if some bloody work
was being done at every rod.

I remained a full hour under cover; but as no fresh
approaches added to my mystery and fear, I sallied forth,
and kept the route to Garlick's, with ears erect and expectant pulses. I had gone but a quarter of a mile, when I
discerned, through the gathering gloom, a black, mis-
shapen object, standing in the middle of the road. As it
seemed motionless, I ventured closer, when the thing resolved to a sutler's wagon, charred and broken, and still
smoking from the incendiaries' torch. Further on, more of
these burned wagons littered the way, and in one place
two slain horses marked the roadside. When I emerged
upon the Hanover road, sounds of shrieks and shot issued
from the landing at Garlick's, and, in a moment, flames
rose from the woody shores and reddened the evening. I
knew by the gliding blaze that vessels had been fired and
set adrift, and from my place could see the devouring element climbing rope and shroud. In a twinkling, a second
light appeared behind the woods to my right, and the
intelligence dawned upon me that the cars and houses at

Tunstall's Station had been burned. By the fitful illumination, I rode tremulously to the old headquarters at Black Creek, and as I conjectured, the depot and train were luridly consuming. The vicinity was marked by wrecked sutlers' stores, the embers of wagons, and toppled steeds. Below Black Creek the ruin did not extend; but when I came to White House the greatest confusion existed. Sutlers were taking down their booths, transports were slipping their cables, steamers moving down the stream. Stuart had made the circuit of the Grand Army to show Lee where the infantry could follow.

CHAPTER XIII

Fever Dreams

———

A SUBTLE enemy had of late joined the Confederate cause against the invaders. He was known as Pestilence, and his footsteps were so soft that neither scout nor picket could bar his entrance. His paths were subterranean—through the tepid swamp water, the shallow graves of the dead; and aerial—through the stench of rotting animals, the nightly miasms of bog and fen. His victims were not pierced, or crushed, or mangled, but their deaths were not less terrible, because more lingering. They seemed to wither and shrivel away; their eyes became at first very bright, and afterward lustreless; their skins grew hard and sallow; their lips faded to a dry whiteness; all the fluids of the body were consumed; and they crumbled to corruption before life had fairly gone from them.

This visitation has been, by common consent, dubbed "the Chickahominy fever," and some have called it the typhus fever. The troops called it the "camp fever," and it was frequently aggravated by affections of the bowels and throat. The number of persons that died with it was fabulous. Some have gone so far as to say that the army could have better afforded the slaughter of twenty thousand men, than the delay on the Chickahominy. The embalmers were now enjoying their millennium, and a steam coffin manufactory was erected at White House, where twenty men worked day and night, turning out hundreds of pine boxes. I had occasion, in one of my visits to the depot, to repair to the tent of one of the embalmers. He was a sedate, grave person, and when I saw him, standing over the nude, hard corpse, he reminded me of the implacable vulture, looking into the eyes of Prometheus. His battery and tube were pulsing, like one's heart and lungs, and the subject was being drained at the neck. I compared the discolored body with the figure of *Ianthe*, as revealed in Queen Mab, but failed to see the beautifulness of death.

"If you could only make him breathe, Professor," said an officer standing by.

The dry skin of the embalmer broke into chalky dimples, and he grinned very much as a corpse might do:

"Ah!" he said, "*then* there would be money made."

To hear these embalmers converse with each other was like listening to the witch sayings in *Macbeth*. It appeared that the arch-fiend of embalming was a Frenchman named Sonça, or something of that kind, and all these worthies professed to have purchased his "system." They told grisly anecdotes of "operations," and experimented with chemicals, and congratulated each other upon the fever. They would, I think, have piled the whole earth with catacombs of stony corpses, and we should have no more green graves, but keep our dead with us as household ornaments.

The Negroes did not suffer with the fever, although their quarters were close and filthy. Their Elysium had come; there was no more work. They slept and danced and grinned, and these three actions made up the sum of their existence. Such people to increase and multiply I never beheld. There were scores of new babies every day; they appeared to be born by twins and triplets; they learned to walk in twenty-four hours; and their mothers were strong and hearty in less time. Such soulless, lost, degraded men and women did nowhere else exist. The divinity they never had; the human they had forgotten; they did no great wrongs—thieving, quarrelling, deceiving—but they failed to do any rights, and their worship was animal, and almost profane. They sang incongruous mixtures of hymns and field songs:

> Oh! bruddern, watch an' pray, *watch* an' pray!
> De harvest am a ripenin' our Lord an' Marser say!
> Oh! ho! yo! dat ole coon, de serpent, ho! oh!
> Watch an' pray!

I have heard them sing such medleys with tears in their eyes, apparently fervid and rapt. A very gray old man would lead off, keeping time to the words with his head and hands; the mass joining in at intervals, and raising a screaming alleluja. Directly they would all rise, link hands, and proceed to dance the accompaniment. The motion would be slow at first, and the method of singing maintained; after a time they would move more rapidly, shouting the lines together; and suddenly becoming convulsed with strange excitement, they would toss up their arms, leap, fall, groan, and, seemingly, lose consciousness. Their prayers were earnest and vehement, but often degenerated to mere howls and noises. Some of both sexes had grand voices, that rang like bugles, and the very impropriety of their music made it fascinating. It used to seem to me that any of the great composers might have borrowed advantageously some of those original Negro airs. In many cases, their owners came within the lines, registered their allegiance, and recovered the Negroes. These were often veritable Shylocks, that claimed their pounds of flesh, with unblushing reference to the law. The poor Africs went back cowed and tearful, and it is probable that they were afterward sent to the far South, that terrible *terra incognita* to a border slave.

Among the houses to which I resorted was that of a Mr. Hill, one mile from White House. He had a thousand acres of land and a valuable fishery on the Pamunkey. The latter was worth, in good seasons, two thousand dollars a year. He had fished and farmed with Negroes; but these had leagued to run away, and he sent them across the river to a second farm that he owned in King William County. It was at Hill's house that the widow Custis was visiting when young Washington reined at the gate, on his road to Williamsburg. With reverent feelings I used to regard the old place, and Hill frequently stole away from his formidable military household to talk with me on the front porch. Perhaps in the same moonlights, with the river shimmering at their feet, and the grapevine shadowing the creaky corners—their voices softened, their chairs drawn

very close, their hands touching with a thrill—the young
soldier and his affianced had made their courtship. I sometimes sat breathless, thinking that their figures had come
back, and that I heard them whispering.

Hill was a Virginian—large, hospitable, severe, proud—
and once I ventured to speak upon the policy of slavery,
with a view to develop his own relation to the "institution." He said, with the swaggering manner of his class,
that slavery was a "domestic" institution, and that therefore no political law could reach it. I insinuated, quietly,
that no political law should therefore sustain it, and took
exception to the idea that what was domestic was therefore without the province of legislation. When I exampled
polygamy, Hill became passionate, and asked if I was an
abolitionist. I opined that I was not, and he so far relented
as to say that slavery was sanctioned by divine and human
laws; that it was ultimately to be embraced by all white
nationalities, and that the Caucasian was certain, in the
end, to subjugate and possess every other race. He
pointed, with some shrewdness, to the condition of the
Chinese in California and Australia, and epitomized the
gradual enslaving of the Mongol and Malay in various
quarters of the world.

"As to our treatment of niggers," he said, curtly, "I
never prevaricate, as some masters do, in that respect. I
whip my niggers when they want it! If they are saucy,
or careless, or lazy, I have 'em flogged. About twice a
year every nigger has to be punished. If they ain't roped
over twice a year, they take on airs and want to be gentlemen. A nigger is bound by no sentiment of duty or affection. You must keep him in trim by fear."

Among the victims of the swamp fever were Major Larrabee and Lieutenant-Colonel Emory, of the Fifth Wisconsin regiment; I had been indebted to them for many a meal
and draught of spirits. I had talked with each of them,
when the camps were darkened and the soldiery asleep.
Larrabee was a soldier by nature—adventurous, energetic,
intrepid, aggressive. He had been a country judge in Wisconsin, and afterwards a member of Congress. When the

war commenced, he enlisted as a common soldier, but
public sentiment forced the State Government to make
him a major. Emory was a mild, reflective, unimpassioned
gentleman—too modest to be eminent, too scrupulous to
be ambitious. The men were opposites, but both capital
companions, and they were seized with the fever about the
same time. The Major was removed to White House, and
I visited him one day in the hospital quarters. Surgeon
General Watson, hospital commandant, took me through
the quarters; there was quite a town of sick men; they lay
in wall-tents—about twenty in a tent—and there were
daily deaths; those that caught the fever were afterwards
unfit for duty, as they took relapses on resuming the field.
The tents were pitched in a damp cornfield; for the Federals so reverenced their national shrines that they forbade
White House and lawn to be used for hospital purposes.
Under the best circumstances, a field hospital is a comfortless place; but here the sun shone like a furnace upon the
tents, and the rains drowned out the inmates. If a man can
possibly avoid it, let him never go to the hospital; for he
will be called a "skulker," or a "shyster," that desires to
escape the impending battle. Twenty hot, feverish, tossing
men, confined in a small tent, like an oven, and exposed to
contumely and bad food, should get a wholesome horror of
war and glory.

So far as I could observe and learn, the authorities at
White House carried high heads, and covetous hands. In
brief, they lived like princes, and behaved like knaves.
There was one—whose conduct has never been investi-
gated—who furnished one of the deserted mansions near
by, and brought a lady from the North to keep it in order.
He drove a span that rivalled anything in Broadway, and
his wines were luscious. His establishment reminded me
of that of Napoleon III, in the late Italian war, and yet,
this man was receiving merely a colonel's pay. My impression is that everybody at White House robbed the Government, and in the end, to cover their delinquencies, these
scoundrels set fire to an immense quantity of stores, and
squared their accounts thus: "Burned on the Pamunkey,

June 28, commissary, quartermaster's, and hospital stores, one million dollars."

The time was now drawing to a close that I should pass amid the familiar scenes of this region. The good people at Daker's were still kindly; but having climbed into the great bed one night, I found my legs aching, my brain violently throbbing, my chest full of pain and my eyes weak. When I woke in the morning my lips were fevered, I could eat nothing, and when I reached my saddle, it seemed that I should faint. In a word, the Chickahominy fever had seized upon me. My ride to New Bridge was marked by great agony, and during much of the time I was quite blind. I turned off, at Gaines's Mill, to rest at Captain Kingwalt's; but the old gentleman was in the grip of the ague, and I forebore to trouble him with a statement of my grievances. Skyhiski made me a cup of tea, which I could not drink, and Fogg made me lie on his "poncho." It was like old times come back, to hear them all speak cheerfully, and the man Clover said that, if there "warn't" a battle soon, he knew what he'd do, he did! he'd go home, straight as a buck!

"Becoz," said Clover, flourishing his hands, "I volunteered to fight. To *fight*, sir! not to dig and drive team. Here we air, sir, stuck in the mud, burnin' with fever, livin' on hardtack. And thair's Richmond! Just thair! You can chuck a stone at it, if you mind to. A'ter awhile them rebbils'll pop out, and fix us. Why ain't we led up, sa-a-y?"

The man Clover represented common sentiment among the troops at this time; but I told him that in all probability he would soon be gratified with a battle. My prediction was so far correct, that when I met Clover on the James River, a week afterward, he said, with a rueful countenance—

"Sa-a-a-y! It never rains but it pours, does it?"

As I rode from the camp of the Pennsylvania Reserves, at noon, on the 21st of June, I seemed to feel a gloomy premonition of the calamities that were shortly to fall upon the Army of the Potomac. I passed in front of Hogan house; through the wood above the mill; along Gaines's

lane, between his mansion and his barn; across a creek,
tributary to the Chickahominy; and up the ploughed hills
by a military road, toward Grapevine Bridge. Lieutenant-
Colonel Heath, of the Fifth Maine Regiment, was riding
with me, and we stopped at the tip of an elevated field to
look back upon the scene. I was very sick and weary, and
I lay my head upon the mane of my nag, while Heath
threw a leg across his saddle pommel, and straightened his
slight figure; we both gazed earnestly.

The river lay in the hollow or ravine to the left, and a
few farm-houses sat among the trees on the hill-tops
beyond. A battery was planted at each house, and we
could see the lines of red-clay parapets marking the sites.
From the roof of one of the houses floated a speck of canvas—the revolutionary flag. A horseman or two moved
shadow-like across a slope of yellow grain. Before and
back the woods belted the landscape, and some pickets of
both sides paced the river brink: they did not fire upon
each other.

Our side of the Chickahominy was not less peaceful. A
couple of batteries lay below us, in the meadows; but the
horses were dozing in the harness, and the gunners, standing bolt upright at the breech, seemed parts of their
pieces; the teamsters lay grouped in the long grass. Immediately in front, Gaines's mansion and outhouses spotted a hillside, and we could note beyond a few white tents
shining through the trees. The roof of the old mill
crouched between a medley of wavy fields and woods to
our right, and just at our feet a tiny rill divided Gaines's
mill from our own. Behind us, over the wilderness of
swamp and bog-timber, rose Smith's redoubt, with the
Federal flag flaunting from the rampart.

"Townsend," said Heath, as he swept the whole country
with his keen eye, "do you know that we are standing upon
historic ground?"

He had been a poet and an orator, and he seemed to feel
the solemnity of the place.

"It may become historic tomorrow," I replied.

"It is so today," he said, earnestly; "not from battle as

yet; *that* may or may not happen; but in the pause before the storm there is something grand; and this is the pause."

He took his soft beaver in his hand, and his short red hair stood pugnaciously back from his fine forehead.

"The men that have been here already," he added, "consecrated the place; young McClellan, and bluff, bull-headed Franklin; the one-armed devil, Kearny, and handsome Joe Hooker; gray, grisly Heintzelman; white-bearded, insane Sumner; Stuart, Lee, Johnston, the Hills——"

"Why not," said I, laughingly, "Eric the red—the redoubtable Heath!"

"Why not?" he said, with a flourish; "Fate may have something in store for me, as well as for these."

I have thought, since, how terribly our light conversation found verification in fact. If I had said to Heath, that, at the very moment, Jefferson Davis and his Commander-in-chief were sitting in the dwelling opposite, reconnoitring and consulting; that, even now, their telescopes were directed upon us; that the effect of their counsel was to be manifest in less than a week; that one of the bloodiest battles of modern times was to be fought beside and around us; that six days of the most terrible fighting known in history were to ensue; that my friend and comrade was standing upon the same clods which would be reddened, at his next coming, with his heart's blood; and that the trenches were to yawn beneath his hoofs, to swallow himself and his steed—if I had foretold these things as they were to occur, I wonder if the "pause before the storm" would have been less awful, and our ride campward less sedate. Poor Heath! Gallant New Englander! he called at my bedside, the sixth day following, as I lay full of pain, fear, and fever, and after he bade me good-bye, I heard his horse's hoofs ringing down the lane. Ten minutes afterward he was shot through the head.

When I reached Michie's, at three o'clock, I had to be helped from the saddle, and the fever was raging in my whole body before nightfall. My hands were flushed, my face hot, but my feet were quite cold, and I was seized with chills that seemed to shake my teeth from my head. Mrs. Michie made me a bowl of scorching tea, and one of the black girls bathed my limbs in boiling water. The fever dreams came to me that night, in snatches of burning sleep, and toward morning I lay restlessly awake, moving from side to side, famishing for drink, but rejecting it, when they brought it to my lips. The next day, my kind hostess gave me some nourishing soup, but after a vain effort to partake of it, I was compelled to put it aside. O'Ganlon procured some pickled fruit and vegetables from a sutler, which I ate voraciously, quaffing the vinegar like wine. Some of my regimental friends heard of my illness, and they sent me quiet luxuries, which gladdened me, though I did not eat. During the day I had some moments of ease, when I tried to read. There was a copy of Wordsworth's poems in the house, and I used to repeat stanzas from "Peter Bell," till they rang, in eddies of rhyme, through my weak brain, and continued to scan and jangle far into the nights. Some of these fever-dreams were like delusions in delirium: peopled with monsters, that grinned and growled. Little black globules used to leer from corners, and after a time they began to revolve toward me, increasing as they came, and at length rolling like mountains of surge. I frequently woke with a scream, and found my body in profuse perspiration. There were fiery snakes, also, that, at first, moved slowly around me, and I followed them with red and terrified eyes. After awhile they flashed in circles of lightning, and hissed showers of sparks, until I became quite crazed with fear. The most horrible apparitions used to come to my bedside, and if I dropped to sleep with any thought half formed or half developed, the odd half of that thought became impregnated, somehow, and straightway loomed up a goblin, or a giant, or a grotesque something, that proceeded to torture me, like a sort of Frankenstein, for having made it. Amid all these ghastly things, there came beautiful glimpses of form, scene, and sensation, that straightway changed to horrors. I remember, for example, that I was gliding down a stream, where the boughs overhead were as shady as the waters, and there were holy eyes that seemed to cool my fever; but suddenly the stream became choked with corpses, that entangled their dead limbs with mine, until I strangled and called aloud—waking up O'Ganlon and some reporters who proposed to give me morphine, that I might not alarm the house.

How the poor soldiers fared, in the hot hospitals, I shudder to think; but a more merciful decree spared my life, and kind treatment met me at every hand. Otherwise, I believe, I should not be alive today to write this story; for the fever had seized me in its severest form, and I had almost tutored myself to look upon my end, far from my home and on the very eve of my manhood.

O'Ganlon at last resolved to send me to White House, and started thither one day, to obtain a berth for me upon a Sanitary steamer. The next day an ambulance came to the door. I tried to sit up in bed, and succeeded; I feebly robed myself and staggered to the stairs. I crawled, rather than walked, to the hall below; but when I took a chair, and felt the cool breeze from the oaks fanning my hair, I seemed to know that I should get well.

"Boom! Boom! Boom!" pealed some cannon at the moment, and all the windows shook with the concussion.

Directly we heard volleys of musketry, and then the camps were astir. Horses went hither and thither; signal flags flashed to-and-fro; a battery of the Reserve Artillery dashed down the lane.

I felt my strength coming back with the excitement; I even smiled feebly as the guns thundered past.

"Take away your ambulance, old fellow," I said, "I shan't go home till I see a battle."

CHAPTER XIV

Two Days of Battle

THE Confederates had been waiting two months for McClellan's advance. Emboldened by his delay they had gathered the whole of their available strength from remote Tennessee, from the Mississippi, and from the coast, until, confident and powerful, they crossed Meadow Bridge on the 26th of June, 1862, and drove in our right wing at Mechanicsville. The reserves of General McCall were stationed here; they made a wavering resistance—wherein four companies of Bucktails were captured bodily—and fell back at nightfall upon Porter's Corps, at Gaines's Mill. Fitz John Porter commanded the brigades of Generals Sykes and Morrell—the former made up solely of regulars. He appeared to have been ignorant of the strength of the attacking party, and he telegraphed to McClellan, early on Thursday evening, that he required no reinforcements, and that he could hold his ground. The next morning, the 27th, he was attacked in front and flank; Stuart's cavalry fell on his right, and turned it at Old Church. He formed at noon in new line of battle, from Gaines's house, along the Mill Road to New Cold Harbor; but stubbornly persisted in the belief that he could not be beaten. By three o'clock he had been driven back two miles, and all his energies were unavailing to recover a foot of ground. He hurled lancers and cavalry upon the masses of Stonewall Jackson and the Hills, but the butternut infantry formed impenetrable squares, hemmed in with rods of steel, and as the horsemen galloped around them, searching for pervious points, they were swept from their sad-

dles with volleys of musketry. He directed the terrible
fire of his artillery upon them, but though the gray foot-
men fell in heaps, they steadily advanced, closing up the
gaps, and their lines were like long stretches of blaze and
ball. Their fire never slackened nor abated. They loaded
and moved forward, column on column, like so many im-
mortals that could not be vanquished. The scene from the
balloon, as Lowe informed me, was awful beyond all comparison—of puffing shells and shrieking shrapnel, with volleys that shattered the hills and filled the air with deathly
whispers. Infantry, artillery, and horse turned the Federal
right from time to time, and to preserve their order of
battle the whole line fell back toward Grapevine Bridge.
At five o'clock Slocum's Division of volunteers crossed the
creek from the south side, and made a desperate dash
upon the solid columns of the Confederates. At the same
time Brigadier General Robert Toombs's Georgia Brigade
charged Smith's redoubt from the south side, and there was
a probability of the whole of both armies engaging before
dark.

My fever of body had so much relinquished to my fever
of mind, that at three o'clock I called for my horse, and
determined to cross the bridge, that I might witness the
battle.

It was with difficulty that I could make my way along
the narrow corduroy, for hundreds of wounded were limping from the field to the safe side, and ammunition wagons
were passing the other way, driven by reckless drivers who
should have been blown up momentarily. Before I had
reached the north side of the creek, an immense throng of
panic-stricken people came surging down the slippery
bridge. A few carried muskets, but I saw several wantonly
throw their pieces into the flood, and as the mass were
unarmed, I inferred that they had made similar disposi-
tions. Fear, anguish, cowardice, despair, disgust were the
predominant expressions of the upturned faces. The gaunt
trees, towering from the current, cast a solemn shadow
upon the moving throng, and as the evening dimness was
falling around them, it almost seemed that they were en-

gulfed in some cataract. I reined my horse close to the side
of a team, that I might not be borne backward by the
crowd; but some of the lawless fugitives seized him by the
bridle, and others attempted to pull me from the saddle.

"Gi' up that hoss!" said one, "what business you got
wi' a hoss?"

"That's my critter, and I am in for a ride; so you get
off!" said another.

I spurred my pony vigorously with the left foot, and
with the right struck the man at the bridle under the chin.
The thick column parted left and right, and though a howl
of hate pursued me, I kept straight to the bank, cleared the
swamp, and took the military route parallel with the
creek, toward the nearest eminence. At every step of the
way I met wounded persons. A horseman rode past me,
leaning over his pommel, with blood streaming from his
mouth and hanging in gouts from his saturated beard. The
day had been intensely hot and black boys were besetting
the wounded with buckets of cool lemonade. It was a common occurrence for the couples that carried the wounded
on stretchers to stop on the way, purchase a glass of the
beverage, and drink it. Sometimes the blankets on the
stretchers were closely folded, and then I knew that the
man within was dead. A little fellow, who used his sword
for a cane, stopped me on the road, and said—

"See yer! This is the ball that jes' fell out o' my boot."

He handed me a lump of lead as big as my thumb, and
pointed to a rent in his pantaloons, whence the drops
rolled down his boots.

"I wouldn't part with that for suthin' handsome," he
said; "it'll be nice to hev to hum."

As I cantered away he shouted after me—

"Be sure you spell my name right! it's Smith, with an
'E'—S-M-I-T-H-E."

In one place I met five drunken men escorting a
wounded sergeant; the latter had been shot in the jaw,
and when he attempted to speak, the blood choked his
articulation.

"You let go him, pardner," said one of the staggering brutes, "he's not your sergeant. Go 'way!"

"Now, sergeant," said the other, idiotically, "I'll see you all right, sergeant. Come, Bill, fetch him over to the corncrib and we'll give him a drink."

Here the first speaker struck the second, and the sergeant, in wrath, knocked them both down. All this time the enemy's cannon were booming close at hand.

I came to an officer of rank, whose shoulder-emblem I could not distinguish, riding upon a limping field-horse. Four men held him to his seat, and a fifth led the animal. The officer was evidently wounded, though he did not seem to be bleeding, and the dust of battle had settled upon his blanched, stiffening face, like grave-mould upon a corpse. He was swaying in the saddle, and his hair—for he was bare-headed—shook across his white eyeballs. He reminded me of the famous Cid, whose body was sent forth to scare the Saracens.

A mile or more from Grapevine Bridge, on a hill-top, lay a frame farm-house, with cherry trees encircling it, and along the declivity of the hill were some cabins, corn-sheds, and corn-bins. The house was now a surgeon's head-quarters, and the wounded lay in the yard and lane, under the shade, waiting their turns to be hacked and maimed. I caught a glimpse through the door, of the butchers and their victims; some curious people were peeping through the windows at the operation. As the processions of freshly wounded went by, the poor fellows, lying on their backs, looked mutely at me, and their great eyes smote my heart.

Something has been written in the course of the war upon straggling from the ranks, during battle. But I have seen nothing that conveys an adequate idea of the number of cowards and idlers that so stroll off. In this instance, I met squads, companies, almost regiments of them. Some came boldly along the road; others skulked in woods, and made long detours to escape detection; a few were composedly playing cards, or heating their coffee, or discussing the order and consequences of the fight. The rolling drums, the constant clatter of file and volley-firing—nothing could remind them of the requirements of the time and their own infamy. Their appreciation of duty and honor seemed to have been forgotten; neither hate, ambition, nor patriotism could force them back; but when the columns of mounted provosts charged upon them, they sullenly resumed their muskets and returned to the field. At the foot of the hill to which I have referred the ammunition wagons lay in long lines, with the horses' heads turned from the fight. A little beyond stood the ambulances; and between both sets of vehicles, fatigue-parties were going and returning to and from the field. At the top of the next hill sat many of the Federal batteries, and I was admonished by the shriek of shells that passed over my head and burst far behind me, that I was again to look upon carnage and share the perils of the soldier.

The question at once occurred to me: Can I stand fire? Having for some months penned daily paragraphs relative to death, courage, and victory, I was surprised to find that those words were now unusually significant. "Death" was a syllable to me before; it was a whole dictionary now. "Courage" was natural to every man a week ago; it was rarer than genius today. "Victory" was the first word in the lexicon of youth yesterday noon; "discretion" and "safety" were at present of infinitely more consequence. I resolved, notwithstanding these qualms, to venture to the hill-top: but at every step flitting projectiles took my breath. The music of the battle-field, I have often thought, should be introduced in opera. Not the drum, the bugle, or the fife, though these are thrilling, after their fashion; but the music of modern ordnance and projectile, the beautiful whistle of the minie-ball, the howl of shell that makes unearthly havoc with the air, the whiz-z-z of solid shot, the chirp of bullets, the scream of grape and canister, the yell of immense conical cylinders, that fall like red-hot stoves and spout burning coals.

All these passed over, beside, beneath, before, behind me. I seemed to be an invulnerable something at whom some cunning juggler was tossing steel, with an intent to impinge upon, not to strike him. I rode like one with his life in his hand, and, so far as I remember, seemed to think of nothing. No fear, *per se;* no regret; no adventure; only expectancy. It was the expectancy of a shot, a choking, a loud cry, a stiffening, a dead, dull tumble, a quiver, and— blindness. But with this was mingled a sort of enjoyment, like that of the daring gamester, who has played his soul and is waiting for the decision of the cards. I felt all his suspense, *more* than his hope; and withal, there was ex- citement in the play. Now a whistling ball seemed to pass just under my ear, and before I commenced to congratu- late myself upon the escape, a shell, with a showery and revolving fuse, appeared to take the top off my head. Then my heart expanded and contracted, and somehow I found myself conning rhymes. At each clipping ball—for I could hear them coming—a sort of coldness and paleness rose to the very roots of my hair, and was then replaced by a hot flush. I caught myself laughing, syllabically, and shrugging my shoulders, fitfully. Once, the rhyme that came to my lips—for I am sure there was no mind in the iteration—was the simple nursery prayer, "Now I lay me down to sleep," and I continued to say "down to sleep," "down to sleep," "down to sleep," till I discovered myself, when I ceased. Then a shell, apparently just in range, dashed toward me, and the words spasmodically leaped up: "Now's your time. This is your billet." With the same insane pertinacity I con- tinued to repeat "Now's your time, now's your time," and "billet, billet, billet," till at last I came up to the nearest battery, where I could look over the crest of the hill; and as if I had looked into the crater of a volcano, or down the fabled abyss into hell, the whole grand horror of a battle burst upon my sight. For a moment I could neither feel nor think. I scarcely beheld, or beholding did not under- stand or perceive. Only the roar of guns, the blaze that flashed along a zigzag line and was straightway smothered in smoke, the creek lying glassily beneath me, the gather- ing twilight, and the brownish blue of woods! I only knew that some thousands of fiends were playing with fire and tossing brands at heaven—that some pleasant slopes, dells, and highlands were lit as if the conflagration of universes had commenced. There is a passage of Holy Writ that comes to my mind as I write, which explains the sensation of the time better than I can do:

"He opened the bottomless pit; and there arose a smoke out of the pit, as the smoke of a great furnace; and the sun and the air were darkened by reason of the smoke of the pit.

"And there came out of the smoke locusts upon the earth."—Revelation, ix. 2, 3.

In a few moments, when I was able to compose myself, the veil of cloud blew away or dissolved, and I could see fragments of the long columns of infantry. Then from the far end of the lines puffed smoke, and from man to man the puff ran down each line, enveloping the columns again, so that they were alternately visible and invisible. At points between the masses of infantry lay field-pieces, throbbing with rapid deliveries, and emitting volumes of white steam. Now and then the firing slackened for a short time, when I could remark the Federal line, fringed with bayonets, stretching from the low meadow on the left, up the slope, over the ridge, up and down the crest, until its right disappeared in the gloaming of wood and distance. Standards flapped here and there above the column, and I knew, from the fact that the line became momentarily more distinct, that the Federals were falling stubbornly back. At times a battery would dash a hundred yards forward, unlimber, and fire a score of times, and directly would return two hundreds yards and blaze again. I saw a regiment of lancers gather at the foot of a protecting swell of field; the bugle rang thrice, the red pennons went upward like so many song birds, the mass turned the crest and disappeared, then the whole artillery belched and bellowed. In twenty minutes a broken, straggling, feeble group of horsemen returned; the red pennons still fluttered, but I knew that they were redder for the blood that dyed them. Finally, the Federal infantry fell back to the foot of the hill on which I stood; all the batteries were clustering around me, and suddenly a column of men shot up from the long sweep of the abandoned hill, with batteries on the left and right. Their muskets were turned towards us, a crash and a whiff of smoke swept from flank to flank, and the air around me rained buck, slug, bullet, and ball!

The incidents that now occurred in rapid succession were so thrilling and absorbing that my solicitude was lost in their grandeur. I sat like one dumb, with my soul in my eyes and my ears stunned, watching the terrible column of Confederates. Each party was now straining every energy—the one for victory, the other against annihilation. The darkness was closing in, and neither cared to prolong the contest after night. The Confederates, therefore, aimed to finish their success with the rout or capture of the Federals, and the Federals aimed to maintain their ground till nightfall. The musketry was close, accurate, and uninterrupted. Every second was marked by a discharge—the one firing, the other replying promptly. No attempt was now made to remove the wounded; the coolness of the fight had gone by, and we witnessed only its fury. The stragglers seemed to appreciate the desperate emergency, and came voluntarily back to relieve their comrades. The cavalry was massed, and collected for another grand charge. Like a black shadow gliding up the darkening hillside, they precipitated themselves upon the columns: the musketry ceased for the time, and shrieks, steel strokes, the crack of carbines and revolvers succeeded. Shattered, humiliated, sullen, the horse wheeled and returned. Then the guns thundered again, and by the blaze of the pieces, the clods and turf were revealed, fitfully strewn with men and horses.

The vicinity of my position now exhibited traces of the battle. A caisson burst close by, and I heard the howl of dying wretches, as the fires flashed like meteors. A solid shot struck a field-carriage not thirty yards from my feet, and one of the flying splinters spitted a gunner as if he had been pierced by an arrow. An artillery-man was standing with folded arms so near that I could have reached to touch him; a whistle and a thumping shock and he fell beneath my nag's head. I wonder, as I calmly recall these episodes now, how I escaped the death that played about me, chilled me, thrilled me—but spared me! "They are fixing bayonets for a charge. My God! See them come down the hill."

In the gathering darkness, through the thick smoke, I saw or seemed to see the interminable column roll steadily downward. I fancied that I beheld great gaps cut in their ranks though closing solidly up, like the imperishable Gorgon. I may have heard some of this next day, and so confounded the testimonies of eye and ear. But I knew that there was a charge, and that the drivers were ordered to stand by their saddles, to run off the guns at any moment. The descent and bottom below me were now all ablaze, and directly above the din of cannon, rifle, and pistol, I heard a great cheer, as of some salvation achieved.

"The Rebels are repulsed! We have saved the guns!"

A cheer greeted this announcement from the batterymen around me. They reloaded, rammed, swabbed, and fired, with naked arms, and drops of sweat furrowed the powder-stains upon their faces. The horses stood motionless, quivering not half so much as the pieces. The grisly officers held to their match-strings, smothering the excitement of the time. All at once there was a running hither and thither, a pause in the thunder, a quick consultation—

" 'Sdeath! They have flanked us again."

In an instant I seemed overwhelmed with men. For a moment I thought the enemy had surrounded us.

"It's all up," said one; "I shall cross the river."

I wheeled my horse, fell in with the stream of fugitives, and was borne swiftly through field and lane and trampled fence to the swampy margin of the Chickahominy. At every step the shell fell in and among the fugitives, adding to their panic. I saw officers who had forgotten their regiments or had been deserted by them, wending with the mass. The wounded fell and were trodden upon. Personal exhibitions of valor and determination there were; but the main body had lost heart, and were weary and hungry.

As we approached the bridge, there was confusion and

altercation ahead. The people were borne back upon me.
Curses and threats ensued.

"It is the Provost-guard," said a fugitive, "driving back
the boys."

"Go back!" called a voice ahead. "I'll blow you to h—ll,
if you don't go back! Not a man shall cross the bridge
without orders!"

The stragglers were variously affected by this intelligence. Some cursed and threatened; some of the wounded
blubbered as they leaned languidly upon the shoulders of
their comrades. Others stoically threw themselves on the
ground and tried to sleep. One man called aloud that the
"boys" were stronger than the Provosts, and that, therefore, the "boys" ought to "go in and win."

"Where's the man that wants to mutiny?" said the voice
ahead; "let me see him!"

The man slipped away; for the Provost officer spoke as
though he meant all he said.

"Nobody wants to mutiny!" called others.

"Three cheers for the Union."

The wounded and well threw up their hats together,
and made a sickly hurrah. The grim officer relented, and
he shouted stentoriously that he would take the responsibility of passing the wounded. These gathered themselves
up and pushed through the throng; but many skulkers
plead injuries, and so escaped. When I attempted to follow, on horseback, hands were laid upon me and I was refused exit. In that hour of terror and sadness, there were
yet jests and loud laughter. However keenly I felt these
things, I had learned that modesty amounted to little in
the army; so I pushed my nag steadily forward and scattered the camp vernacular, in the shape of imprecations,
left and right.

"Colonel," I called to the officer in command, as the line
of bayonets edged me in, "may I pass out? I am a civilian!"

"No!" said the Colonel, wrathfully. "This is no place for
a civilian."

"That's why I want to get away."

"Pass out!"

I followed the winding of the woods to Woodbury's Bridge—the next above Grapevine Bridge. The approaches were clogged with wagons and field-pieces, and I understood that some panic-stricken people had pulled up some of the timbers to prevent a fancied pursuit. Along the sides of the bridge many of the wounded were washing their wounds in the water; and the cries of the teamsters echoed weirdly through the trees that grew in the river. At nine o'clock, we got under way—horsemen, batteries, ambulances, ammunition teams, infantry, and finally some great siege thirty-twos that had been hauled from Gaines's House. One of these pieces broke down the timbers again, and my impression is that it was cast into the current. When we emerged from the swamp timber, the hills before us were found brilliantly illuminated with burning camps. I made toward headquarters, in one of Trent's fields; but all the tents save one had been taken down, and lines of white-covered wagons stretched southward until they were lost in the shadows. The tent of General McClellan alone remained, and beneath an arbor of pine boughs, close at hand, he sat, with his corps commanders and aides, holding a council of war. A ruddy fire lit up the historical group, and I thought at the time, as I have said a hundred times since, that the consultation might be selected for a grand national painting. The crisis, the hour, the adjuncts, the renowned participants, peculiarly fit it for pictorial commemoration.

The young commander sat in a chair, in full uniform, uncovered. Heintzelman was kneeling upon a fagot, earnestly speaking. De Joinville sat apart, by the fire, examining a map. Fitz John Porter was standing back of McClellan, leaning upon his chair. Keyes, Franklin, and Sumner were listening attentively. Some sentries paced to and fro, to keep out vulgar curiosity. Suddenly, there was a nodding of heads, as of some policy decided; they threw themselves upon their steeds, and galloped off toward Michie's.

As I reined at Michie's porch, at ten o'clock, the bridges behind me were blown up, with a flare that seemed a blazing of the Northern Lights. The family were sitting upon the porch, and Mrs. Michie was greatly alarmed with the idea that a battle would be fought round her house next day.

O'Ganlon, of Meagher's staff, had taken the fever, and sent anxiously for me, to compare our symptoms.

I bade the good people adieu before I went to bed, and gave the man Pat a dollar to stand by my horse while I slept, and to awake me at any disturbance, that I might be ready to scamper. Pat, I am bound to say, woke me up thrice by the exclamation of—

"Sure, yer honor, there's—well—to pay in the yard! I think ye and the Doctor had better ride off."

On each of those occasions, I found that the man Pat had been lonesome, and wanted somebody to speak to.

What a sleep was mine that night! I forgot my fever. But another and a hotter fever burned my temples—the fearful excitement of the time! Whither were we to go, cut off from the York, beaten before Richmond—perhaps even now surrounded—and to be butchered tomorrow, till the clouds should rain blood? Were we to retreat one hundred miles down the hostile Peninsula—a battle at every rod, a grave at every footstep? Then I remembered the wounded heaped at Gaines's Mill, and how they were groaning without remedy, ebbing at every pulse, counting the flashing drops, calling for water, for mercy, for death. So I found heart; for I was not buried yet. And somehow I felt that fate was to take me, as the great poet took Dante, through other and greater horrors.

CHAPTER XV

McClellan's Retreat

THE SCENE presented in Michie's lawn and oak grove, on Saturday morning, June 28, was terribly picturesque, and characteristic of the calamity of war. The well was beset by crowds of wounded men, perishing of thirst, who made frantic efforts to reach the bucket, but were borne back by the stronger desperadoes. The kitchen was swarming with hungry soldiers who begged corn-bread and half-cooked dough from the Negroes. The shady side-yard was dotted with pale, bruised, and bleeding people, who slept out their weariness upon the damp grass, forgetful, for the moment, of their sores. Ambulances poured through the lane, in solemn procession, and now and then, couples of privates bore by some wounded officer, upon a canvas "stretcher." The lane proving too narrow, at length, for the passing vehicles, the gate-posts and fence were torn up, and finally, the soldiers made a footway of the hall of the dwelling.

The retreat had been in progress all night, as I had heard the wagons through my open windows. By daylight the whole army was acquainted with the facts that we were to resign our depot at White House, relinquish the north bank of the river, and retire precipitately to the shores of the James. A rumor—indignantly denied, but as often repeated—prevailed among the teamsters, surgeons, and drivers, that the wounded were to be left in the enemy's hands. It shortly transpired that we were already cut off from the Pamunkey. A train had departed for White House at dawn, and had delivered its cargo of mortality

safely; but a second train, attempting the passage, at seven o'clock had been fired into, and compelled to return. A tremendous explosion, and a shaft of white smoke that flashed to the zenith, informed us, soon afterward, that the railroad bridge had been blown up.

About the same time, the roar of artillery recommenced in front, and regiments that had not slept for twenty hours were hurried past us, to take position at the entrenchments. A universal fear now found expression, and helpless people asked of each other, with pale lips—

"How far have we to walk to reach the James?"

It was doubtful, at this time, that any one knew the route to that river. A few members of the signal corps had adventured thither to open communication with the gunboats, and a small cavalry party of Casey's division had made a foray to New Market and Charles City Court House. But it was rumored that Wise's brigade of Confederates was now posted at Malvern Hill, closing up the avenue of escape, and that the whole right wing of the Confederate army was pushing toward Charles City. Malvern Hill, the nearest point that could be gained, was about twenty miles distant, and Harrison's Landing—presumed to be our final destination—was thirty miles away. To retreat over this distance, encumbered with baggage, the wounded and the sick, was discarded as involving pursuit, and certain calamity. Cavalry might fall upon us at every turning, since the greater portion of our own horse had been scouting between White House and Hanover, when the bridges were destroyed, and was therefore separated from the main army. At eight o'clock, weak with fever and scarcely able to keep in the saddle, I joined Mr. Anderson of the *Herald,* and rode toward the front, that I might discover the whereabouts of the new engagement. Winding through a cart-track in Michie's woods, we came upon fully one third of the whole army, or the remnant of all that portion engaged at Gaines's Mill—the Reserves, Porter's Corps, Slocum's division, and Meagher's brigade— perhaps thirty thousand men. They covered the whole of Trent's farm, and were drawn up in line, heavily equipped,

with their colors in position, field officers dismounted, and
detachments from each regiment preparing hot coffee at
certain fires. A very few wagons—and these containing
only ammunition—stood harnessed beside each regiment.
In many cases the men lay or knelt upon the ground. Such
hot, hungry, weary wretches, I never beheld. During the
whole night long they had been crossing the Chickahominy, and the little sleep vouchsafed them had been taken
in snatches upon the bare clay. Travelling from place to
place, I saw the surviving heroes of the defeat: Meagher
looking very yellow and prosaic; Slocum—small, indomitable, active; Newton—a little gray, a trifle proud, very
mercurial, and curiously enough, a Virginian; Meade—
lithe, spectacled, sanguine; and finally General McCall, as
grave, kindly odd and absent, as I had found him four
months before. The latter worthy was one of the first of
the Federal generals to visit Richmond. He was taken
prisoner the second day afterward, and the half of his
command was slain or disabled.

I went to and fro, obtaining the names of killed,
wounded and missing, with incidents of the battle as well
as its general plan. These I scrawled upon bits of newspaper, upon envelopes, upon the lining of my hat, and
finally upon my shirt wristbands. I was literally filled with
notes before noon, and if I had been shot at that time, endeavors to obtain my name would have been extremely
difficult. I should have had more titles than some of the
Chinese princes; some parts of me would have been found
fatally wounded, and others italicized for gallant behavior.
Indeed, I should have been shot in every part, taken prisoner at every place, killed outright in every skirmish, and
marvellously saved through every peril. My tombstone
would have been some hundreds of muster-rolls and my
obituary a fortune to a newspaper. I recollect, with some
amusement, the credit that each regiment took upon itself
for distinguished behavior. There were few colonels that
did not claim all the honors. I fell in with a New Jersey
brigade, that had been decimated of nearly half its *quota*,
and a spruce young major attempted to convey an idea of

the battle to me. He said, in brief, that the New Jersey brigade, composed mainly of himself and his regiment, and some few organizations of little consequence—although numbering ten thousand odd soldiers—had received the whole shock of a quantity of "Rebels." The said "Rebels" appeared to make up one fourth part of the population of the globe. There was no end to them. They seemed to be several miles deep, longer and more crooked than the Pamunkey, and stood with their rear against Richmond, so that they couldn't fall back, even if they wanted to. In vain did the New Jersey brigade and his regiment attack them with ball and bayonet. How the "Rebels" ever withstood the celebrated charge of his regiment was altogether inexplicable.

In the language of the major—"the New Jersey brigade —and my regiment—fit, and fit, and fit, and give 'em 'get out!' But sir, may I be——, well there (expression inadequate), we couldn't budge 'em. No, sir! (very violently), not budge 'em, sir! *I* told the boys to walk at 'em with cold steel. Says I: 'Boys, steel'ill fetch 'em, or nothin' under heaven!' Well, sir, at 'em we went—me and the boys. There ain't been no sich charge in the whole war! Not in the whole war, sir! (intensely fervid); leave it to any impartial observer if there has been! We went up the hill, square in the face of all their artillery, musketry, cavalry, sharpshooters, riflemen—everything, sir! Everything! (energetically). One o' my men overheard the Rebel General say, as we came up: says he—'that's the gamest thing I ever see.' Well! we butchered 'em frightful. We must a killed a thousand or two of 'em, don't you think so, Adjutant? But, sir—it was all in vain. No go, sir! no, sir, no go! (impressively). And the New Jersey brigade and my regiment fell back, inch by inch, with our feet to the foe (rhetorically). Is that so, boys?"

The "boys," who had meantime gathered around, exclaimed loudly, that it was "true as preachin," and the Major added, in an undertone that his name was spelled ——

"But where were Porter's columns?" said I, "and the Pennsylvania Reserves?"

"I didn't see 'em," said the Major: "I don't think they was there. If they had a been, why wa'nt they on hand to save my regiment, and the New Jersey brigade?"

It would be wrong to infer from these vauntings, that the Federals did not fight bravely and endure defeat unshrinkingly. On the contrary, I have never read of higher exemplifications of personal and moral courage than I witnessed during this memorable retreat. And the young Major's boasting did not a whit reduce my estimate of his efficiency. For in America, swaggering does not necessarily indicate cowardice. I knew a captain of artillery in Smith's division, who was wordier than Gratiano, and who exaggerated like Falstaff. But he was a lion in action, and at Lee's Mill and Williamsburg his battery was handled with consummate skill.

From Trent's farm the roadway led by a strip of corduroy, through sloppy, swampy woods, to an open place, beyond a brook, where Smith's division lay. The firing had almost entirely ceased, and we heard loud cheers running up and down the lines, as we again ventured within cannon range. On this spot, for the second time, the Federals had won a decided success. And in so far as a cosmopolitan could feel elated, I was proud, for a moment, of the valor of my division. The victors had given me meals and a bed, and they had fed my pony when both of us were hungry. But the sight of the prisoners and the collected dead saddened me somewhat.

These two engagements have received the name of the First and Second battles of Golding's Farm. They resulted from an effort of Toombs's Georgia brigade to carry the redoubt and breastworks of General Smith. Toombs was a civilian, and formerly a senator from Georgia. He had no military ability, and his troops were driven back with great slaughter, both on Friday and Saturday. Among the prisoners taken was Colonel Lamar of (I think) the 7th Georgia regiment. He passed me, in a litter, wounded, as I rode toward the redoubt.

Lamar was a beautiful man, shaped like a woman, and his hair was long, glossy, and wavy with ringlets. He was a tiger, in his love of blood, and in character self-willed and vehement. He was of that remarkable class of Southern men, of which the noted "Filibuster" William Walker was the great exponent. I think I may call him an apostle of slavery. He believed it to be the destiny of our pale race to subdue all the dusky tribes of the earth, and to evangelize, with the sword, the whole Western continent, to the uses of master and man. Such people were called disciples of "manifest destiny." He threw his whole heart into the war; but when I saw him, bloodless, panting, quivering, I thought how little the wrath of man availed against the justice of God.

From Smith's on the right, I kept along a military road, in the woods, to John Sedgwick's and Israel Bush Richardson's divisions, at Fair Oaks. Richardson was subsequently slain, at the second battle of Bull Run. He was called "Fighting Dick," and on this particular morning was talking composedly to his wife, as she was about to climb to the saddle. His tent had been taken down, and soldiers were placing his furniture in a wagon. A greater contrast I never remarked, than the ungainly, awkward, and rough General, with his slight, trim, pretty companion. She had come to visit him and had remained until commanded to retire. I fancied, though I was separated some distance, that the little woman wept, as she kissed him good-bye, and he followed her, with frequent gestures of good-hap, till she disappeared behind the woods. I do not know that such prosaic old soldiers are influenced by the blandishments of love; but "Fighting Dick" never wooed death so recklessly as in the succeeding engagements of New Market and Malvern Hill.

From Seven Pines to the right of Richardson's headquarters, ran a line of alternate breastwork, redoubt, and stockade. The best of these redoubts was held by Captain Petit, with a New York Volunteer battery. I had often talked with Petit, for he embodied, as well as any man in the army, the martial qualifications of a volunteer. He despised order. Nobody cared less for dress and dirt. I have seen him, sitting in a hole that he hollowed with his hands, tossing pebbles and dust over his head, like another Job. He had profound contempt for any man and any system that was not "American." I remember asking him, one day, the meaning of the gold lace upon the staff hats of the Irish brigade.

"Means run like shell!" said Petit, covering me with dirt.

"Don't the Irish make the best soldiers?" I ventured.

"No!" said Petit, raining pebbles, "I had rather have one American than ten Irishmen."

The fighting of Petit was contrary to all rule; but I think that he was a splendid artillery-man. He generally mounted the rampart, shook his fist at the enemy, flung up his hat, jumped down, sighted the guns himself, threw shells with wonderful accuracy, screamed at the gunners, mounted the rampart again, halloed, and, in short, managed to do more execution, make more noise, attract more attention and throw more dirt than anybody in the army. His redoubt was small, but beautifully constructed, and the parapet was heaped with double rows of sandbags. It mounted rifled field-pieces, and, at most times, the gunners were lying under the pieces, asleep. Not any of the entrenched posts among the frontier Indians were more enveloped in wilderness than this. The trees had been felled in front to give the cannon play, but behind and on each side belts of dense, dwarf timber covered the boggy soil. To the left of Petit, on the old field of Seven Pines, lay the divisions of Hooker and Kearny, and thither I journeyed, after leaving the redoubtable volunteer.

Joseph Hooker was a New Englander, reputed to be the handsomest man in the army. He fought bravely in the Mexican War, and afterwards retired to San Francisco, where he passed a Bohemian existence at the Union Club House. He disliked McClellan, was beloved by his men, and was generally known as "Old Joe." He has been one of the most successful Federal leaders, and seems to hold a charmed life. In all probability he will become Commander-in-chief of one of the grand armies.

Philip Kearny has passed away since the date of which I speak. He was known as the "one-armed Devil," and was,

by odds, the best educated of all the Federal military
chiefs. But, singularly enough, he departed from all tactics, when hotly afield. His personal energy and courage
have given him renown, and he loved to lead forlorn
hopes, or head storming-parties, or ride upon desperate
adventures. He was rich from childhood, and spent much
of his life in Europe. For a part of this time he served as a
cavalry-man with the French, in Algiers. In private life he
was equally reckless, but his tastes were scholarly, and he
was generous to a fault. Both Kearny and Hooker were
kind to the reporters, and I owe the dead man many a
favor. General Daniel Sickles commanded a brigade in
this corps. To the left, and in the rear of Heintzelman's
corps, lay the divisions of Casey and Couch, that had relapsed into silence since their disgrace at Seven Pines.
General Silas Casey was a thin-haired old gentleman, too
gracious to be a soldier, although I believe that he is still
in the service. His division comprised the extreme left of
the Grand Army, and bordered upon a deep, impenetrable
bog called White Oak Swamp. It was the purpose of Mc-
Clellan to place this swamp between him and the enemy,
and defend its passage till his baggage and siege artillery
had obtained the shelter of the gunboats, on the shores of
the James. I rode along this whole line, to renew my impressions of the position, and found that sharp skirmishing
was going on at every point. When I returned to Savage's,
where McClellan's headquarters had temporarily been
pitched, I found the last of the wagons creaking across the
track, and filing slowly southward. The wounded lay in
the out-houses, in the trains of cars, beside the hedge, and
in the shade of the trees about the dwelling. A little back,
beside a wood, lay Lowe's balloon traps, and the infantry
"guard," and cavalry "escort" of the Commander-in-chief
were encamped close to the new provost quarters, in a
field beyond the orchard. An ambulance passed me, as I
rode into the lane; it was filled with sufferers, and two men
with bloody feet crouched in the trail. From the roof of
Savage's house floated the red hospital flag. Savage him-

self was a quiet Virginia farmer, and a magistrate. His name is now coupled with a grand battle.

I felt very hungry, at four o'clock, but my weak stomach revolted at coarse soldier fare, and I determined to ride back to Michie's. I was counselled to beware; but having learned little discretion afield, I cantered off, through a trampled tillage of wheat and an interminable woods. In a half hour I rode into the familiar yard; but the place was so ruined that I hardly recognized it. Not a panel of fence remained; the lawn was a great pool of slime; the windlass had been wrenched from the well; a few gashed and expiring soldiers lay motionless beneath the oaks, the fields were littered with the remains of camps, and the old dwelling stood like a haunted thing upon a blighted plain. The idlers, the teamsters, and the tents were gone—all was silence—and in the little front porch sat Mrs. Michie, weeping; the old gentleman stared at the desolation with a working face, and two small yellow lads lay dolorously upon the steps. They all seemed to brighten up as I appeared at the gate, and when I staggered from my horse, both of them took my hands. I think that tears came into all our eyes at once, and the little Ethiops fairly bellowed.

"My friends," I said, falteringly, "I see how you have suffered, and sympathize with you, from my heart."

"Our beautiful property is ruined," said Mrs. Michie, welling up.

"Yer's five years of labor—my children's heritage—the home of our old age—look at it!"

The old gentleman stood up gravely, and cast his eyes mournfully around.

"I have nobody to accuse," he said; "my grief is too deep for any hate. This is war!"

"What will the girls say when they come back?" was the mother's next sob; "they loved the place: do you think they will know it?"

I did not know how to reply. They retained my hands, and for a moment none of us spoke.

"Don't think, Mr. Townsend," said the chivalrous old gentleman again, "that we like you less because some of your country people have stripped us. Mother, where is the gruel you made for him?"

The good lady, expecting my return, had prepared some nourishing chicken soup, and directly she produced it. I think she took heart when I ate so plentifully, and we all spoke hopefully again. Their kindness so touched me that as the evening came quietly about us, lengthening the shadows, and I knew that I must depart, I took both their hands again, doubtful what to say.

"My friends—may I say, almost my parents? for you have been as kind—good-bye! In a day, perhaps, you will be with your children again. Richmond will be open to you. You may freely go and come. Be comforted by these assurances. And when the war is over—God speed the time!—we may see each other under happier auspices."

"Good-bye!" said Mr. Michie; "if I have a house at that time, you shall be welcome."

"Good-bye," said Mrs. Michie; "tell your mother that a strange lady in Virginia took good care of you when you were sick."

I waved a final adieu, vaulted down the lane, and the wood gathered its solemn darkness about me. When I emerged upon Savage's fields, a succession of terrible explosions shook the night, and then the flames flared up, at points along the railroad. They were blowing up the locomotives and burning the cars. At the same hour, though I could not see it, White House was wrapped in fire, and the last sutler, teamster, and cavalry-man had disappeared from the shores of the Pamunkey.

I tossed through another night of fever, in the captain's tent of the Sturgis Rifles—McClellan's body guard. And somehow, again, I dreamed fitfully of the unburied corpses on the field of Gaines's Mill.

CHAPTER XVI

A Battle Sunday

IN THE dim of the morning of our Lord's Sabbath, the twenty-ninth of June, 1862, I sat in my saddle at Savage's. The gloom was very cheerless. A feeling of hopeless vagabondism oppressed me. I remembered the Disinherited Knight, the Wandering Jew, Robinson Crusoe, and other poor errants in the wide world, and wondered if any of them ever looked so ruefully as I, when the last wagon of the Grand Army disappeared through the shadow.

The tent had been taken down at midnight. I had been dozing in the saddle, with parched lips and throbbing temples, waiting for my comrade. Headquarters had been intending to move, without doing it, for four hours, and he informed me that it was well to stay with the Commanding General, as the Commanding General kept out of danger, and also kept in provisions. I was sick and petulant, and finally quarrelled with my friend. He told me, quietly, that I would regret my harshness when I should be well again. I set off for White Oak, but repented at Burnt Chimneys, and turned back. In the misty dawn I saw the maimed still lying on the ground, wrapped in relics of blankets, and in one of the outhouses a grim embalmer stood amid a family of nude corpses. He dealt with the bodies of high officers only; for, said he—

"I used to be glad to prepare private soldiers. They were wuth a five dollar bill apiece. But, Lord bless you, a colonel pays a hundred, and a brigadier-general two hundred. There's lots of them now, and I have cut the acquaintance of everything below a major. I might," he added, "as a great favor, do a captain, but he must pay a major's price. I insist upon that! Such windfalls don't come every day. There won't be another such killing for a century."

A few horsemen of the escort loitered around headquarters. All the tents but one had been removed, and the staff crouched sleepily upon the refuse straw. The rain began to drizzle at this time, and I unbuckled a blanket to wrap about my shoulders. Several people were lying upon dry places, here and there, and espying some planks a little remote, I tied my horse to a peach tree, and stretched myself languidly upon my back. The bridal couch or the throne were never so soft as those knotty planks, and the drops that fell upon my forehead seemed to cool my fever.

I had passed into a sort of cognizant sleep when a harsh, loud, cruel voice awakened me, and I seemed to see a great Polyphemus, stretching his hands into the clouds, and gaping like an earthquake.

"Boy," I heard him say, to a slight figure, near at hand, "boy, what are you standing there for? What in —— do you want?"

"Nothing!"

"Take it, and go, —— —— you! Take it, and go!"

I peeped timorously from my place, and recognized the Provost-General of the Grand Army. He had been sleeping upon a camp chest, and did not appear to be refreshed thereby.

"I feel sulky as ——!" he said to an officer adjoining; "I feel —— bad-humored! Orderly!"

"General!"

"Whose horses are these?"

"I don't know, General!"

"Cut every —— —— one of 'em loose. Wake up these —— —— loafers with the point of your sabre! Every —— —— one of 'em! That's what I call —— —— boldness!"

He strutted off like the great Bomba or the Czar, and I thought I never beheld a more exceptional person in any high position.

With a last look at Savage's white house, the abandoned

wretches in the lawn, the blood-red hospital flag, the torn track and smouldering cars, I turned my face southward, crossed some bare plains, that had once been fields, and at eight o'clock passed down the Williamsburg road, toward Bottom's Bridge. The original roadway was now a bottom-less stretch of sand, full of stranded wheels, dead horses, shreds of blankets, discarded haversacks, and mounds of spilled crackers. Other routes for wagons had been opened across fields, over bluffs, around pits and bogs, and through thickets and woods. The whole country was crossed with deeply-rutted roads, as if some immense city had been lifted away, and only its interminably sinuous streets remained. Near Burnt Chimneys, a creek crossing the road made a ravine, and here I overtook the hindmost of the wagons. They had been stalled in the gorge, and a provost guard was hurrying the laggard teamsters. The creek was muddy beyond comparison, and at the next hill-top I passed Burnt Chimneys, a few dumb witnesses that pointed to heaven. A mile or two further, I came to some of the retreating regiments, and also to five of the siege thirty-twos with which Richmond was to have been bom-barded. The main army still lay back at their entrench-ments to cover the retreat, and at ten o'clock I heard the roar of field guns; the pursuit had commenced, and the Confederates were pouring over the ramparts at Fair Oaks. I did not go back; battles were of no consequence to me. I wanted some breakfast. If I could only obtain a cup of warm coffee and a fragment of meat, I thought that I might recover strength. But nothing could be obtained anywhere, for money or charity. The soldiers that I passed looked worn and hungry, for their predecessors had swept the country like herds of locusts; but one cheerful fellow, whom I addressed, produced a lump of fat pork that I tried to eat, but made a signal failure. All my baggage had been left at Michie's, where it remains to this moment. None cared to be hospitable to correspondents at this de-spondent hour, and a horrible idea of starvation took pos-session of my mind. A mile from White Oak Swamp, some distance back of the road, lay the Engineer Brigade. They were now on the eve of breaking camp, and when I reached Colonel McCloud Murphy's, his chests were packed, and all his provisions had gone ahead. He gave me, however, a couple of hard crackers and a draught of whiskey and quinine, whereby I rallied for a moment. At General Woodbury's I observed a middle-aged lady, making her toilet by a looking-glass hung against the tent-pole. She seemed as careful of her personal appearance, in this trying time, as if she had been at some luxurious court. There were several women on the retreat, and though the guns thundered steadily behind, they were never flurried, but could have received company, or accepted offers of marriage, with the utmost complacency. If there was any one that rouged, I am sure that no personal danger would have disturbed her while she heightened her roses; and she would have tied up her back hair in defiance of shell or grape.

At Casey's ancient headquarters, on the bluff facing White Oak Swamp, I found five correspondents. We fraternized immediately, and they all pooh-poohed the battle, as such an old story that it would be absurd to ride back to the field. We knew, however, that it was occurring at Peach Orchard, on a part of the old ground at Fair Oaks. These gentlemen were in rather despondent moods, and there was one who opined that we were all to be made prisoners of war. In his own expressive way of putting it, we were to be "gobbled up." This person was stout and inclined to panting and perspiration. He wore glasses upon a most pugnacious nose, and his large, round head was covered with short, bristly, jetty hair.

"I promised my wife," said this person, who may be called Cindrey, "to stay at home after the Burnside business. The Burnside job was very nearly enough for me. In fact I should have quite starved on the Burnside job, if I hadn't took the fever. And the fever kept me so busy that I forgot how hungry I was. So I lived over that."

At this point he took off his glasses and wiped his face; the water was running down his cheeks like a miniature cataract, and his great neck seemed to emit jets of perspiration.

"Well," he continued, "the Burnside job wasn't enough for me; I must come out again. I must follow the young Napoleon. And the young Napoleon has made a pretty mess of it. I never expect to get home any more; I know I shall be gobbled up!"

A youngish, oldish, oddish fellow, whom they called "Pop," here told Mr. Cindrey to keep his pulse up and take a drink. A tall, large person, in semi-quaker garb, who did not look unlike George Fox, run to seed, said, with a flourish, that these battles were nothing to Shiloh. He was attached to the provincial press, and had been with the army of the West until recently. Without any exception, he was the "fussiest," most impertinent, most disagreeable man that I ever knew. He always made a hero of himself in his reports, and if I remember rightly, their headings ran after this fashion:

Tremendous Battle at Roanoke! *The Correspondent of* THE Blunderbuss *hoists the* National Flag above the REBEL RAMPARTS ! ! ! or again—*Grand Victory at* Shiloh! *Mr. Twaddle, our Special Correspondent,* TAKEN PRISONER ! ! ! *He* escapes ! ! ! *He is* fired upon ! ! ! *He wriggles through* four swamps *and* SEVEN HOSTILE CAMPS! *He is* again captured! *He STRANGLES the sentry! He drinks the Rebel Commander, Philpot, BLIND! Philpot gives him* THE password ! ! *Philpot compliments the Blunderbuss.* OUR *Correspondent gains the Gunboats! He is* taken aboard! *His welcome! Description of* HIS BOOTS! *Remarks, etc.,* etc., ETC ! ! !

This man was anxious to regulate not only his own newspaper, but he aspired to control the entire press. And his self adulation was incessant. He rang all the changes upon Shiloh. Every remark suggested some incident of Shiloh. He was a thorough Shilohite, and I regretted in my heart that the "Rebels" had not shut him away at Shiloh, that he might have enjoyed it to the end of his days.

The man Pop produced some apple whiskey, and we repaired to a spring, at the foot of the hill, where Pop mixed a cold punch, and we drank in rotation. I don't think that Cindrey enjoyed his draught, for it filtered through his neck as if he had sprung a leak there; but the man Twaddle might have taken a tun, and, as Pop said, the effect would have been that of "pouring whiskey through a knot-hole." It was arranged among our own reporters, that I, being sick, should be the first of the staff to go to New York. The man Pop said jocosely, that I might be allowed to die in the bosom of my family. The others gave me their notes and lists, but none could give me what I most needed—a morsel of food. At eleven o'clock our little party crossed White Oak Creek. There was a corduroy bridge upon which the teams travelled, and a log bridge of perilous unsteadiness for foot passengers. But the soldiers were fording the stream in great numbers, and I plunged my horse into the current so that he spattered a group of fellows, and one of them lunged at me with a bayonet. Beyond the creek and swamp, on the hillsides, baggage wagons and batteries were parked in immense numbers. The troops were taking positions along the edge of the bottom, to oppose incursions of the enemy, when they attempted pursuit, and I was told that the line extended several miles westward, to New Market Cross Roads, where, it was thought, the Confederates would march out from Richmond to offer battle. The roadway, beyond the swamp, was densely massed with horse, foot, cannon, and teams. The latter still kept toward the James, but the nags suffered greatly from lack of corn. Only indispensable material had been hauled from the Chickahominy, and the soldiers who fought the ensuing protracted battles were exhausted from hunger. Everything had an uncomfortable, transient, expectant appearance, and the feeble people that limped toward the *ultima thule* looked fagged and wretched.

There were some with balls in the groin, thigh, leg, or ankle, that made the whole journey dropping blood at every step. They were afraid to lie down, as the wounded limbs might then grow rigid and stop their progress. While I pitied these maimed persons, I held the sick in greater sympathy. The troubles of the one were local; the others were pained in every bone. Bullets are fearful tenants, but fevers are worse. And some of the flushed, staggering folk, that reeled along the roadside, were literally out of their minds. They muttered and talked incoherently, and shouted ribald songs till my blood curdled to see them. At the first house on the right of the road, a half-mile past the Creek, I noticed many idle soldiers climbing the white palings, to watch something that lay in the yard. A gray-haired man was expiring, under the coolness of a spreading tree, and he was even now in the closing pangs. A comrade at his side bathed his brow with cool water, but I saw that he would shortly be with Lazarus or Dives. His hands were stretched stiffly by his sides, his feet were rigidly extended, and death was hardening into his bleached face. The white eyeballs glared sightlessly upward: he was looking into the other world.

The heat at this time was so intolerable that our party, in lieu of any other place of resort, resolved to go to the woods. The sun set in heaven like a fiery furnace, and we sweated at every pore. I was afraid, momentarily, of sunstroke, and my horse was bathed in foam. Some companies of cavalry were sheltered in the edges of the woods, and, having secured our nags, we penetrated the depths, and spread out our blankets that we might lie down. But no breath of air stirred the foliage. The "hot and copper sky" found counterpart in the burning earth, and innumerable flies and insects fastened their fangs in our flesh. Cindrey was upon the rack, and it seemed to me that he possessed a sort of capillary perspiration, for the drops stood at tips of each separate bristle. He appeared to be passing from the solid to the fluid state, and I said, ungenerously, that the existing temperature was his liquifying point.

"Then," said the man Pop, with a youngish, oldish smile, "we may as well liquor up."

"I don't drink!" said Twaddle, with a flourish. "During

all the perilous hours of Shiloh, I abstained. But I am willing to admit, in respect to heat, that Shiloh is nowhere at present. And, therefore, I drink with a protest."

"No man can drink from my bottle, with a protest," said Pop. "It isn't regular, and implies coercion. Now I don't coerce anybody, particularly you."

"Oh!" said Twaddle, drinking like a fish, or, as Pop remarked, enough to float a gunboat; "oh! we often chaffed each other at Shiloh."

"If you persist in reminding me of Shiloh," blurted Cindrey, "you'll be the ruin of me—you and the heat and the flies. You'll have me dissolving into a dew."

Here he wiped his forehead, and killed a large blue fly, that was probing his ear. We all resolved to go to sleep, and Twaddle said that *he* slept like a top, in the heat of action, at Shiloh. Pop asked him, youngishly, to be kind enough to capture no redoubts while we slumbered, and not to raise the national flag over any ramparts for fifteen minutes. Then he grinned oldishly, and commenced to snore, with his flask in his bosom. I am certain that nobody ever felt a tithe of the pain, hunger, heat, and weariness, which agonized me, when I awoke from a half-hour's sweltering nap. My clothing was soaking with water; I was almost blind; somebody seemed to be sawing a section out of my head; my throat was hot and crackling; my stomach knew all the pangs of emptiness; I had scarcely strength to motion away the pertinacious insects. A soldier gave me a trifle of boiling water from his canteen; but I gasped for air; we were living in a vacuum. Sahara could not have been so fierce and burning. Two of us started off to find a spring. We made our way from shade to shade, expiring at every step, and finally, at the base of the hill, on the brink of the swamp, discovered a rill of tepid water, that evaporated before it had trickled a hundred yards. If a sleek and venomous water-snake—for there were thousands of them hereabout—had coiled in the channel, I would still have sucked the draught, bending down as I did. Then I bethought me of my pony. He had neither been fed nor watered for twenty hours, and I hastened to obtain him from his place along the woodside. To my terror, he was gone. Forgetful of my weakness, I passed rapidly, hither and thither, inquiring of cavalry-men, and entertaining suspicions of every person in the vicinity. Finally, I espied him in charge of a rough, thievish sabreman, who affected not to see me. I went up to the animal, and pulled the reins from his shoulder, to discover the brand mark—"U. S." As I surmised, he had not been branded, and I turned indignantly upon the fellow:

"My friend, how came you by this horse?"

"Quartermaster!" said the man, guiltily.

"No sir! He belongs to me. Take off that cavalry-saddle, and find mine, immediately."

"Not if the court knows itself," said the man—"and it thinks it do!"

"Then," said I, white with rage, "I shall report you at once, for theft."

"You may, if you want to," replied the man, carelessly.

I struck off at once for the new provost quarters, at a farm-house, close by. The possible failure to regain my animal filled me with rueful thoughts. How was I, so dismounted, to reach the distant river? I should die, or starve, on the way. I thought I should faint, when I came to the end of the first field, and leaned, tremblingly, against a tree. I caught myself sobbing, directly, like a girl, and my mind ran upon the coolness of my home with my own breezy bedroom, soft paintings, and pleasant books. These themes tortured me with a consciousness of my folly. I had forsaken them for the wickednesses of this un-happy campaign. And my body was to blacken by the road-side—the sable birds of prey were to be my mourners.

But, looking through my tears, a moving something passed between me and the sky. A brownish bay pony, trailing a fence-rail by his halter, and browsing upon patches of oats. I whistled thrice and the faithful animal trotted to my feet, and extended his great nose to be rubbed. I believe that this horse was the only living thing in the army that sympathized with me. He knew that I was sick, and I thought once, that, like the great dogs of

Saint Bernard, he was about to get upon his knees, that I might the more readily climb upon his back. He did, however, stand quietly, while I mounted, and I gave him a drink at the foot of the hill. Returning, I saw the soldier, wrongfully accused, eyeing me from his haunt beneath the trees. I at once rode over to him, and apologized for my mistake.

"Never mind," said the man, complacently. "You was all right. I might a done the same thing. Fact is," he added, "I did hook this hoss, but I knew you wan't the party."

During the rest of the day I travelled disconsolately, up and down the road, winding in and out of the lines of teams.

I was assured that it would be impossible to get to the James till next day, as no portion of that army had yet advanced so far. The moody minutes of that afternoon made the longest part of my life, while the cannon at Peach Orchard and Savage's roared and growled incessantly. Toward the close of the day I fell in with Captain Hill, of the New York Saratoga regiment, who gave me the outline of the fight.

The Confederates had discovered that we were falling back, by means of a balloon of home manufacture—the first they had been able to employ during the entire war. They appeared at our entrenchments on Sunday morning, and finding them deserted, commenced an irregular pursuit, whereby they received terrible volleys of musketry from ambuscaded regiments, and retired, in disorder, to the ramparts. This was the battle of Peach Orchard, and was disastrous to the Southerners. In the afternoon, they again essayed to advance, but more cautiously. The Federals, meantime, lay in order of battle upon Savage's, Dudley's, and Crouch's farms, their right resting on the Chickahominy, their centre on the railroad, and their left beyond the Williamsburg turnpike. For a time, an artillery contest ensued, and the hospitals at Savage's, where the wounded lay, were thrice fired upon. The Confederates finally penetrated the dense woods that belted this country, and the battle, at nightfall, became fervid and sanguinary. The Federals held their ground obstinately, and fell back, covered by artillery, at midnight. The woods were set on fire, in the darkness, and conflagration painted fiery terrors on the sky. The dead littered all the fields and woods. The retreating army had marked its route with corpses. This was the battle of Savage's, and neither party has called it a victory.

During the rest of the night the weary fugitives were crossing White Oak Creek and Swamp. Toward daybreak, the last battery had accomplished the passage; the bridge was destroyed; and preparations were made to dispute the pursuit in the morning.

I noted these particulars and added to my lists of dead and captured. At dusk I was about to sleep, supperless, upon the bare ground, when my patron, Colonel Murphy, again came in sight, and invited me to occupy a shelter-tent, on the brow of the hill at White Oak. To my great joy, he was able to offer me some stewed beef, bread and butter, and hot coffee. I ate voraciously, seizing the food in my naked fingers, and rending it like a beast.

The regiment of Colonel Murphy was composed of laborers, and artificers of every possible description. There were blacksmiths, moulders, masons, carpenters, boat-builders, joiners, miners, machinists, riggers, and rope-makers. They could have bridged the Mississippi, rebuilt the Tredegar iron works, finished the Tower of Babel, drained the Chesapeake, constructed the Great Eastern, paved Broadway, replaced the Grand Trunk railroad, or tunnelled the Straits of Dover. I have often thought that the real greatness of the Northern army lay in its ingenuity and industry, not in its military qualifications.

Our conversation turned upon these matters, as we sat before the Colonel's tent in the evening, and a chaplain represented the feelings of the North in this manner: "We must whip them. We have got more money, more men, more ships, more ingenuity. They are bound to knuckle at last. If we have to lose man for man with them, their host will die out before ours. And we won't give up the Union—not a piece of it big enough for a bird or a bee to cover

—though we reduce these thirty millions one half, and leave only the women and children to inherit the land."

The heart of the army was now cast down, though a large portion of the soldiers did not know why we were falling back. I heard moody, despondent, accusing mutterings, around the camp-fires, and my own mind was full of grief and bitterness. It seemed that our old flag had descended to a degenerate people. It was not now, as formerly, a proud recollection that I was an American. If I survived the retreat, it would become my mission to herald the evil tidings through the length and breadth of the land. If I fainted in their pursuit, a loathsome prison, or a grave in the trenches, were to be my awards. When I lay down in a shelter-tent, rolling from side to side, I remembered that this was the Sabbath day. A battle Sabbath! How this din and slaughter contrasted with my dear old Lord's days in the prayerful parsonage! The chimes in the white spire, where the pigeons cooed in the hush of the singing, were changed to cannon peals; and the boys that dozed in the "Amen corner," were asleep forever in the trampled grainfields. The good parson, whose clauses were not less truthful, because spoken through his nose, now blew the loud trumpet for the babes he had baptized, to join the captains of fifties and thousands; and while the feeble old women in the side pews made tremulous responses to the prayer for "thy soldiers fighting in thy cause," the banners of the Republic were craped, dusty, and bloody, and the scattered regiments were resting upon their arms for the shock of the coming dawn.

Thus I thought, tossing and talking through the long watches, and toward morning, when sleep brought fever-dreams, a monstrous something leered at me from the blackness, saying, in a sort of music—

"Gobbled up! Gobbled up!"

CHAPTER XVII

By the Riverside

A CRASH and a stunning shock, as of a falling sphere, aroused me at nine o'clock. A shell had burst in front of our tent, and the enemy's artillery was thundering from Casey's old hill, beyond the swamp. As I hastily drew on my boots—for I had not otherwise undressed—I had opportunity to remark one of those unaccountable panics which develop among civilian soldiers. The camps were plunged into disorder. As the shells dropped here and there, among the tents and teams, the wildest and most fearful deeds were enacted. Here a caisson blew up, tearing the horses to pieces, and whirling a cannoneer among the clouds. Then an ammunition wagon exploded, and the air seemed to be filled with fragments of wood, iron, and flesh. A boy stood at one of the fires, combing out his matted hair; suddenly his head flew off, spattering the brains, and the shell—which we could not see—exploded in a piece of woods, mutilating the trees. The effect upon the people around me was instantaneous and appalling. Some, that were partially dressed, took to their heels, hugging a medley of clothing. The teamsters climbed into the saddles, and shouted to their nags, whipping them the while. If the heavy wheels hesitated to revolve, they left horses and vehicles to their fate, taking themselves to the woods; or, as in some cases, cut traces and harness, and galloped away like madmen. In a twinkling our camps were almost deserted, and the fields, woods, and roads were alive with fugitives, rushing, swearing, falling, and trampling, while the fierce bolts fell momentarily among them, making havoc at every rod.

To join this flying, dying mass was my first impulse; but after-thought reminded me that it would be better to remain. I must not leave my horse, for I could not walk the whole long way to the James, and the fever had so reduced me that I hardly cared to keep the little life remaining. I almost marvelled at my coolness; since, in the fulness of strength and health, I should have been one of the first of the fugitives; whereas, I now looked interestedly upon the exciting spectacle, and wished that it could be daguerreotyped.

Before our artillery could be brought to play, the enemy, emboldened at his success, pushed a column of infantry down the hill, to cross the creek, and engage us on our camping-ground. For a time I believed that he would be successful, and in that event, confusion and ruin would have overtaken the Unionists. The gray and butternut lines appeared over the brow of the hill—they wound at double quick through the narrow defile—they poured a volley into our camps when half-way down, and under cover of the smoke they dashed forward impetuously, with a loud huzza. The artillery beyond them kept up a steady fire, raining shell, grape, and canister over their heads, and ploughing the ground on our side, into zigzag furrows— rending the trees, shattering the ambulances, tearing the tents to tatters, slaying the horses, butchering the men. Directly Captain Mott's battery was brought to bear; but before he could open fire, a solid shot struck one of his twelve-pounders, breaking the trunnion and splintering the wheels. In like manner one of his caissons blew up, and I do not think that he was able to make any practice whatever. A division of infantry was now marched forward, to engage the Confederates at the creek side; but two of the regiments—and I think that one was the 20th New York—turned bodily, and could not be rallied. The moment was full of significance, and I beheld these failures with breathless suspense. In five minutes the pursuers would gain the creek, and in ten, drive our dismayed battalions, like chaff before the wind. I hurried to my horse, that I might be ready to escape. The shell and ball still made music around me. I buckled up my saddle with tremulous fingers, and put my foot upon the stirrup. But a cheer recalled me and a great clapping of hands, as at some clever performance in the amphitheatre. I looked again. A battery from our position across the road had opened upon the Confederate infantry, as they reached the very brink of the swamp. For a moment the bayonets tossed wildly, the dense column staggered like a drunken man, the flags rose and fell, and then the line fell back disorderly. At that instant a body of Federal infantry, that I had not seen, appeared, as by invocation; their steel fell flashingly, a column of smoke enveloped them, the hills and skies seemed to split asunder with the shock—and when I looked again, the road was strewn with the dying and dead; the pass had been defended.

As the batteries still continued to play, and as the prospect of uninterrupted battle during the day was not a whit abated, I decided to resume my saddle, and, if possible, make my way to the James. The geography of the country, as I had deciphered it, satisfied me that I must pass New Market, before I could rely upon my personal safety. New Market was a paltry cross-road's hamlet, some miles ahead, but as near to Richmond as White Oak Creek. The probabilities were that the Confederates would endeavor to intercept us at this point, and so attack us in flank and rear. As I did not witness either of these battles, though I heard the discharge of every musket, it may be as well to state, in brief, that June 30 was marked by the bloodiest of all the Richmond struggles, excepting, possibly, Gaines's Mill. While the Southern artillery engaged Franklin's corps, at White Oak Crossing, and their left made several unavailing attempts to ford the creek with infantry, their entire right and centre marched out the Charles City Road, and gave impetuous battle at New Market. The accounts and the results indicate that the Federals won the day at New Market, sheerly by good fighting. They were parching with thirst, weak with hun-

ger, and it might have been supposed that reverses had
broken their spirit. On the contrary they did not fall back
a rod, during the whole day, and at evening Heintzelman's
corps crowned their success by a grand charge, whereat
the Confederates broke and were pursued three miles
toward Richmond. The gunboats *Galena* and *Aroostook,*
lying in the James at Turkey Bend, opened fire at three
o'clock, and killed promiscuously Federals and Confederates. But the Southern soldiers were superstitious as to
gunboats, and they could not be made to approach within
range of the *Galena's* monstrous projectiles.

I shall always recall my journey from White Oak to Harrison's Bar as marked by constantly increasing beauties of
scenery, and terrors of event. At every hoof-fall I was
leaving the low, boggy, sparsely settled Chickahominy
region, for the high farm-lands of the James. The dwellings, as I progressed, became handsome; the Negro quarters were less like huts and cattle-sheds; the ripe wheatfields stretched almost to the horizon; the lawns and lanes
were lined with ancient shade-trees; there were picturesque gates and lodges; the fences were straight and
whitewashed, there were orchards, heavy with crimson
apples, where the pumpkins lay beneath, like globes of
gold, in the rows of amber corn. Into this patriarchal and
luxuriant country, the retreating army wound like a great
devouring serpent. It was to me the coming back of the
beaten *jetters* through *Midgards,* or the repulse of the
fallen angels from heaven, trampling down the river-sides
of Eden. They rode their team-horses into the wavy wheat,
and in some places, where the reapers had been at work,
they dragged the sheaves from the stacks, and rested
upon them. Hearing of the coming of the army, the pro-
prietors had vainly endeavored to gather their crops, but
the Negroes would not work, and they had not modern
implements, whereby to mow the grain rapidly. The pro-
fanations of those glorious stretches of corn and rye were
to me some of the most melancholy episodes of the war.
No mind can realize how the grain-fields used to ripple,
when the fresh breezes blew up and down the furrows,

and the hot suns of that almost tropical climate had yielded each separate head till the whole landscape was like a bright cloud, or a golden sea. The tall, shapely stalks seemed to reach out imploringly, like sunny-haired virgins, waiting to be gathered into the arms of the farmer. They were the Sabine women, on the eve of the bridal, when the insatiate Romans tore them away and trampled them. The Indian corn was yet green, but so tall that the tasselled tops showed how cunningly the young ears were ripening. There were melons in the corn-rows, that a week would have developed, but the soldiers dashed them open and sucked the sweet water. They threw clubs at the hanging apples till the ground was littered with them, and the hogs came afield to gorge; they slew the hogs and divided the fresh pork among themselves. As I saw, in one place, dozens of huge German cavalry-men, asleep upon bundles of wheat, I recalled their Frankish fore-fathers, swarming down the Apennines, upon Italy.

The air was so sultry during a part of the day, that one was constantly athirst. But there was a belt of country, four miles or more in width, where there seemed to be neither rills nor wells. Happily, the roads were, in great part, enveloped in stately timber, and the shade was very grateful to men and horses. The wounded still kept with us, and many that were fevered. They did not complain with words; but their red eyes and painful pace told all the story. If we came to rivulets, they used to lie upon their bellies, along the margins, with their heads in the flowing water. The nags were so stiff and hot, that, when they were reined into creeks, they refused to go forward, and my brown animal once dropped upon his knees, and quietly surveyed me, as I pitched upon my hands, floundering in the pool.

I remember a stone dairy, such as are found upon Pennsylvania grazing farms, where I stopped to drink. It lay up a lane, some distance from the road, and two enormous tulip poplar trees sheltered and half-concealed it. A tiny creek ran through the dairy, over cool granite slabs, and dozens of earthen milk-bowls lay in the water, with the mould of the cream brimming at the surface. A pewter drinking-mug hung to a peg at the side, and there were wooden spoons for skimming, straining pails, and great ladles of gourd and cocoanut. A cooler, tidier, trimmer dairy I had not seen, and I stretched out my body upon the dry slabs, to drink from one of the milk-bowls. The cream was sweet, rich, and nourishing, and I was so absorbed directly, that I did not heed the footfalls of a tall, broad, vigorous man, who said in a quiet way, but with a deep, sonorous voice, and a decided Northern twang—

"Friend, you might take the mug. Some of your comrades will want to drink from that bowl."

I begged his pardon hastily, and said that I supposed he was the proprietor.

"I reckon that I must give over my ownership, while the army hangs around here," said the man; "but I must endure what I can't cure."

Here he smiled grimly, and reached down the pewter cup. Then he bent over a fresh bowl, and dexterously dipped the cup full of milk, without seeming to break the cream.

"Drink that," he said; "and if there's any better milk in these parts, I want to know the man."

He looked at me critically, while I emptied the vessel, and seemed to enjoy my heartiness.

"If you had been smart enough to come this way, victorious," added the man, straightforwardly, "instead of being out-generalled, whipped, and driven, I should enjoy the loss of my property a great deal more!"

There was an irresistible heartiness in his tone and manner. He had, evidently, resolved to bear the misfortunes of war bravely.

"You are a Northern man?" I said, inquiringly.

"How do you know?"

"There are no such dairies in Virginia; a Virginian never dipped a mug of milk after your fashion; you haven't the Virginia inflection, and very weak Virginia principles."

The man laughed dryly, and filled himself a cup, which he drank sedately.

"I reckon you are correct," he said; "pretty much correct, any way. I'm a New Yorker, from the Mohawk Valley, and I have been showing these folks how they can't farm. If there's anybody that farms better than I do, I want to know the man!"

He looked at the flowing water, the clean slabs and walls, the shining tins, and smacked his lips satisfactorily. I asked him if he farmed with Negroes, and if the prejudices of the country affected either his social or industrial interests. He answered that he was obliged to employ Negroes, as he had thrice tried the experiment of working with whites, but with ill success.

"*I* would have kept 'em," he added, in his great voice, closing a prodigious fist, "but the men would not stay. I couldn't make the neighbors respect them. There was nobody for 'em to associate with. They were looked upon as niggers, and they got to feel it after a while. So I have had only niggers latterly; but I get more work from them than any other man in these parts. If there's anybody that gets more work out of niggers than I do, I want to know the man!"

There was a sort of hard, hearty defiance about him, typical of his severe, angular race, and I studied his large limbs and grim, full face with curious admiration. He told me that he hired his Negro hands from the surrounding slaveowners, and that he gave them premiums upon excess of work, approximating to wages. In this way they were encouraged to habits of economy, perseverance, and sprightliness.

"I don't own a nigger," he said, "not one! But I don't think a nigger's much too good to be a slave. I won't be bothered with owning 'em. And I won't be conquered into 'the institution.' I said, when I commenced, that I should not buy niggers, and I won't buy niggers, because I said so! As to social disadvantages, every Northern man has 'em here. They called me an abolitionist; and a fellow at the hotel in Richmond did so to my face. I knocked him into a heap, and nobody has meddled with me since. Of course," he said, after a moment, "it won't do to inflame these people. These people are like my bulls, and you mustn't shake a red stick at 'em. Besides, I'm not a fanatic. I never was. My wife's one of these people, and I let her think as she likes. But, if there's anybody in these parts that wants to interfere with me, I should like to know the man!"

The contemptuous tone in which he mentioned "these people" amused me infinitely, and I believed that his resolute, indomitable manner would have made him popular in any society. He was shrewd, withal, and walked beside me to his gate. When the regiments halted to rest, by the wayside, he invited the field officers to the dairy, and so obtained guards to rid him of depredators. He would have escaped very handsomely, but the hand of war was not always so merciful, and a part of the battle of Malvern Hill was fought upon his property. I have no doubt that he submitted unflinchingly, and sat more stolidly amid the wreck than old Marius in battered Carthage.

Until two o'clock in the afternoon I rode leisurely southward, under a scorching sky, but still bearing up, though aflame with fever. The guns thundered continuously behind, and the narrow roads were filled, all the way, with hurrying teams, cavalry, cannon, and foot soldiers. I stopped a while by a white frame church—primly, squarely built—and read the inscriptions upon the tombs uninterestedly. Some of the soldiers had pried open the doors, and a wounded Zouave was delivering a mock sermon from the pulpit. Some of his comrades broke up the meeting by singing—"John Brown's body lies a mouldering in the grave," and then a major ordered them out, and put a guard upon the building. The guard played cards upon the door sills.

I was frequently obliged, by the crowded state of the roads, to turn aside into woods, fens, and fields, and so make precarious progress. Sometimes I strayed, unwittingly, a good way from the army, and recovered the route with difficulty. On one of these occasions, I was surprised by a person in civil dress, who seemed to shoot up out of the ground. He was the queerest, grimmest, fearfulest man

that I have ever known, and, at first, I thought that the
arch fiend had appeared before me. The wood was very
deep here, and there were no wayfarers but we two. It
was quite still; but now and then we heard the rumble of
wagons, and the crack of teamsters' whips. The man in
question wore a dead black beard, and his eyebrows were
of the same intense, lustreless hue. So were his eyes and his
hair; but the latter formed a circle or cowl around his
head. He had a pale skin, his fingers were long and bony,
and he rode dexterously in and out among the tree boles
with his hat in his hand. His horse was as black as himself,
and, together, they made a half-brigandish, half-satanic
appearance.

I reined in sharply, when I saw this person, and he
looked at me like the evil-eye, through his great owlish
orbs.

"Good day," he said, in profound basso, as low I think
as "double G," and when he opened his mouth, I saw that
his teeth were very white.

I saluted him gravely, and, not without a shudder, rode
beside him. He proved to be a sort of missionary, from
the evangelical religious denominations of the North, to inquire into the spiritual condition of the soldiers. Camps
were full of such people, but I had not found any man who
appeared to be less qualified for his vocation; to have such
a figure at one's deathbed would be like a foretaste of the
great fiend. He had a fashion of working his scalp half
way down to his eyes, as he spoke, and when he smiled—
though he never laughed aloud—his eyelashes did not con-
tract, as with most people, but rather expanded, till his
eyeballs projected from his head. On such occasions, his
white teeth were revealed like a row of fangs, and his lep-
rous skin grew yet paler.

"The army has not even the form of godliness," said
this man. In the course of his remarks, he had discovered
that I was a correspondent, and at once turned the conversation into a politico-religious channel.

"The form of godliness is gone," said the man again in
double G. "This is a calamitous fact! I would it were not

so! I grieve to state it! But inquiry into the fact has satisfied me that the form of godliness does not exist. Ah!"

When the man said "Ah!" I thought that my horse
would run away, and really, the tone was like the deep
conjuration in Hamlet: "*swear-r-r-r!*"

"For example," said the man, who told me that his
name was Dimpdin—"I made some remarks to the 1st
New Jersey, on Sabbath week. The field officers directed
the men to attend; I opened divine service with a feeling
hymn; a very feeling hymn! A long measure hymn! By
Montgomery! I commenced earnestly in prayer. In appro-
priate prayer! I spoke advisedly for a short hour. What
were the results? The deplorable results? There were men,
sir, in that assembly, who went to sleep. To sleep!"

He must have gone a great way below double G this
time, and I did not see how he could get back. He drew
his scalp quite down to the bridge of his nose, and, seeing
that my horse pricked up his ears, timorously smiled like
the idol of Baal.

"There were men, sir, who did worse. Not simply failing to be hearers of the word! But doers of evil! Men
who played cards during the service. Played cards! Gambled! Gambled! And some—abandoned wretches!—who
mocked me! Lifted up their voices and mocked! Mockers,
gamblers, slumberers!"

I never heard anything so awful as the man Dimpdin's
voice, at the iteration of these three words. They seemed
to come from the bowels of the earth, and rang through
the wood like the growl of a lion. He told me that he was
engaged upon a memorial to the Evangelical Union, which
should state the number of unconverted men in the ranks,
and the number of castaways. He accredited the loss of
the campaign to the prevailing wickedness, but was unwilling to admit that the Southern troops were more
religious. His theory of reform, if I remember it, embraced
the raising of chaplains to the rank of major, with proportionate pay and perquisites, the establishment of a military
religious bureau, and a chaplain-general with aides. Each
soldier, officer, teamster, and drummer-boy was to have a

testament in his knapsack, and services should be held on the eve of every battle, and at roll-call in the mornings. There was to be an inspection of testaments as of muskets. For swearing, a certain sum should be subtracted from the soldier's pay, and conferred upon the chaplains.

"In fact," said Dimpdin, tragically—scalping himself meanwhile—"the church must be recognized in every department, and if my memorial be acted upon favorably, we shall have such victories, in three months, as will sweep Rebellion into the grave. Yes! Into the grave! The grave!"

I was obliged to say, here, that my horse could not stand these sepulchral noises, and that my nerves, being shattered by the fever, were inadequate to bear the shock. So the man Dimpdin smiled, like a window-mummy, and contented himself with looking like Apollyon. We reached a rill directly, and he produced a wicker flask, with a britannia drinking-case.

"Young men love stimulating drinks," said Dimpdin—"strong drinks! alcoholic drinks! Here is a portion of Monongahela! old Monongahela! We will refresh ourselves!"

He found a lemon, accidentally, in his saddle-bag, and contrived an informal punch, with wonderful dexterity. I took a draught modestly, and he emptied the rest, with an "Ah!" that shook the woods.

I wondered if the man Dimpdin would suggest the apportionment of flasks to soldiers, in his evangelical report!

He left me, when we regained the road, to ride with a lithe, bronchial person, in white neckcloth and coat cut close at the collar. They looked like the fox and the fiend, in the fable, and I seemed to hear the man Dimpdin's voice for three succeeding weeks.

At three o'clock, I climbed a gentle hill—and I was now very weary and weak—and from the summit, looked upon the river James, flowing far off to the right, through woods, and bluffs, and grainfields, and reedy islands. At last, I had gained the haven. The bright waters below me seemed to cool my red, fiery eyes, and a sort of blessed blindness fell for a time upon me, so that, when I looked again my lashes were wet. The prospect was truly beautiful. Far to the west, standing out from the chalky bluffs, were scattered the white camps of Wise's Confederate brigade. Beyond, on the remote bank of the river, lay farm-lands, and stately mansions, and some one showed me, rising faintly in the distance, Drury's Bluff, the site of Fort Darling, where the gunboats were repulsed in the middle of May. Below, in the river, lay the *Galena*, and a little way astern, the *Aroostook*. Signal-men, with flags, were elevated upon the masts of each, and the gunners stood upon the decks, as waiting some emergency. The vessels had steam up, and seemed to be ready for action at any moment. This was Grand Turkey Bend, and the rising ground on which I stood was known as Malvern Hill. A farm-house lay to my left, and repairing thither, I cast myself from the nag, and lay down in the shady yard, thankful that I had reached the haven, and only solicitous now to escape the further privations of McClellan's Peninsular campaign.

CHAPTER XVIII

The Hospital Transport

AN earnest desire now took possession of me, to be the first of the correspondents to reach New York. The scenes just transpired had been unparalleled in the war, and if, through me, my newspaper should be the first to make them public, it would greatly redound to my credit. Perhaps no profession imparts an enthusiasm in any measure kindred to that of the American newsgatherer. I was careless of the lost lives and imperilled interests, the suffering, the defeat: no emotions either of the patriot or the man influenced me. I only thought of the *éclat* of giving the story to the world, and nurtured an insane desire to make to Fortress Monroe, by some other than the common expedient. That this was a paltry ambition I know; but I write what happened, and to the completion of my sketch of a correspondent, this is necessary to be said. I found Glumley at the old mansion referred to, and stealthily suggested to him the seizing of an open boat, whereby we might row down to the Fortress. He rejected it as impracticable, but was willing to hazard a horseback ride down the Peninsula. I knew that this would not do, and after a short time I continued my journey down the riverside, hopeful of finding some transport or despatch boat. I was now in Charles City County, and the river below me was dotted with woodland islands. I soon got upon the main road to Harrison's Point or Bar, and followed the stream of ambulances and supply teams for more than an hour. At last we reached a diverging lane, through which we passed to a landing, close to a fine dwelling, whose style of architecture I may denominate the "Gothic run mad." An old cider-press was falling into rottenness on the lawn; four soldiers were guarding the well, that the mob might not exhaust its precious contents, and between some Negro huts and the brink of the bluff stood a cluster of broad-armed trees, beneath whose shade the ambulance-drivers were depositing the wounded.

I have made these chapters sufficiently hideous, without venturing to transcribe these new horrors. Suffice it to say that the men whom I now beheld had been freshly brought from the fight of New Market, and were suffering the first agonies of their wounds. One hour before, they had felt all the lustiness of life and adventure. Now, they were whining like babes, and some had expired in the ambulances. The act of lifting them to the ground so irritated their wounds that they howled dismally, and yet were so exhausted that after lying upon the ground awhile, they quietly passed into sleep. Such are the hardening results of war, that some soldiers, who were unhurt, actually refused to give a trifle of river water from their canteens to their expiring comrades. At one time a brutal wrangle occurred at the well, and the guard was compelled to seek reinforcement, or the thirsty people would have massacred them.

I was now momentarily adding to my notes of the battles, and the wounded men very readily gave me their names; for they were anxious that the account of their misfortunes should reach their families, and I think also, that some martial vanity lingered, even among those who were shortly to crumble away. A longboat came in from the *Galena*, after a time, and General McClellan, who had ridden down to the pier, was taken aboard. He looked to be very hot and anxious, and while he remained aboard the vessel, his staff dispersed themselves around the banks and talked over the issues of the contest. As the General receded from the strand, every sweep of the long oars was responded to from the hoarse cannon of the battle-field, and when he climbed upon deck, the steamer moved slowly up the narrow channel, and the signal-man in the foretop flourished his crossed flag sturdily. Directly, the *Galena* opened fire from her immense pieces of ordnance, and the roar was so great that the explosions of field-guns were fairly drowned. She fired altogether by the direction of the signals, as nothing could be seen of the battle-field from her decks. I ascertained afterward that she played havoc with our own columns as well as the enemy's, but she brought hope to the one, and terror to the other. The very name of gunboat affrighted the Confederates, and they were assured, in this case, that the retreating invaders had at length reached a haven. The *Galena* kept up a steady fire till nightfall, and the Federals, taking courage, drove their adversaries toward Richmond, at eve. Meanwhile the Commanding General's escort and body-guard had encamped around us, and during the night the teams and much of the field cannon fell back. I obtained shelter and meals from Quartermaster Le Duke of Iowa, whose canvas was pitched a mile or more below, and as I tossed through the watches I heard the splashing of water in the river beneath, where the tired soldiers were washing away the powder of the battle.

In the morning I retraced to headquarters, and vainly endeavored to learn something as to the means of going down the river. Commanders are always anxious to grant correspondents passes after a victory; but they wish to defer the unwelcome publication of a defeat. I was advised by Quartermaster-General Van Vliet, however, to proceed to Harrison's Bar, and, as I passed thither, the last day's encounters—those of Malvern Hill—occurred. The scenes along the way were reiterations of terrors already described—creaking ambulances, staggering foot soldiers, profane wagoners, skulking officers and privates, officious provost guards, defiles, pools and steeps packed with teams and cannon, wayside houses beset with begging, gossiping, or malicious soldiers, and wavy fields of wheat and rye thrown open to man and beast. I was amused at one point, to see some soldiers attack a beehive that they might seize the honey. But the insects fastened themselves

upon some of the marauders, and after indescribable curs-
ing and struggling, the bright nectar and comb were relinquished by the toilers, and the ravishers gorged upon
sweetness.

Harrison's Bar is simply a long wharf, extending into the
river, close by the famous mansion where William Henry
Harrison, a President of the United States, was born, and
where, for two centuries, the scions of a fine old Virginia
family have made their homestead. The house had now
become a hospital, and the wounded were being conveyed
to the pier, whence they were delivered over to some
Sanitary steamers, for passage to Northern cities. I tied
my horse to the spokes of a wagon-wheel, and asked a
soldier to watch him, while I repaired to the quay. A half
drunken officer was guarding the wharf with a squad of
men, and he denied me admittance, at first, but when I had
said something in adulation of his regiment—a trick common to correspondents—he passed me readily. The ocean
steamer *Daniel Webster* was about being cast adrift when
I stepped on board, and Colonel Ingalls, Quartermaster in
charge, who freely gave me permission to take passage in
her, advised me not to risk returning to shore. So, reluctantly, I resigned my pony, endeared to me by a hundred
adventures, and directly I was floating down the James,
with the white teams and the tattered groups of men re-
ceding from me, and each moment the guns of Malvern
Hill growing fainter. Away! praised be a merciful God!
away from the accursed din, and terror, and agony, of my
second campaign—away forever from the Chickahominy.

For awhile I sat meditatively in the bow of the boat, full
of strange perplexities and thankfulness. I had escaped
the bullet, and fever, and captivity, and a great success in
my profession was about to be accorded to me, but there
was much work yet to be done. The rough material I had
for a grand account of the closing of the campaign; but
these fragmentary figures and notes must be wrought into
narrative, and to avail myself of their full significance, I
must lose no moment of application. I found that I was
one of four correspondents on board, and we resolved to

district the boat, each correspondent taking one fourth of
the names of the sick and wounded. The spacious saloons,
the clean deck, the stairways, the gangways, the hold, the
halls—all were filled with victims. They lay in rows upon
straw beds, they limped feverishly here and there; some
were crazed from sunstroke, or gashes; and one man that I
remember counted the rivets in the boilers over the whole
hundred miles of the journey, while another—a teamster
—whipped and cursed his horses as if he had mistaken the
motion of the boat for that of his vehicle.

The *Daniel Webster* was one of a series of transports
supplied for the uses of the wounded by a national committee of private citizens. Her wood work was shining and
glossy, her steel shone like mirrors, and she was cool as
Paradise. Out of the smoke, and turmoil, and suffocation
of battle these wretched men had emerged, to enjoy the
blessedness, unappreciated before, of shelter, and free air
and cleanliness. There was ice in abundance on board,
and savory lemonade lay glassily around in great buckets.
Women flitted from group to group with jellies, bonbons,
cigars, and oranges, and the grateful eyes of the prostrate
people might have melted one to tears. These women were
enthusiasts of all ages and degrees, who proffered themselves, at the beginning of the war, as stewardesses and
nurses. From the fact that some of them were of mascu-
line natures, or, in the vocabulary of the times, "strong-
minded," they were the recipients of many coarse jests,
and imputations were made upon both their modesty and
their virtue. But I would that any satirist had watched
with me the good offices of these Florence Nightingales of
the West, as they tripped upon merciful errands, like good
angels, and left paths of sunshine behind them. The soldiers had seen none of their countrywomen for months,
and they followed these ambassadors with looks half-
idolatrous, half-downcast, as if consciously unworthy of so
tender regard.

"If I could jest die, now," said one of the poor fellows
to me, "with one prayer for my country, and one for that
dear young lady!"

There was one of these daughters of the good Samaritan whose face was so full of coolness, and her robes so airy, flowing, and graceful, that it would have been no miracle had she transmuted herself to something divine. She was very handsome, and her features bore the imprint of that high enthusiasm which may have animated the maid of Arc. One of the more forward of the correspondents said to her, as she bore soothing delicacies to the invalids, that he missed the satisfaction of being wounded, at which she presented an orange and a cigar to each of us in turn. Among the females on board, I remarked one, very large, angular, and sanguine, who sat at a small table, dispensing luxuries with the manners of a despot and the charity of a child. She had a large vessel of boiling coffee, from which she drew spicy quantities at intervals; and when the troops thronged around eagerly, she rebuked the more forward, and called up some emaciated, bashful fellows, giving them the preference. Every soldier who accepted coffee was obliged to take a religious tract, and she gave them away with a grim satisfaction that was infinitely amusing and interesting. I ventured to ask this imperative person for a bottle of ink, and after some difficulty—arising out of a mistaken notion on her part that I was dangerously wounded—she vaulted over a chair, and disappeared into a state-room. When she returned, her arms were filled with a perfect wilderness of stationery, and having supplied each of us in turn, she addressed herself to me in the following sententious manner:

"See here! You reporter! (There's ink!) I want to be put in the newspapers! Look at me! Now! Right straight! (Pens?) Here I am; thirteen months at work; been everywhere; done good; country; church; never noticed. Never! —Now! I want to be put in newspapers."

At this point the Imperatress was called off by some soldiers, who presumed to draw coffee without her consent. She slapped one of them soundly, and at once overpowered him with kindnesses, and tracts; then she returned and gave me a photograph, representing herself with a basket of fruit, and a quantity of good books. I took note of her name, but unfortunately lost the memorandum, and unless she has been honored by some more careful scribe, I fear that her labors are still unrecognized.

During much of the trip, I wrote material parts of my report, copied portions of my lists, and managed before dusk, to get fairly underway with my narrative. From the deck of the steamer I beheld at five o'clock, what I had long wished to see—the famous island of Jamestown, celebrated in the early annals of the New World, as the home of John Smith, and of Nathaniel Bacon, and as the resort of the Indian Princess, Pocahontas. A single fragment of a tower, the remnant of the Colonial church, was the only ruin that I could see.

At seven o'clock we dropped anchor in Hampton Roads, and a boat let down from the davits. Some of my wily compeers endeavored to fill all the stern seats, that I might not be pulled to shore; but I swung down by a rope, and made havoc with their shins, so that they gained nothing; the surf beat so vehemently against the pier at Old Point that we were compelled to beach the boat, and I ran rapidly through the ordnance yard to the Hygeia House, where our agent boarded; he had gone into the Fortress to pass the night, and when I attempted to follow him thither, a knot of anxious idlers, who knew that I had just returned from the battle-fields, attempted to detain me by sheer force. I dashed rapidly up the plank walk, reached the portal, and had just vaulted into the area, when the great gates swung to, and the tattoo beat; at the same instant the sergeant of guard challenged me:

"Who comes there? Stand fast! Guard prime!"

A dozen bright musket-barrels were levelled upon me, and I heard the click of the cocks as the fingers were laid upon the triggers. When I had explained, I was shown the Commandant's room, and hastening in that direction, encountered Major Charles Hathaway Larrabee, my old patron of the Fifth Wisconsin regiment. He took me to the barracks, where a German officer, commanding a battery, lodged, and the latter accommodated me with a camp bedstead. Here I related the incidents of the engagements, and before I concluded, the room was crowded with people. I think that I gave a sombre narration, and the hearts of those who heard me were cast down. Still, they lingered; for the bloody story possessed a hideous fascination, and I was cross-examined so pertinaciously that my host finally arose, protesting that I needed rest, and turned the party out of the place. The old fever-dreams returned to me that night, and my brain spun round for hours before I could close my eyes.

CHAPTER XIX

On Furlough Awhile

COUNTER winds and tides had so delayed the *Adelaide,* on which I departed for New York with my despatches, that it became a doubtful question as to whether we could make connection with the early train for New York. The Captain shook his head distrustfully when he had looked at his watch, and told me that he frequently failed to land his passengers in time. The bitterness of the doubt so troubled me, that I paced the decks, looking at the approaching city, and thinking that all my labor was to be disappointed in the end. I could not telegraph my narrative and lists, for Government controlled the wires; and moreover, the Associated Press regulations forbade any newspaper to telegraph exclusive news from any point but Washington. I half resolved to hire a special locomotive, but it was doubtful that the railway authorities could procure one, at so short notice. Unless I overtook the eight o'clock A. M. train, I could not get to New York before two o'clock next morning—too late for the press. Besides, how did I know that some correspondent had not reached Washington, by way of one of the Potomac vessels, and so forestalled me? Here was an opportunity to be the first of all our correspondents to publish the incidents and results of six days' stupendous warfare—but escaping at the very moment of realization. The seconds were hours as we swept past Fort Carroll, rounded Fort McHenry, and swung toward our moorings, under Fort Federal Hill.

"If we make a prompt landing," said the Captain, "you may barely get the train."

I stood with my bundles of notes upon the high deck, and signalled a cab-driver. He caught the precious manuscript, and bolted for his cab. In another second he was dashing like a runaway up the pier, over the bridge, through Pratt Street, and—out of sight. Slowly the great hulk turned awkwardly about; one turn of her paddles brought us close enough to fling a rope, a second drew her very near the shore; the distance was fearful, but I braced myself for the leap.

"Stand clear!" I called to the score of hackmen.

A little run, a spring—and I fell upon my feet, rolled over upon my face, gathered myself to the arms of all the Jehus, and was carried off bodily by a man with a great knob on his forehead as big as the end of his whip-handle.

"G'lang! Who-o-o-oh! Swis-s-s!"

I think that I promised that man everything under the sun to catch the train. I recollect that the knob on his forehead grew black and bulging as he lashed his horse. I found myself standing up in the cab, screaming like the driver. We were both insane, and the horse must have been of the breed of Pegasus, for I could feel the vehicle gyrating in the air. Now we turned a lamp-post, and the glass splintered somewhere; a dog howled as we drove over his appendage; a woman with a baby gave a short scream and disappeared into the earth; a policeman gave chase, but we laughed him to scorn.

Huzza! Here we are! The train stands puffing at the long platform. "Your bundle, yer honor! Wasn't I the boy to make the keers? Didn't I projuce yer honor in good time, sur?" I only know that I flung a greenback to the two—that I vainly besought the ticket agent to give me no change, but consign it to the first engineer who failed to make time—that I wrote on the back of my hat for four hours—that I devoured a chicken and as many eggs as she had laid in a lifetime, at Havre de Grace—that I leaped upon the platform at Broad and Prime streets, Philadelphia, at noon—that I plunged into a cab, and said, significantly—

"New York Ferry!"

It chafed me to pass through the promenade street of my home-city, without a moment to spare for my family or friends. The cab-horse slipped in Chestnut Street, and I went over the rest of the route on foot, at a dog-trot pace, passing in various quarters for a sportsman, a professional runner, and a lunatic. I was greatly aggravated between Amboy and Camden, by persons making inquiries for brothers, sons, and acquaintances. At last, when I attained the steamer, the Captain kindly shut me up in his office, and I went on with my narrative till my eyes were burning and my hands failed in their function. Kill von Kull and its picturesque shores went by; we emerged into the beautiful bay, and winding among its buoys, harbor lights and shipping, came to, at length, at the foot of Christopher Street. I repaired to the office at once, and wrote far into the night, refraining, finally, from sheer blindness and exhaustion, and dropped asleep in the carriage as I was taken toward the Metropolitan Hotel.

The next day was Friday, July 4, the anniversary of American Independence, and my version of the six-days' battles caused universal gloom and grief. I had furnished five pages or forty columns of closely printed matter, and thousands of tremulous fingers were tracing out the names of their dead dear ones, while I sipped my wine and rehearsed for the hundredth time, the incidents of the retreat to a multitude of men. Cards and letters came to me by the gross, from bereaved countrymen, and I was obliged, finally, to add a postscript to my account, and a protest that I knew no more, and could answer no interrogatories. A bath, fresh clothing, and rich food so far improved my appearance in a few days, that I presented no other traces of sickness and travel than a sunburnt face, and a rheumatic walk.

With restoration came a revival of old desires, appetites, and attachments. It required one additional campaign to sober me in these respects, and I was not a little relieved to receive an order on the fourth day to proceed to Washington, and attach myself to the "Army of Virginia" at the head of which Major General John Pope had just been

placed. After two quieter days' enjoyment, in the Quaker
City, I reported myself at the Capital, but was debarred
from taking the field at once, owing to the tardiness of the
new Commander. For two weeks or more, I loitered
around Washington, and although the time passed monot-
onously, I saw many persons and events which have much
to do with the history of the Rebellion. The story of
"Washington During the War" has yet to be written in all
its vividness of enterprise, devotion, and infamy. It has
been, in periods of peace, a dull, dolorous town, of mam-
moth hotels, paltry dwellings, empty lots, prodigiously
wide avenues, a fossil population, and a series of gigantic
public buildings which seemed dropped by accident into
a fifth-rate backwoods settlement. During the sessions
Washington was overrun with "smartness": smart pages,
smart messengers, smart cabmen, smart publicans, smart
politicians, smart women, smart scoundrels! Greatness
became commonplace here, and Mr. Douglas might drink
at Willard's Bar, with none so poor to do him reverence,
or General Winfield Scott strut like a colossus along "the
Avenue," and the sleepy Negroes upon their hacks would
give him the attention of only one eye. It was interesting,
to notice how rapidly provincial eminence lost caste here.
Slipkins, who was "Honorable" at home, and of whom his
county newspaper said that "this distinguished fellow citizen of ours will be heard from, among the greatest of the
free,"—Slipkins moved to and fro unnoticed, and voted
with his party, and drank much brandy and water, and left
no other record at the Capital than some unpaid bills, and
perhaps an unacknowledged heir. A gaping rustic and
his new bride, or a strolling foreigner, marvelling and
making notes at every turn, might be observed in the
Patent Office examining General Washington's breeches,
but these were at once called "greenies," and people put
out their tongues and winked at them. The Secretaries'
ladies gave parties now and then, attended by the folks
who sold them horses, or carpets, or wines; the President
gave a "levee," whereat a wonderfully Democratic horde
gathered to pinch his hands and ogle his lady; the Marine

band (in *red* coats), played twice a week in the Capital
grounds, and Senators, Cyprians, Ethiops, and children
rallied to enjoy; a theatre or two played time-honored
dramas with Thespian companies; a couple of scholars lec-
tured in the sombre Smithsonian Institution; an intrigue
and a duel filled some most doleful hiatus; and a clerk ab-
sconded with half a million, or an Indian agent robbed the
red men and fell back to the protection of his "party." A
very dismal, a very dirty, and a very Democratic settlement was the American Capital, till the war came.

Even the war lost half its interest in Washington. A
regiment marching down Broadway was something to see,
but the same regiment on Pennsylvania Avenue looked
mean and matter-of-fact. A general in the field, or riding
uncovered through Boston or Baltimore, or even lounging
at the bar of the Continental or the Astor House or the
Tremont, was invested with an atmosphere half heroic,
half poetic; but generals in Washington may be counted
by pairs, and I used to sit at dinner with eight or a dozen
of them in my eye. There was the new Commander-in-
Chief, Henry W. Halleck, a short, countrified person,
whose blue coat was either threadbare or dusty, or lacked
some buttons, and who picked his teeth walking up and
down the halls at Willard's, and argued through a white,
bilious eye and a huge mouth. There was General O. M.
Mitchel, also, who has since passed away—a little, knotty
gentleman, with stiff, gray, Jacksonian hair. And General
Samuel D. Sturgis passed in and out perpetually, with im-
pressive, individual Major General N. P. Banks, or some
less prominent person, all of them wearing the gold star
upon their shoulders, and absolute masters of some thousands of souls. The town, in fact, was overrun with troops.
Slovenly guards were planted on horseback at crossings,
and now and then they dashed, as out of a profound sleep,
to chase some galloping cavalier. Gin and Jews swarmed
along the Avenue, and I have seen gangs of soldiers of
rival regiments, but oftener of rival nationalities, pum-
melling each other in the highways, until they were
marched off by the Provosts. The number of houses of ill-

fame was very great, and I have been told that generals
and lieutenants of the same organization often encountered and recognized each other in them. Contractors and
"jobbers" used to besiege the offices of the Secretaries of
War and Navy, and the venerable Welles (who reminded
me of Abraham in the lithographs), and the barnacled
Stanton, seldom appeared in public. Simple-minded,
straightforward A. Lincoln, and his ambitious, clever lady,
were often seen of afternoons in their barouche; the little
old-fashioned Vice-President walked unconcernedly up
and down; and when some of the Richmond captives came
home to the Capital, immense meetings were held, where
patriotism bawled itself hoarse. A dining hour at Willard's
was often wondrously adapted for a historic picture, when
accoutred officers, and their beautiful wives—or otherwise
—sat at the *table d'hôte*, and sumptuous dishes flitted here
and there, while corks popped like so many Chinese crackers, and champagne bubbled up like blood. At night, the
Provost Guard enacted the farce of coming by deputations
to each public bar, which was at once closed, but reopened
five minutes afterward. Congress water was in great demand for weak heads of mornings, and many a young lad,
girt up for war, wasted his strength in dissipation here, so
that he was worthless afield, and perhaps died in the hospital. The curse of civil war was apparent everywhere.
One had but to turn his eye from the bare Heights of Arlington, where the soldiers of the Republic lay demoralized, to the fattening vultures who smoked and swore at
the National, to see the true cause of the North's short-
comings—its inherent and almost universal corruption. Human nature was here so depraved, that man lost faith in
his kind. Death lurked behind ambuscades and fortifications over the river, but Sin, its mother, coquetted *here,*
and as an American, I often went to bed loathing the Capital, as but little better than Sodom, though its danger had
called forth thousands of great hearts to throb out, in its
defence. For every stone in the Capitol building, a man
has laid down his life. For every ripple on the Potomac,
some equivalent of blood has been shed.

I lodged for some time in Tenth Street, and took my meals at Willard's. The legitimate expenses of living in this manner were fourteen dollars a week; but one could board at Kirkwood's or Brown's for seven or eight dollars, very handsomely. A favorite place of excursion, near the city, was "Crystal Spring," where some afternoon orgies were enacted which should have made the sun go into eclipse. I repaired once to Mount Vernon, and looked dolorously at the tomb of the *Pater Patrae*, and once to Annapolis, on the Chesapeake, which the war has elevated into a fine naval station.

At length Pope's forces were being massed along the line of the Rappahannock, below the Occoquan River, and upon the "Piedmont" highlands. Piedmont is the name applied to the fine table-lands of northern Virginia, and the ensuing campaign has received the designation of the "Piedmont Campaign." Pope's army proper was composed of three corps, commanded respectively by Generals Irvin McDowell, Franz Sigel, and Nathaniel P. Banks. But a portion of General McClellan's peninsular army had meantime returned to the Potomac, and the corps of General A. E. Burnside was stationed at Fredericksburg, thirty miles or more below Pope's headquarters at Warrenton.

I presented myself to General Pope on the 12th of July, at noon. His Washington quarters consisted of a quiet brick house, convenient to the War Office, and the only tokens of its importance were some guards at the threshold, and a number of officers' horses, saddled in the shade of some trees at the curb. The lower floor of the dwelling was appropriated to quartermasters' and inspectors' clerks, before whom a number of people were constantly presenting themselves, with applications for passes—sutlers, in great quantities, idlers, relic-hunters, and adventurers in still greater ratio, and, last of all, citizens of Virginia, solicitous to return to their farms and families. The mass of these were rebuffed, as Pope had inaugurated his campaign with a show of severity, even threatening to drive all the non-combatants out of his lines, unless they took the Federal oath of allegiance. He gave me a pass willingly, and chatted pleasantly for a time. In person he was dark, martial, and handsome—inclined to obesity, richly garbed in civil cloth, and possessing a fiery black eye, with luxuriant beard and hair. He smoked incessantly, and talked imprudently. Had he commenced his career more modestly, his final discomfiture would not have been so galling; but his vanity was apparent to the most shallow observer, and although he was brave, clever, and educated, he inspired distrust by his much promising and general love of gossip and story-telling. He had all of Mr. Lincoln's garrulity (which I suspect to be the cause of their affinity), and none of that good old man's unassuming common sense.

The next morning, at seven o'clock, I embarked for Alexandria, and passed the better half of the forenoon in negotiating for a pony. At eleven o'clock, I took my seat in a bare, filthy car, and was soon whirled due southward, over the line of the Orange and Alexandria railroad. The country between Alexandria and Warrenton Junction, or, indeed, between Washington and Richmond, was not unlike those masterly descriptions of Gibbon, detailing the regions overrun by Hyder Ali. The towns stood like ruins in a vast desert, and one might write musing epitaphs at every wind-beaten dwelling, whence the wretched denizens had fled in cold and poverty to a doubtful hospitality in the far South. Fences there were none, nor any living animals save the braying hybrids which limped across the naked plains to eke out existence upon some secluded patches of grass. These had been discharged from the army, and they added rather than detracted from the lonesomeness of the wild. Their great mournful eyes and shaggy heads glared from copses, and in places where they had lain down beside the track to expire. If we sometimes pity these dumb beasts as they drag loaded wains, or heavy omnibuses, or sub-soil ploughs, we may also bestow a tender sentiment upon the army mules. Flogged by teamsters, cursed by quartermasters, ridiculed by roaring regiments of soldiers, strained and spavined by fearful draughts, stalled in bogs and fainting upon hillsides—their bones will evidence the sites of armies, when the skeletons of men have crumbled and become reabsorbed. I have seen them die like martyrs, when the inquisitor, with his bloody lash, stood over them in the closing pangs, and their last tremulous howl has almost moved to tears.

Some of the dwellings seemed to be occupied, but the tidiness of old times was gone. The women seemed sunburnt and hardened by toil. They looked from their thresholds upon the flying train, with their hair unbraided and their garters ungyved—not a Negro left to till the fields, nor a son or brother who had not travelled to the wars. They must be now hewers of wood, and drawers of water, and the fingers whereon diamonds used to sparkle must clench the axe and the hoe.

At last we came to Bull Run, the dark and bloody ground where the first grand armies fought and fled, and again to be consecrated by a baptism of fire. The railway crossed the gorge upon a tall trestle bridge, and for some distance the track followed the windings of the stream. A black, deep, turgid current, flowing between gaunt hills, lined with cedar and beech, crossed here and there by a ford, and vanishing, above and below, in the windings of wood and rock; while directly beyond, lie the wide plains of Manassas Junction, stretching in the far horizon, to the undulating boundary of the Blue Ridge. As the Junction remains today, the reader must imagine this splendid prospect, unbroken by fences, dwellings, or fields, as if intended primevally to be a place for the shock of columns, with redoubts to the left and right, and fragments of stockades, dry rifle pits, unfinished or fallen breastworks, and, close in the foreground, a medley of log huts for the winter quartering of troops. The woods to the north mark the course of Bull Run; a line of telegraph poles going westward points to Manassas Gap; while the Junction proper is simply a point where two single track railways unite, and a few frame "shanties" or sheds stand contiguous. These are, for example, the "New York Headquarters," kept by a person with a hooked nose, who trades in cakes, lemonade, and (probably) whiskey, of the brand called "rotgut"; or the "Union Stores," where a person in semi-military dress deals in India-rubber overcoats, under-clothing, and boots. As the train halts, lads and Negroes propose to sell sandwiches to passengers, and soldiers ride up to take mail-bags and bundles for imperceptible camps. In the distance some teams are seen, and a solitary horse-man, visiting vestiges of the battle; sidelings beside the track are packed with freight cars, and a small mountain of pork barrels towers near by; there are blackened re-mains of locomotives a little way off, but these have per-haps hauled regiments of Confederates to the Junction; and over all—men, idlers, ruins, railway, huts, entrench-ments—floats the star-spangled banner from the roof of a plank depot.

The people in the train were rollicking and well-dis-posed, and black bottles circulated freely. I was invited to drink by many persons, but the beverage proffered was intolerably bad, and several convivials became stupidly drunk. A woman in search of her husband was one of the passengers, and those contiguous to her were as gentle-manly as they knew how to be. "A pretty woman, in war-time," said a Captain, aside, to me, "is not to be sneezed at." At Catlett's, a station near Warrenton Junction, we narrowly escaped a collision with a train behind, and the occupants of our train, women included, leaped down an embankment with marvellous agility. Here we switched off to the right, and at four o'clock dismounted at the pleasant village of Warrenton.

CHAPTER XX

Campaigning with General Pope

———

THE court-house village of Fauquier County contained a population of twelve or fifteen hundred at the commencement of the war. Its people embraced the revolutionary cause at the outstart, and furnished some companies of foot to the Confederate service, as well as a mounted company known as the "Black Horse Cavalry." The guns of Bull Run were heard here on the day of battle, and hundreds of the wounded came into town at nightfall. Thenceforward Warrenton became prominently identified with the struggle, and the churches and public buildings were transmuted to hospitals. After the Confederates retired from Manassas Junction, the vicinity of Warrenton was a sort of neutral ground. At one time the Southern cavalry would ride through the main street, and next day a body of mounted Federals would pounce upon the town, the inhabitants, meanwhile, being apprehensive of a sabre combat in the heart of the place. Some people were ruined by the war; some made fortunes. The mayor of the village was named Bragg, and he was a trader in horses, as well as a wagon-builder. There were two taverns, denominated respectively, the "Warrenton Inn," and the "Warren Green Hotel." I obtained a room at the former. A young man named Dashiell kept it. He was a fair-complexioned, clever, high-strung Virginian, and managed to obtain a great deal of paper money from both republics. It is an encomium in America, to say that a man "Can keep a hotel," but what shall be said of the man who can keep a hotel in war-time? I observed young Dashiell's move-

ments from day to day, and I am satisfied that his popularity arose from his fairness and frankness. He charged
nine dollars a week for room and board of three meals, but
could, with difficulty, obtain meat and vegetables for the
table. His mother and his brother-in-law lived in the house.
The latter was a son of Mayor Bragg, and had been twice
in the Confederate service. He was engaged both at Bull
Run and at Fairfax Court House, and made no secret of
his activity at either place. But he was treated considerately, though he vaunted intolerably. The "Inn" was a
frame dwelling, with a first floor of stone, surrounded by a
double portico. The first room (entering from the street)
was the office, consisting of a bare floor, some creaking
benches, some chairs with whittled and broken arms, a
high desk, where accounts were kept, a row of bells, numbered, communicating with the rooms. Hand-bills were
pinned to the walls, announcing that William Higgins was
paying good prices for "likely" field hands, that Timothy
Ingersoll's stock of dry goods was the finest in Piedmont,
that James Mason's mulatto woman, named Rachel, had
decamped on the night of Whitsuntide, and that one hundred dollars would be paid by the subscriber for her return. Most of these bills were out of date, but some recent
ones were exhibited to me calling for volunteers, labelled,
"Ho! for winter-quarters in Washington"; "Sons of the
South arise!"—"Liberty, glory, and no Yankeedom!" A bell-
cord hung against the "office" door, communicating with
the stables, where a deaf hostler might *not* be rung up. In
the back yard, suspended from a beam, and upright, hung
a large bell, which called the boarders to meals. It commonly rang thrice, and I was told on inquiry, by the cook—
"De fust bell, sah, is to prepah to prepah for de table;
dat bell, when de fust cook don't miss it, is rung one hour
befo' mealtime. De second bell, sah, is to *prepah* for de
table; de last bell, to *come* to de table."

I should have been better pleased with the ceremony, if
the food had been more cleanly, more wholesome, and
more abundant. We used to clear the plates in a twinkling,
and if a person asked twice for beef, or butter, he was

stared at by the Negroes, as if he had eaten an entire cow. I soon brought the head-waiter to terms by promising him a dollar a week for extra attendance, and could even get ice after a time, which was a luxury. There was a bar upon the premises, which opened stealthily, when there were liquors to be sold. Cider (called champagne) could be purchased for three dollars a bottle, and whiskey came to hand occasionally. There were cigars in abundance, and I used to sit on the upper porch of evenings, puffing long after midnight, and watching the sentinels below.

There was some female society in Warrenton, but the blue-coats engrossed it all. The young women were ardent partisans, but also very pretty; and treason somehow heightened their beauty. Disloyalty is always pardonable in a woman, and these ladies appreciated the fact. They refused to walk under Federal flags, and stopped their ears when the bands played national music; but every evening they walked through the main street, arm in arm with dashing lieutenants and captains. Many flirtations ensued, and a great deal of gossip was elicited. In the end, some of the misses fell out among themselves, and hated each other more than the common enemy. I overheard a young lady talking in a low tone one evening, to a Captain in the Ninth New York regiment.

"If you knew my brother," she said, "I am sure you would not fire upon *him*."

As there were plain, square, prim porches to all the dwellings, the ladies commonly took positions therein of evenings, and a grand promenade commenced of all the young Federals in the town. The streets were pleasantly shaded, and a leafy coolness pervaded the days, though sometimes, of afternoons, the still heat was almost stifling. A jaunt after supper often took me far into the country, and the starlights were softer than one's peaceful thoughts. To be a civilian was a distinguished honor now, and I enjoyed the staring of the citizens, who pondered as to my purposes and pursuits, as only villagers can do. There is a quiet pleasure in being a strange person in a country town, and so far from objecting to the inquisitiveness of the folk,

I rather like it. One may be passing for a young duke, or
tourist, or clergyman, or what not?

The Ninth New York (militia) regiment guarded Warrenton, and it was composed of clever, polite young fellows, who had taken to volunteering before there was any
promise of war, and who turned out, pluckily, when the
strife began. Perhaps public sentiment or pride of organization influenced them. They were all good-looking and
tidy, and their dress-parades, held in the main street, were
handsome affairs. I have never seen better disciplined columns, and the youthful faces of the soldiers, with the staid
locality of the exhibition—young women, Negroes, dogs
and babies, and old men looking on—seemed to contradict
the bloody mission of the troops. The old men, referred to,
were villagers of such long standing that had the Court of
Saint James, or the Vatican, or the battle of Waterloo been
moved into their country, they would have still been villagers to the last. They met beside the Warrenton Inn, under the shade of the trees, at eleven o'clock every morning,
and borrowed the New York papers of the latest date. One
individual, slightly bald, would read aloud, and the rest
crouched or stood about him, making grunts and remarks
at intervals. They did not wish to believe the Federal reports, but they must needs read, and as most of them had
sons in the other army, their pulses were constantly tremulous with anxiety. I think that Pope's resolve to transport
these harmless old people beyond his lines was very bar-
barous, and the soldiers denounced it in similar terms. The
old men spoke of Pope as of some terrible despot, and
wished to know when he was coming to town, as they had
appointed a committee, and drafted a petition, asking his
forbearance and charity. When these villagers found me
out to be a newspaper correspondent, they regarded me
with amusing interest, and marvelled what I would say of
their town. A villager is very sensitive as to his place of
residence, and these good people read the —— daily, confounding me with all the paper—editorial, correspondence,
and, I verily believe, advertisements. One of them wished

me to board at his residence, and I was, after a time, invited out to dinner and tea frequently.

The Negroes remained in Warrenton in great numbers, and held carnival of evenings when the bands played. "Contrabands" were coming daily into town, and idleness and vice soon characterized the mass of them. They were ignorant, degraded, animal beings, and many of them loved rum; it was the last link that bound them to human kind. Servants could be hired for four dollars a month and "keep"; but they were "shiftless" and unprofitable. The Provost-Marshal of the place was a Captain Hendrickson. His quarters were in the Court House building, and he kept a zealous eye upon sutlers and citizens. The former trespassed in the sales of liquors to soldiers, and the latter were accused of maintaining a contraband mail, and of conspiring to commit divers offences. There were a number of churches in the village, all of which served as hospitals, and in the quiet cemetery west of the town, two hundred slain soldiers were interred. A stake of white pine was driven at the head of each grave. Here lay some of the men who had helped to change the destinies of a continent. No public worship was held in the place. The Sundays were busy as other days: trains came and went, teams made dust in the streets, cavalry passed through the village, music arose from all the outlying camps; parades and inspections were made, and all the preparations for killing men were relentlessly forwarded. A pleasant entertainment occurred one evening, when a plot of ground adjoining the Warrenton Inn was appropriated for a camp theatre. Candle footlights were arranged, and the stage was canopied with national flags. The citizens congregated, and the performers deferred to their prejudices by singing no Federal songs. The Negroes climbed the trees to listen, and their gratified guffaws made the night quiver. The war lost half its bitterness at such times; but I thought with a shudder of Stuart's thundering horsemen, charging into the village, and closing the night's mimicry with a horrible tragedy.

Some of the dwellings about the place were elegant and

spacious, but many of these were closed and the owners removed. Two newspapers had been published here of old, and while ransacking the office of one of them, I discovered that the type had been buried under the floor. The planks were speedily torn away, and the cases dragged to light. I obtained some curious relics, in the shape of "cuts" of recruiting officers, runaway Negroes, etc., as well as a column of a leader, in type, describing the first battle of Bull Run. For two weeks I had little to do, as the campaign had not yet fairly commenced, and I passed many hours every day reading. A young lawyer, in the Confederate service, had left an ample library behind him, and the books passed into the hands of every invader in the town.

Pope finally arrived at Warrenton, and as the troops seemed to be rapidly concentrating, I judged it expedient to procure a horse at once, and canvassed the country with that object. By paying a quartermaster the Government price ($130), I could select a steed from the pound, but inspection satisfied me that a good saddle nag could not be obtained in this way. After much parleying with Hebrews and chaffing with country people, I heard that Mayor Bragg kept some fair animals, and when I stated my purpose at his house, he commenced the business after a fashion immemorial at the South, by producing some whiskey.

When Mayor Bragg had asked me pertinently if I knew much about the "pints of a hoss," and what "figger in the way of price" would suit me, he told an erudite Negro named "Jeems" to trot out the black colt. The black colt made his appearance by vaulting over a gate, and playfully shivering a panel of fence with his "off" hoof. Then he executed a flourish with his tail, leaped thrice in the air, and bit savagely at the man "Jeems."

When I asked Mayor Bragg if the black colt was sufficiently gentle to stand fire, he replied that he was gentle as a lamb and offered to put me astride him. I had no sooner taken my seat, however, than the black colt backed, neighed, flourished, and stood erect, and finally ran away.

A second animal was produced, less mettlesome, but

also black, finely strung, daintily hoofed, and as Mayor Bragg said, "just turned four year." The price of this charger was one hundred and ninety dollars; but in consideration of my youth and pursuit, Mayor Bragg proposed to take one hundred and seventy-five; we compromised upon a hundred and fifty dollars, Mayor Bragg throwing in a halter, and by good luck I procured a saddle the same evening, so that I rode triumphantly through the streets of Warrenton, and fancied that all the citizens were admiring my new purchase.

I was struck with the fact that Mayor Bragg, though an ardent patriot, would accept of neither Confederate nor Virginia money; he required payment for his animal in Father Chase's "greenbacks."

Mounted anew, I fell into my former active habits, and made two journeys, to Sperryville and Little Washington, in one direction, to Madison in another; each place was probably twenty miles distant; the latter was merely a cavalry outpost, where Generals John P. Hatch and George D. Bayard were stationed, and the former villages were the headquarters, respectively, of General Nathaniel P. Banks and General Franz Sigel.

Madison was, at this time, a precarious place for a long tarrying. I went to sleep in the inn on the night of my arrival, and at that time the place was thronged with cavalry and artillery-men. Next morning, when I aroused, not a blue-coat could be seen. They had fallen back in the darkness, and prudently abstaining from breakfast, I galloped northward, as if the whole Confederate army was at my heels. These old turnpike roads were now marked by daily chases and rencontres. A few Virginians, fleetly mounted, would provoke pursuit from a squad of Federals, and the latter would be led into ambuscades. A quaint incident happened in this manner, near Madison.

Captain T. was chasing a party of Confederates one afternoon, when his company was suddenly fired upon from a wheatfield, parties rising up on both sides of the road, and discharging carbines through the fence rails. Three or four men, and as many horses were slain; but the ambushing body was outnumbered, and several of its members killed. Among others, a young lieutenant took deliberate aim at Captain T. at the distance of twelve yards; and, seeing that he had missed, threw up his carbine to surrender. The captain had already drawn his revolver, and, amazed at the murderous purpose, he shot the assassin in the head, killing him instantly. Nobody blamed Captain T., but he was said to be a humane person, and the affair preyed so continually upon his mind, that he committed suicide one night in camp.

At Sperryville I saw and talked with Franz Sigel, the idol of the German Americans. He had been a lieutenant in his native country, but subsided, in St. Louis, to the rank of publican, keeping a beer saloon. When the war commenced, he was appointed to a colonelcy, in deference to the large German Republican population of Missouri. His abilities were speedily manifested in a series of engagements which redeemed the Southern border, and he finally fought the terrible battle of Pea Ridge, Arkansas, which broke the spirit of the Confederates west of the Mississippi. The man who fought "mit Sigel" in those days, was always told in St. Louis: "Py tam! you pays not'ing for your lager." Sigel now commanded one of Pope's corps. He was a diminutive person, but well-knit, emaciated by his active career, feverish and sanguine of face, and, as it appeared to me, consuming with energy and ambition. As a general he was prompt to decide and do, and his manner of dealing with Confederate property was severer than that of any American. He battered the splendid mansion hotel of White Sulphur Springs to the ground, for example, when somebody discharged a rifle from its window. He preferred to fight by retreating, and if pursued, generally unmasked his guns and made massacre with the scattered opponents. Another German commander was Blenker, whose corps of Germans might have belonged to the free bands of the Black Forest. They were the most lawless men in the Federal service, and what they did not steal they destroyed. Such volunteers were mercenaries, in every sense of the word. I have been told that they slaugh-

tered sheep and cattle in pure wantonness, and the rats of
Ehrenfels did not make a cleaner sweep of provisions. The
Germans, as a rule, lacked the dash of the Irish troops and
the tact of the Americans. They thought and fought in
masses, had little individuality, and were thick-skulled;
but they were persevering and had their hearts in the
cause.

General Banks was a fine representative of the higher
order of Yankee. Originally a machinist in a small manu-
facturing town near Boston, he educated himself, and was
elected successively Legislator, Governor, Congressman,
and General of volunteers. His personal graces were
equalled by his energy, and his ability was considerable.
He has been very successful in the field, and has conducted a retreat unparalleled in the war; these things being always reckoned among American successes. The
country hereabout was mountainous, healthy, and well
adapted for campaigning. Streams and springs were numerous, and there were fine sites for camps. The deserted
toll-houses along the way glowered mournfully through
the rent windows, and I fancied them, sometimes, as I
rode at night, haunted by the shambling tollman.

> Ancient road that wind'st deserted,
>   Through the level of the vale,—
> Sweeping toward the crowded market,
>   Like a stream without a sail,
>
> Standing by thee, I look backward,
>   And, as in the light of dreams,
> See the years descend and vanish,
>   Like thy tented wains and teams.
>   —T. B. READ

To provide myself with thorough equipment for Pope's
campaign, I returned to Washington, and purchased a
patent camp-bed which strapped to my saddle, saddle
bags of large capacity, India-rubber blankets, and a full
suit of waterproof cloth—hat, coat, *genoullieres*, and gaunt-

lets. I had my horse newly shod, I drew upon my establishment for an ample sum of money, and, to properly inaugurate the campaign, I gave an entertainment in the parlor of the inn.

Pipes, cold ham, a keg of beer, and a demijohn of whiskey comprised the attractions of the night. The guests were three captains, two adjutants, two majors, a colonel, four correspondents, several lieutenants, and a signal officer. There was some jesting, and much laughing, considerable story-telling, and (toward the small hours) a great deal of singing. Much heroism was evolved; all the guests were devoted to death and their country; and there was one person who took off his coat to fight an imaginary something, but changed his mind, and dropped asleep directly. At length, a gallant captain, to demonstrate his warlike propensities, fired a pistol through the front window; and somebody blowing out the candles, the whole party retired to rest upon the floor. In this delightful way my third campaign commenced, and next evening I set off for the advance.

CHAPTER XXI

Army Morals

———————

Some of General McDowell's aides had invited me to pass a night with them at Warrenton Springs. Fully equipped, I joined Captain Ball, of Cincinnati, and we rode southward, over a hard, picturesque turnpike, under a clear moonlight. The distance was seven miles, and a part of this route was enlivened by the fires, halloos, and the music of camps. Volunteers are fond of serenading their officers; and this particular evening was the occasion of much merry-making, since a majority of the brass bands were to be mustered out of the service tomorrow. We could hear the roll of drums from imperceptible localities, and the sharp winding of bugles broke upon the silence like the trumpet of the Archangel. Stalwart shapes of horsemen galloped past us, and their hoofs made monotone behind, till the cadence died so gradually away that we did not know when the sound ceased and when the silence began. The streams had a talk to themselves, as they strolled away into the meadow, and an owl or two challenged us, calling up a corporal hawk. This latter fellow bantered and blustered, and finally we fell into an ambush of wild pigs, which charged across the road and plunged into the woods. There were despatch stations at intervals, where horses stood saddled, and the couriers waited for hoof-beats, to be ready to ride fleetly toward headquarters. Anon, we saw wizard lights, as of Arctic skies, where remote camps built conflagration; and trudging wearily down the stony road, poor ragged, flying Negroes, with their families and their worldly all, came and

205

went—God help them!—and touched their hats so obsequiously that my heart was wrung, and I felt a nervous
impulse to put them upon my steed and take their burdens
upon my back. Little sable folk, asleep and ahungered,
drawn to that barefoot woman's breast; and the tired boy,
weeping as he held to his father's hand; and the father
with the sweat of fatigue and doubt upon his forehead—
children of Ishmael all; war raging in the land, but God
overhead! These are the "wandering Jews" of our day,
hated North and South, because they are poor and blind,
and do no harm; but out of their wrongs has arisen the
abasement of their wrongers. Is there nothing over all?

We entered the beautiful lawn of the Springs' hotel, at
ten o'clock, and a Negro came up to take our horses. By
the lamplight and moonlight I saw McDowell's tent, a
sentry pacing up and down before it, and the thick, powerful figure of the General seated at a writing-table within.
Irvin McDowell was one of the oldest officers in the service, and when the war commenced he became a leading
commander in the Eastern army. At Bull Run he had a
responsible place, and the ill success of that battle brought
him into unpleasant notoriety. Though he retained a leading position he was still mistrusted and disliked. None
bore ingratitude so stolidly. He may have flinched, but he
never replied; and though ambitious, he tried to content
himself with subordinate commands. Some called him a
traitor, others an incompetent, others a plotter. If McClellan failed, McDowell was cursed. If Pope blundered, Mc-
Dowell received half the contumely. But he loosened no
cord of discipline to make good will. Implacable, dutiful,
soldierly, rigorous in discipline, sententious, brave—the
most unpopular man in America went on his way, and I
think that he is recovering public favor again. The General
of a republic has a thorny path to tread, and almost every
public man has been at one time disgraced during the
Civil War. McDowell, I think, has been treated worse than
any other.

Our nags being removed, we repaired to one of the rustic cottages which bounded the lawn, and I was intro-

duced to several members of the staff; among others, to a
Count Saint Alb, an Austrian. He had been an officer in his
native country; but came to America, anxious for active
service, and was appointed to General McDowell's staff
with the rank of captain. I understood that he was writing
a book upon America. There are many such adventurers in
the Federal service, but the present one was clever and
amusing, and he spoke English fluently.

Our tea was plain but abundant, consisting of broiled
beef, fresh bread, butter, and cheese; and the inveterate
whiskey was produced afterward, when we assembled on
the piazza, so that the hours passed by pleasantly, if not
profitably, and we retired at two o'clock.

In the morning I bathed in the clear, cold sulphur
spring, where thousands of invalid people had come for
healing waters. A canopy covered the spring, and a soldier
stood on guard at the top of the descending steps, to preserve the property in its original cleanliness. This was one
of the most famous medical springs on the American continent; the water was so densely impregnated that its peculiarly offensive smell could be detected at the distance
of a mile. The place was going to ruin now. All the bath-
ing-rooms were falling apart, the pipes had been carried
off to be moulded into bullets, and the great hotel was
desolate. I walked into the ball-room; but the large gilded
mirrors had been splintered, and lewd writings defaced
the wall. Some idlers were asleep upon the piazzas, and
the furniture was removed or broken. Some rustic cottages
dotted the lawn, but these were now inhabited by officers
and their servants. A few days were to finish the work of
rapine, and a heap of ashes was to mark the scene of
tournament, coquetry, and betrothal. I witnessed a review
of troops in a field contiguous, at nine o'clock. The heat
was so intense that many men fell out of line and were
carried off to their camps. McDowell passed exactingly
from man to man, examined muskets, clothing, and knapsacks, and the inspection was proceeding, when I bade
my friends good-bye and set out for Culpeper.

I crossed the North Rappahannock, or Hedgemain

River, upon a precarious bridge of planks. A new bridge
for artillery was being constructed close by; for the river
beneath had a swift, deep current, and could with difficulty be forded. Patches of wagons, squads of horse, and
now and then a regiment of infantry, varied the monotony
of the journey. The country was high, woody, and sparsely
settled. At noon I overtook Tower's brigade, and observing the 94th N. Y. Regiment resting in the woods, I dismounted and made the acquaintance of its colonel. He
was at this juncture greatly enraged with some of his soldiers who had been plucking green apples.

"Boy," he said to one, "put down that fruit! Drop it, or
I'll blow your head off! Directly you'll double up, pucker,
and say that you have the 'di-o-ree,' and require an ambulance. Orderly!"

A sergeant came up and touched his cap.

"Take your musket," said the Colonel; "go out to that
orchard, and order those men away. If they hesitate or
object, shoot them!"

A few such colonels would marvellously improve the
volunteer organization.

The Hazel or North Anna River, a branch of the Hedgemain, interposed a few miles further on, and passing
through a covered bridge, I turned down the north bank,
crossed some spongy fields, and at length came to a dry
place in the edge of a woods, where I tied my nag, spread
out my bed, and prepared to dine. A box of sardines, a
lemon, and some fresh sandwiches constituted the repast,
and being dusty and parched I stripped afterward and
swam across the river. Seeing that my horse plunged and
neighed, with swollen eyeballs and every evidence of
terror, I hastened toward him and discovered a black
snake, six feet or more in length, which seemed about to
coil itself around the nag's leg. The size and contiguity of
the reptile at first appalled me, and my mind was not more
composed when the serpent, at my approach, manifested
an inclination to assume the offensive. Its folds were
thicker than my arm, and it commenced to revolve rapidly,
at length running up a sapling, suspending itself by the

tail, and hissing vehemently. It belonged to the family of "racers," and was hideous and powerful beyond any specimen that I had seen. I blew it into halves at the second discharge of my pistol, and at once resumed my saddle, indisposed to remain longer amidst such acquaintances.

At four o'clock I saw Culpeper, a trim little village, lying in the hollow of several hills. A couple of steeples added to its picturesqueness, and a swift creek, crossed by a small bridge, interposed between myself and the main part of the place. It looked like Sunday when I rode through the principal street. The shutters were closed in the shop windows, the dwellings seemed tenantless, no citizens were abroad, no sutlers had invaded the country; only a few cavalry-men clustered about an ancient pump to water their nags, and some military idlers were sitting upon the long porch of a public house, called the Virginia Hotel. I tied my horse to a tree, the bole of which had been gnawed bare, and found the landlord to be an old gentleman named Paine, who appeared to be somewhat out of his head. Two days before the Confederate cavalry had vacated the village, and the army had been encamped about the town for many months. A sabre conflict had taken place in the streets; and these events, happening in rapid succession, combined with the insolence of some Federal outriders, had so agitated the host that his memory was quite gone, and he could not perform even the slightest function. There is a panacea for all these things, which the faculty and philanthropy alike forbid, but which my experience in war-matters has invariably found unfailing. I produced my flask, and gently insinuated it to the old gentleman's lips. He possessed instinct sufficient to uncork and apply it, and the results were directly apparent, in a partial recovery of memory. He said that meals were one dollar each, board four dollars a day, or by the week twenty-five dollars. These terms are unknown in America; but when Mr. Paine added that horse provender was one dollar per "feed," I looked aghast, and required some stimulant myself to appreciate the enormity of the reckoning. I discovered, however, that the people of the

village were almost starving; that beef had been fifty cents
a pound during the whole winter, flour twenty-five dollars
per barrel, coffee one dollar and a quarter a pound, and
corn one dollar per bushel. The army had swept the country like famine, and the citizens had pinched, pining faces,
with little to eat today and nothing for tomorrow.

I acquiesced in the charge, as no choice remained, and
asked to be shown to my room. A burly Negro, apparently
suffering *delirium tremens,* seized my baggage with quaking hands, and lifting a pair of red eyes upon me, shuffled
through a bare hall, up a stairway, and into a bedroom. I
never saw a more hideous being in my life, and when he
had flung my luggage upon the floor, he sank into a chair,
and glared woefully into my face, breathing like one about
to expire.

"Young Moss," said he, "can't you give a po' soul a drop
o' sperits? Do for de good Lord's sake! Do, Moss, fo' de po'
nigga's life. Do! do! Moss."

I poured him out a little in a tumbler, less from charity
than from fear; for he knew that I was provided with a
bottle, and I seemed to read murder in his eyes.

He drank like one athirst and scant of breath, making a
dry, chuckling noise with his throat. When he had finished, he leaned his powerful neck and head upon the bed
and groaned terribly.

"Moss," he said again, "ain't you got no tobacco, Moss?
I hain't had none since Christmas. I's mos' dead. I'm po'
sinful nigga'. Do give some tobacco to po' creature, do!"

I told him that I did not chew the weed, but gave him a
crushed cigar, and he thrust it into his mouth, as if it was
food and he was perishing. This wretched animal performed the duties of a chambermaid upon the premises;
he made the beds, attended to the toilets, answered the
bells, etc. He finally become so offensive that I forbade
him my room, and he revenged himself by paltry thefts.
There were two other servants, a woman with a baby, and
a shrewd, dishonest mulatto man, who was the steward
and carver. This fellow secreted provender in the kitchen
and sold it stealthily to hungry soldiers. A public house so

mismanaged I had nowhere met. Sometimes we could get
no breakfast till noon, and finally the price of dinner went
up to one dollar and a half, with nothing to eat. The table
was protected from flies by a series of paper fans, pendant
from the ceiling and connected by a cord, which an ebony
boy pulled, at the foot of the room to keep them in motion. This boy being worked day and night, often fell
asleep upon his stool, when the yellow man boxed his ears,
or knocked him down; and then he would fan with such
vigor that a perfect gale swept down the table. The landlord was a kindly old man, but he could not "keep a hotel,"
and the strong-minded part of the house consisted of his
wife and four daughters. General Ben Butler would have
sent these young women to Ship Island, five times of a day.
They were very bad-mannered and always sat apart at
one end of the cloth, talking against the "Yankees." As
there was no direct provocation to do so, this boldness was
gratuitous, and detracted rather than added to my estimate of the heroism of Southern women. I have known
them to burst into the office, crowded with blue-coats, and
scream—

"Pop, Yankees thieving in garden!" or, "Pop, drive these
Yankees out of parlor!"

Every afternoon when the pavement was unusually pa-
tronized by young officers, these women would sally out,
promenade in crinoline, silk stockings, and saucy hoods,
and the crowd would fall respectfully back to let them
pass. A flag hung from a hospital over the sidewalk, and
with a pert flourish, the landlord's daughters filed off the
pavement, around the ensign, and back again. This was
amusing, I thought, but not very clever, and rather im-
modest. Had they been handsome, some romance might
have attached to the act; but being homely and not mar-
riageable, I smiled at the occurrence and entered it in my
diary as "patriotism run mad." The stable arrangements
were, if possible, worse. One had to be certain, from actual
presence, that his horse was fed at all, and during the first
three days of my tenure, the black hostler lost me a breast

strap, a halter, a crupper strap, and finally emptied my saddlebags.

Now and then a woman made her appearance at a front window, stealthily peeping into the street, or a neighboring farmer ventured into town upon a lean consumptive mule. The very dogs were skinny and savage for want of sustenance, and when a long, cadaverous hog emerged from nowhere one day, and tottered up the main street, he was chased, killed, and quartered so rapidly, that the famous steam process seemed to have been applied to him, of being dropped into a hopper, and tumbling out, a medley of hams, ribs, lard, and penknives. The stock of provisions at the hotel finally gave out, and I was compelled to purchase morsels of meat from the steward. Dreadful visions of famishing ensued, but ultimately the railway was opened to town, and a sutler started a shop in the village. I lived upon sardines and crackers for two days, and a Major Fifield, Superintendent of Military Railroads, gave me savory breakfasts of ham afterward.

Troops were now concentrating in the neighborhood of Culpeper, and a bevy of camps encircled the little village. Crawford's Brigade, of Banks's Corps, garrisoned the place, and a provost marshal occupied the quaint Court House. Reconnoissances were made southward daily, and I joined one of these, which left the village on the second of August, at three o'clock, for Orange Court House, seventeen miles on the way to Richmond. Detachments of a Vermont and a New York cavalry regiment composed the reconnoitring party, and the whole was commanded by General Crawford, a clever and unostentatious soldier. We bivouacked that night near Raccoon Ford, on the river Rapidan. No fires were built; for we knew that the enemy was all around us, and we slept coldly and imperfectly till the gray of Sunday morning. At daylight we galloped into the main street of Orange Court House, having first sent a squadron around the village, to ride in at the other end. At the very moment of our entry, a company or more of Confederate horses was also trotting into town. Both parties sounded the charge simultaneously, and the carbines exploded in the very heart of the village. For a minute or more a sabre fight ensued, alternated by the firing of revolvers; but the defenders were overmatched, and several of them having been slain, they turned to escape. At that moment, however, our other squadron charged upon them, effectually blocking up the street, and the whole party surrendered. A major, who exhibited some obstinacy, was felled from the saddle by a terrible cut, which clove his skull, and a very dexterous young fellow who attempted to escape by a side street dodged a bevy of pursuers and saved his head by the loss of both his ears. The disfigured corpses of those freshly slain were laid along the sidewalk in a row; and after some invasion of henroosts and private pantries, we remounted, and with fifty or more prisoners crossed the Rapidan, and were welcomed into Culpeper with cheers. The prisoners were lodged in the loft of the courthouse, and their officers were paroled, and boarded among the neighbors. They complied with the terms of their parole very honorably, and bore testimony to the courtesy of their captors. I talked with them often upon the tavern porch, but an undue intimacy with any of them might have brought me into disrepute. Although the larders of the village were supposed to be empty, savory meals were nevertheless sent daily to these cavalry-men, and it was evident that the people on all hands sympathized with their soldiery.

The stringent orders of Pope, relative to removing the disaffected beyond his lines, were never enforced. I doubt if the veritable commander himself meant to do more than intimidate evil doers; but I saw frequent evidences of scrupulous humanity on the part of his general officers.

One day when I was negotiating with the provost for the purchase of some port wine, stored upon the premises of a village druggist, a sergeant elbowed his way into the presence of the Marshal, and pushed forward two very dirty lads, who gave their ages respectively, as ten and thirteen years. They were of Hibernian parentage, and belonged to the class of newsboys trading with the different brigades. The younger lad was wiping his nose and eyes with a relic of a coat sleeve, and the elder was studying the point of the case, with a view to an elaborate defence. The sergeant produced a thick roll of bills and laid them upon the desk.

"Gineral Crawford," said he, "orders these boys to be locked up in the jail. They have been passing this stuff upon the country folks, and belong to a gang of young varmints who follers the 'lay.' The Gineral is going to have 'em brought up at the proper time and punished."

The bills were fair imitations of Confederate currency, and were openly sold in the streets of Northern cities at the rate of thousands of dollars for a penny. These lads probably purchased horses, swine, or fowls with them, or perhaps paid some impoverished widow for board in the worthless counterfeit.

The younger lad sobbed and howled when the order for his incarceration had been announced, but the elder made a stout remonstrance.

He didn't know the Gineral would arrest him. Everybody else passed the bills. He thought they wos good bills; some man gave 'em to him. They wan't passed, nohow, upon nobody but *Rebels!* He could prove that! He "know'd" a quartermaster that passed 'em. Wouldn't they let him and Sam off this wunst?

They were both sent to Coventry, despite their years, and down to the last day of our tenure in Culpeper, I saw these wicked urchins peeping through the grates of the old brick jail, where they lay in the steam and vapor, among Negroes, drunkards, and thieves—an evidence of justice, which it is a pleasure to record, in this free narrative.

I joined a mess in the Ninth New York regiment finally, and contrived to exist till the fifth of the month, when Pope moved his headquarters to a hill back of Culpeper, and thereafter I lived daintily for a little while. On the 8th of August, however, an event occurred, which disturbed the wisest calculations of the correspondent and the Generals: THE BATTLE OF CEDAR MOUNTAIN.

CHAPTER XXII

Going into Action

————

While General Pope's army was concentrating between the Rappahannock and Rapidan rivers, the army of General "Stonewall" Jackson was lying upon the south bank of the Rapidan, and that renowned commander's headquarters were at Gordonsville, about thirty miles from Culpeper. It was generally presumed that Jackson had fortified Gordonsville, intending to lie in wait there, or possibly to oppose the crossing of Pope upon the banks of the river. It was not believed that Jackson's force was very great, because the main body of the Confederates were held below Richmond, where McClellan's army still remained. The Southern capital seemed to be menaced both from the North and the South; but in reality, the Grand Army was re-embarking at Harrison's Bar, and sailing up the Chesapeake in detachments, to effect a junction with Pope on the plains of Piedmont. So important a movement could not be concealed from the Confederates, and they had resolved to annihilate Pope before McClellan's reinforcements could arrive. It was the work of two weeks to transport eighty or a hundred thousand men three hundred miles, and finding that Burnside's corps had already landed upon the Potomac, Stonewall Jackson determined to cross the Rapidan and cripple the fragment of Pope's forces stationed at Culpeper.

Stonewall Jackson is one of the many men whose extraordinary military genius has been developed by the Civil War. But unlike the mass who have become famous in a day and lost their laurels in a week, Jackson's glory has steadily increased. He was first brought into notice at Winchester, where he fought a fierce battle with Banks, and derived the *sobriquet* which he has retained to the present time. Soon afterward, he chased Banks's army down the Shenandoah Valley, and across the Potomac. Afterward, he bore a conspicuous part in the engagement below Richmond, and was now to become prominent in the most daring episodes of the whole war. His excellence was *activity*. He scrupled at no fatigue, marched his troops over steep and circuitous roads, was everywhere when unexpected, and nowhere when sought, and his boldness was equal to his energy. He did not fear to attack overpowering numbers, if the situation demanded it. All that General Lee might plan, General Jackson would dare to execute; and he has been, above all others, the Soult of the Southern war, while Stuart was its Murat, and Lee its Napoleon.

We first had intimation of the advance of Jackson on the afternoon of the 7th of August. Two regiments of cavalry, picketed upon the Rapidan, rode pell-mell into Culpeper, reporting a large Southern force at the fords, and rapidly advancing. Pope at once ordered the whole of one of these regiments under arrest, and it was the opinion of the army that the approach was a feint, or, at most, a reconnoissance in force. Subsequent information satisfied the incredulous, however, that a considerable body of troops were marching northward, and their outriding scouts had been seen at Cedar Mountain, only six miles from Culpeper. The latter is one of the many woody knobs or heights that environ the village, but it is nearer than any other, and should have been occupied by Pope, simultaneously with his arrival. It is scarcely a mountain in elevation, but so high that the clouds often envelope its crest, and it commands a view of all the surrounding country. There are cleared patches up its sides, and the highest of these constitutes the farm of a clergyman, after whom the eminence is sometimes called "Slaughter's Mountain." At its base lie a few pleasant farms; and a shallow rivulet or creek, called Cedar Run, crosses the road between the mountain and Culpeper. Upon the mountain side Jackson had placed his batteries, and his infantry lay in dense thickets and belts of woods before the hill and on each side of it. The position was a powerful, though not an impregnable one; for batteries might readily be pushed up the slope, and our infantry had often ascended steeper eminences. But an opposing army scattered about the meadow lands below, would find its several components exposed to shot and shell, thrown from points three or four hundred feet above them.

When it had been discovered that the enemy had anticipated us in seizing this strong position, word was at once despatched to Banks and Sigel to bring up their columns without delay. The brigade of General Crawford was marched through Culpeper at noon on Friday; and that afternon, foot-sore, but enthusiastic, regiments began to arrive in rapid succession.

I had been passing the morning of Friday with Colonel Bowman, a modest and capable gentleman, when the serenity of our converse was disturbed by a sergeant, who rode into camp with orders for a prompt advance in light marching order. In a twinkling all the camps in the vicinity were deserted, and the roads were so blocked with soldiers on my return, that I was obliged to ride through fields.

I trotted rapidly into the village, and witnessed a scene exciting and martial beyond anything which I had remarked with the Army of Virginia. Regiments were pouring by all the roads and lanes into the main street, and the spectacle of thousands of bayonets, extending as far as the eye could reach, was enhanced by the music of a score of bands, throbbing all at the same moment with wild music. The orders of officers rang out fitfully in the din, and when the steel shifted from shoulder to shoulder, it was like looking down a long sparkling wave. Above the confusion of the time, the various nativities of volunteers roared their national ballads. "St. Patrick's Day," intermingled with the weird refrain of "Bonnie Dundee," and snatches of German sword-songs were drowned by the thrilling chorus of the "Star-Spangled Banner." Then some stentor would strike a stave of "John Brown's body lies a mouldering in the grave," and the wild, mournful music would be caught up by all—Germans, Celts, Saxons, till the little town rang with the thunder of voices, all uttering the name of the grim old Moloch, whom—more than any one save Hunter —Virginia hates. Suddenly, as if by rehearsal, all hats would go up, all bayonets toss and glisten, and huzzas would deafen the winds, while the horses reared upon their haunches and the sabres rose and fell. Then, column by column, the masses passed eastward, while the prisoners in the courthouse cupola looked down, and the citizens peeped in fear through crevices of windows.

Being unattached to the staff of any general at the time, and therefore at liberty as a mere spectator, I rode rapidly after the troops, passed the foremost regiments, and unwittingly kept to the left, which I did not discover in the excitement of the ride, till my horse was foaming and my face furrowed with heat drops. I saw that the way had been little travelled, and inquiry at a log farm-house, some distance further, satisfied me that I had mistaken the way. Two men in coarse brown suits were chopping wood here, and they informed me, with an oath, that the last soldiers seen in the neighborhood had been Confederate pickets. A by-road enabled me to recover the proper route, and from the top of a hill overlooking Culpeper, I had a view of the hamlet, nestling in its hollow; the roads entering it, black with troops, and all the slopes covered with wagontrains, whose white canopies seemed infinite. The skies were gorgeously dyed over the snug cottages and modest spires; some far woods were folded in a pleasant haze; and the blue mountains lifted their huge backs, voluming in the distance, like some boundary for humanity, with a happier land beyond. Here I might have stood, a few months before, and heard the church bells; and the trees around me might have been musical with birds. But now the parsons and the choristers were gone; the scaffold was erected, the axe bare, and with a good-bye glance at the world and man, some hundreds of wretches were to drop into eternity. We have all read of the guillotine in other lands; it was now before me in my own.

As I passed into the highway again, and riding through narrow passages, grazing officers' knees, turning vicious battery horses, winding in and out of woods, making detours through pasture fields, leaping ditches, and so making perilous progress, I passed many friends who hailed me cheerfully—here a brigadier-general who waved his hand, or a colonel who saluted, or a staff officer who rode out and exchanged inquiries or greetings, or a sergeant who winked and laughed. These were some of the men whose bodies I was to stir tomorrow with my foot, when the eyes that shone upon me now would be swollen and ghastly.

Some of the privates seeing me in plain clothes, as I had joined the army merely as a visitor and with no idea of seeing immediate service there, mistook me for a newspaper correspondent, which in one sense I was; and I was greeted with such cries as—

"Our Special Artist!"

"Our Own Correspondent!"

"Give our Captain a setting up, you sir!"

"Puff our Colonel!"

"Give me a good obituary!"

"Where's your pass, bub?"

"Halloo! Jenkins. Three cheers for Jenkins!"

I shall not soon forget one fellow, who planted himself in my path (his regiment had halted), and leaning upon his musket looked steadily into my eyes.

"Ef I had a warrant for the devil," he said, "I'd arrest that feller."

Many of the soldiers were pensive and thoughtful; but the mass were marching to their funerals with boyish outcries, apparently anxious to forget the responsibilities of the time.

"Let's sing, boys." "Oh! Get out, or I'll belt you over the snout." "Halloo! Pardner, is there water over there?" "Three groans for old Jeff!" "Hip-hip—hoo-roar! Hi! Hi!"

A continual explosion of small arms, in the shape of epithets, jests, imitations of the cries of sheep, cows, mules, and roosters, and snatches of songs, enlivened the march. If something interposed, or a halt was ordered, the men would throw themselves in the dust, wipe their foreheads, drink from their canteens, gossip, grin, and shout confusedly, and some sought opportunities to straggle off, so that the regiments were materially decimated before they reached the field. The leading officers maintained a dignity and a reserve, and reined their horses together in places, to confer. At one time, a private soldier came out to me, presenting a scrap of paper, and asked me to scrawl him a line, which he would dictate. It was as follows:

"My dear Mary, we are going into action soon, and I send you my love. Kiss baby, and if I am not killed I will write to you after the fight."

The man asked me to mail the scrap at the first opportunity; but the same post which carried his simple billet, carried also his name among the rolls of the dead.

At five o'clock I overtook Crawford's brigade, drawn up in front of a fine girdle of timber, in a grass field, and on the edge of Cedar Creek. Their ambulances had been unhitched and ranged in a row against the woods, and the soldiers were soon formed in line of battle, extending across the road, with their faces toward the mountain. In this order they moved through the creek, and disappeared behind the ridge of a cornfield. The hill towered in front, but with the naked eye I could distinguish only a speck of floating something above the roof of Slaughter's white house. This was said to be a flag, though I did not believe it; and as there were no evidences of any enemy, which I could determine, I turned my attention to the immediate necessities of myself and my horse. A granary lay at a little distance, and as I was hastening thither, a trooper came along with a blanket full of corn. Fortuitously, he dropped about a dozen ears, which I secured, and hitched my animal to a tree, where he munched until I had fallen asleep. The latter event happened in this wise.

I had observed a slight person in the uniform of a surgeon. He was dividing a large lump of pork at the time, and three great crackers lay before him. I approached and introduced myself, and in a few minutes I was a partial proprietor of the meat, and he a recipient of some drink. The same person directed me to occupy a shelf of the ambulance, and when we lay down together he narrated some of his experiences in Martinsburg, when the Confederates occupied the place after Banks's retreat. He had charge of a hospital at that time, and witnessed the entrance of the Confederate army. The wildness of the people was unbounded, he said, and all who had given so much as a drop of cold water to the invaders were pointed out and execrated. The properties of a few, said to be Unionists, were endangered; and ruffianly soldiers climbed to the windows of the hospital, hooting and taunting the sick. Not to be outdone in bitterness, the tenants flung up their crutches and cheered for the Union, that darling idea, which has marshalled a million of men and filled hecatombs with its champions. In a few days the Federals took possession of the town anew, and the Southern element was in turn oppressed. This is civil war—more cruel than the excesses of hereditary enemies. A year before these people of the Shenandoah were fellow-countrymen of the soldiery they contemned.

CHAPTER XXIII

The Battle of Cedar Mountain

THERE being nothing to eat in the vicinity of the ambulances, I mounted anew at five o'clock and rode back toward Culpeper. No portion of the troops of Crawford were visible now, and only some gray smoke moved up the side of the mountain. A few stragglers were bathing their faces in Cedar Creek, and some miles in the rear lay several of McDowell's brigades under arms. Their muskets were stacked along the sides of the road, the men lay sleepily upon the ground—company by company, each in its proper place—the field-officers gossiping together, and the colors upright and unfurled. I was stopped all the way along the lines and interrogated as to what was happening in front.

"Any Reb-bils out yonder?" asked a grim, snappish colonel.

"Guess they don't mean to fight before breakfast!" blurted a captain.

"Wish they'd cut away, anyway, if they goin' to!" muttered a chorus of privates.

At the village there was nothing to be purchased, although some sutlers' stores lay at the depot, guarded by provost officers. I persuaded a Negro to give me a mess of almost raw pork, and a woman, with a child at the breast, cooked me some biscuit. There were many civilians and idle officers in the town, and the streets were lined with cavalry. Mr. Paine, the landlord, was losing the remnant of his wits, and the young ladies were playing the "Bonnie Blue Flag," and laughing satirically at some young officers who listened. The correspondents began to show themselves in force, and a young fellow whom I may call Chitty, representing a provincial journal, greatly amused me with the expression of fears that there might be no engagement after all. Chitty was an attorney who had forsaken a very moderate practice for a press connection, and he informed me, in confidence, that he was gathering materials for a history of the war. By reason of his attention to this weighty project, he failed to do any reporting, and as his mind was not very well balanced, he was commonly taken to be a simpleton. As there was nobody else to talk to, I amused myself with Chitty during the forenoon, and he narrated to me some doubtful intrigues which had varied his career in Piedmont. But Chitty had mingled in no battles, and now that a contest was about to take place, his heart warmed in anticipation. He asked me if the hottest fighting would not probably occur on the right, and intimated, in that event, his desire to carry despatches through the thickest of the fray. Death was welcome to Chitty if he could so distinguish himself. Between Chitty and a nap in a wagon, I managed to loiter out the morning, and at three o'clock a cannon peal, so close that it shook the houses, brought my horse upon his haunches. For awhile I did not leave the village. Cannon upon cannon exploded; the young ladies ceased their mirth; the landlord staggered with white lips into the air, and after a couple of hours, I heard the signal that I knew so well—a volley of musketry. Full of all the old impulses, I climbed into the saddle, and spurred my horse towards the battlefield.

The ride over six miles of clay road was a capital school for my pony. Every hoof-fall brought him closer to the cannon, and the sound had become familiar when he reached the scene. At four o'clock, the musketry was close and effective beyond anything I had known, and now and then I could see, from secure places, the spurts of white cannon-smoke far up the side of the mountain. The action was commenced by emulous skirmishers, who crawled from the woodsides, and annoyed each other from coverts of ridge, stump, and stone heap. A large number of Southern riflemen then threw themselves into a corner of wood, considerably advanced from their main position. Their fire was so destructive that General Banks felt it necessary to order a charge. Two brigades, when the signal was given, marched in line of battle, out of a wood, and charged across a field of broken ground toward the projecting corner. As soon as they appeared, sharpshooters darted up from a stretch of scrub cedars on their right, and a battery mowed them down by an oblique fire from the left. The guns up the mountainside threw shells with beautiful exactness, and the concealed rifle-men in front poured in deadly showers of bullet and ball. As the men fell by dozens out of line, the survivors closed up the gaps, and pressed forward gallantly. The ground was uneven, however, and solid order could not be observed throughout. At length, when they had gained a brookside at the very edge of the wood, the column staggered, quailed, fell into disorder, and then fell back. Some of the more desperate dashed singly into the thicket, bayoneting their enemies, and falling in turn in the fierce grapple. Others of the Confederates ran from the wood, and engaged hand to hand with antagonists, and, in places, a score of combatants met sturdily upon the plain, lunging with knife and sabre bayonet, striking with clubbed musket, or discharging revolvers. But at last the broken lines regained the shelter of the timber, and there was a momentary lull in the thunder.

For a time, each party kept in the edges of the timber, firing at will, but the Confederates were moving forward in masses by detours, until some thousands of them stood in the places of the few who were at first isolated. Distinct charges were now made, and a large body of Federals attempted to capture the battery before Slaughter's house, while separate brigades charged by front and flank upon the impenetrable timber. The horrible results of the previous effort were repeated; the Confederates preserved their position, and, at nightfall, the Federals fell back a mile or more. From fifteen hundred to two thousand of the latter were slain or wounded, and, though the heat of the battle had lasted not more than two hours, nearly four thousand men upon both sides were maimed or dead. The valor of the combatants in either cause was unquestionable. But no troops in the world could have driven the Confederates out of the impregnable mazes of the wood. It was an error to expose columns of troops upon an open plain, in the face of imperceptible sharpshooters. The batteries should have shelled the thickets, and the infantry should have retained their concealment. The most disciplined troops of Europe would not have availed in a country of bog, barren, ditch, creek, forest, and mountain. Compared to the bare plain of Waterloo, Cedar Mountain was like the antediluvian world, when the surface was broken by volcanic fire into chasms and abysses. In this battle, the Confederate batteries, along the mountainside, were arranged in the form of a crescent, and, when the solid masses charged up the hill, they were butchered by enfilading fires. On the Confederate part, a thorough knowledge of the country was manifest, and the best possible disposition of forces and means; on the side of the Federals, there was zeal without discretion, and gallantry without generalship.

During the action, Stonewall Jackson occupied a commanding position on the side of the mountain, where, glass in hand, he observed every change of position, and directed all the operations. General Banks was indefatigable and courageous; but he was left to fight the whole battle, and not a regiment of the large reserve in his rear came forward to succor or relieve him. As usual, McDowell was cursed by all sides, and some of Banks's soldiers threatened to shoot him. But the unpopular Commander had no defence to make, and said nothing to clear up the doubts relative to him. He exposed himself repeatedly, and so did Pope. The latter rode to the front at nightfall—for what purpose no one could say, as he had been in Culpeper during the whole afternoon—and he barely escaped being captured. The loss of Federal officers was very heavy. Fourteen commissioned officers were killed and captured out of one regiment. Sixteen commissioned officers only remained in four regiments. One general was taken prisoner and several were wounded. A large number of field-officers were slain.

During the progress of the fight I galloped from point to point along the rear, but could nowhere obtain a panoramic view. The common sentiment of civilians, that it is always possible to see a battle, is true of isolated contests only. Even the troops engaged know little of the occurrences around them, and I have been assured by many soldiers that they have fought a whole day without so much as a glimpse of an enemy. The smoke and dust conceal objects, and where the greatest execution is done, the antagonists have frequently fired at a line of smoke, behind which columns may or may not have been posted.

It was not till nightfall, when the Federals gave up the contested ground and fell back to some cleared fields, that I heard anything of the manner of action and the resulting losses. As soon as the firing ceased, the ambulance corps went ahead and began to gather up the wounded. As many of these as could walk passed to the rear on foot, and the spectacle at eight o'clock was of a terrible character. The roads were packed with ambulances, creaking under fearful weights, and rod by rod the teams were stopped to accommodate other sufferers who had fallen or fainted on the walk. A crippled man would cling to the tail of a wagon, while the tongue would be burdened with two, sustaining themselves by the backs of the horses. Water was sought for everywhere, and all were hungry. I met at sundry times friends who had passed me hopeful and humorous the day before, now crawling wearily with a shattered leg or dumb with a stiff and dripping jaw. To realize the horror of the night, imagine a common clay road, in a quiet, rolling country, packed with bleeding people—the fences down, horsemen riding through the fields, wagons blocking the way, reinforcements in dark columns hurrying up, the shouting of the well to the ill, and the feeble replies—in a word, recall that elder time when the "earth was filled with violence," and add to the idea that the time was in the night.

I assumed my old rôle of writing the names of the

wounded, but when, at nine o'clock, the 10th Maine regiment—a fragment of the proud column which passed me in the morning—returned, I hailed Colonel Beale, and reined with him into a clover-field, the files following wearily. Tramping through the tall garbage, with a few words, and those spoken in low tones, we stopped at length in a sort of basin, with the ground rising on every side of us. The men were placed in line, and the Company Sergeants called the rolls. Some of the replies were thrilling, but all were prosaic:

"Smith!"

"Smithe fell at the first fire, Sergeant. Bill, here, saw him go down."

"Sturgis!"

"Sam's in the ambulance, wi' his thigh broke. I don't believe he'll live, Sergeant!"

"Thompson!"

"Dead."

"Vinton!"

"Yar!" (feebly said). "Four fingers shot off."

In this way, the long lists were read over, while the survivors chatted, laughed, and disputed, talking of the incidents of the day. Most of the men lay down in the clover, and some started off in couples to procure water. The field-officers gave me some items relative to the conflict, and as they were ordered to remain here, I resolved to pass the night with them. Obtaining a great fence-rail, I lashed my horse to it by his halter, and, removing his saddle and bridle, left him free to graze in the vicinity. Then I unfolded my camp-bed, covered myself with a rubber blanket, and continued to listen to the conversation. Of course, accusations, bitter mutterings, moodiness, and melancholy prevailed. I heard these for some time, interspersed with sententious eulogies upon particular persons, and references to isolated events. The evening was one of the pleasantest of the year, in all that nature could contribute; a fine starlight, a transparent atmosphere, a coolness, and a fragrance of sweet-clover blossoms. I had laid my head upon my arm, and shut my eyes, and felt drowsiness come upon

me, when something hurtled through the air, and another
gun boomed in the stillness. A shell, describing an arc of
fire, fell some distance to our left, and in a moment a second shell passed directly over our heads.

"——!" said an officer; "have they moved a battery so
close? See! it is just at the end of this field!"

I looked back. At the top of the basin in which we lay,
something flashed up, throwing a glare upon the woody
background, and a shell, followed by a shock, crashed rico-
chetting, directly in a line with us, but leaped, fortunately,
above us, and continued its course far beyond.

"They mean 'em for us," said the same voice; "they see
these lights where the fools have been warming their coffee. Halloo!"

Another glare of fire revealed the grouped men and
horses around the battery, and for a moment I thought the
missile had struck among us. There was a splutter, as of
shivering metal flying about, and, with a sort of intuition,
the whole regiment rose and ran. I started to my feet and
looked for my horse. His ears were erect, his eyeballs dis-
tended, and his nostrils were tremulous with fright. A
fifth shell, so perfectly in range that I held my breath and
felt my heart grow cold, came toward and passed me, and,
with a toss of his head, the nag flung up the rail as if it
had been a feather. He seemed literally to juggle it, and
it flitted here and there, so that I dared not approach him.
A favorable opportunity at length ensued, and I seized
the animal by his halter. He was now wild with panic,
and sprang toward me as if to trample me. In vain I endeavored to pull him toward the saddle. Fresh projectiles
darted beside and above us, and the last of these seemed
to pass so close that I could have reached and touched it.
Panic took possession of me. I grasped my camp-bed,
rather by instinct than by choice, and, holding it desperately under my arm, took to my heels.

It was a long distance to the bottom of the clover-field,
and the swift iron followed me remorselessly. At one moment, when a shell burst full in my face, half blinding me,
I felt weak to faintness, but still I ran. I had wit enough to

avoid the high road, which I knew to be packed with fugitives, and down which, I properly surmised, the enemy would send his steady messengers. Once I fell into a ditch, and the breath was knocked out of my body, but I rolled over upon my feet with marvellous sprightliness, till, at last, when I gained a corn-field, my attention was diverted to a strange, rattling noise behind me. I turned and looked. It was my horse, the rail dangling between his legs, his eyes on fire in the night. As we regarded each other, a shell burst between us. He dashed away across the inhospitable fields, and I fell into the high road among the routed. Expletives like these ensued:

"Sa-a-ay! Hoss! Pardner! Are you going to ride over this wounded feller?"

"Friend, have you a drop of water for a man that's fainted here?"

"Halloo! Buster! Keep that bayonit out o' my eye, if you please!"

"Where's General Banks? I hearn say he's a prisoner."

"I do' know!"

"Was we licked, do you think?"

"No! We warn't nothin' o' the kind. Sigel's outflanked 'em and okkepies the field. A man jus' told me so."

"Huzza! Hearties, cheer up! Sigel's took the field, and Stonewall Jackson's dead."

"Three cheers for Sigel."

"Hoorooar, hoor——"

"Oh! Get out! That's all blow. Don't try stuff me! We're lathered; that's the long and shawt of it."

"Is that so? Boys, I guess we're beat!"

Such was the character of exclamations that ran here and there, and after a little volley of them had been let off, a long pause succeeded, when only the sighs of the injured and the tramp of men and nags broke the silence. Overhead the starlight and the blue sky; on either side the rolling, shadowy fields; and wrapping the horizon in a gray, grisly girdle, the reposing woods plentiful with dew. Nature was putting forth all her still, sweet charms, as if to make men witness the damned contrasts of their own wrath, violence, and murder. Even thus, perhaps—I reasoned—in the days of old, did the broken multitudes of Xerxes return by the shores of the golden Archipelago; and the Hellespont shone as peacefully as these silvernesses of earth and firmament. The dulness of history became invested with new intelligence. I filled in the details of a thousand routs conned in school-days, when only the dry outlines lay before me. They were mysteries before, and lacked the warmness of life and truth; but now I *saw* them! The armor and the helmets fell away, with all other trappings of custom, language, and ceremony. This pale giant, who walked behind the ambulance, leaning upon the footboard, was the limping Achilles, with the arrow of Paris festering in his heel. This ancient veteran, with his back to the field, was the fugitive Aeneas, leaving Troy behind. And these, around me, belonged to the columns of Barbazona, scattered at Legnano by the revengeful Milanese. Cobweb and thick dust and faded parchment had somewhat softened those elder events; but in their day they were tangible, practical, and prosaic, like this scene. Years will roll over this, as over those, and folks will read at firesides, half doubtfully, half wonderingly, the story of this bafflement, when no fragment of its ruin remains. It was a profound feeling that I should thus be walking down the great retreat of time, and that the occurrences around me should be remembered forever!

There were a few prisoners in the mass, walking before cavalry-men. Nobody interfered with them, and they were not in a position to feel elated. Now and then, when we reached an ambulance, the fugitives would press around it to inquire if any of their friends were within. Rough recognitions would ensue, as thus:

"Bobby, is that you, back there?—Bobby Baker?"

"Who is it?" (feebly uttered).

"Me, Bobby—Josh Wiggins. Are you shot bad, Bobby?"

"Shot in the thigh; think the bone's broke. You haven't got a drop of water, have you?"

"No, Bobby; wish I had. Have any more of our boys been hurt that you know of?"

"Switzer is dead; Bill Cringle and Jonesy are prisoners; 'Pud' White is in the ambulance ahead; 'Fol' Thompson's lost an arm; that's all I know."

When we had gone two miles or more, we found a provost column drawn across the road, and a mounted officer interrogating all who attempted to pass:

"Stop there! You're not wounded."

"Yes, I am."

"Pass on! Halt boy! Go back. Men, close up there. Stop that boy."

"I am sun-struck, Major."

"You lie! Drive him back. Go back, now!"

Beyond this the way was comparatively clear; but as I knew that other guards held the road further on, I passed to the right, and with the hope of finding a rill of water, went across some grass fields, keeping toward the low places. The fields were very still, and I heard only the subdued noises wafted from the road; but suddenly I found myself surrounded by men. They were lying in groups in the tall grass, and started up suddenly, like the clansmen of Roderick Dhu. At first I thought myself a prisoner, and these some cunning Confederates who had lain in wait. But, to my surprise, they wore Federal uniforms, and were simply skulkers from various regiments, who had been hiding here during the hours of battle. Some of these miserable wretches asked me the particulars of the fight, and when told of the defeat, muttered that they were not to be hood-winked and slaughtered.

"I was sick, anyway," said one fellow, "and felt like droppin' on the road."

"I didn't trust my colonel," said another; "he ain't no soldier."

"I'm tired of the war, anyhow," said a third, "and my time's up soon; so I shan't have my head blown off."

As I progressed, dozens of these men appeared; the fields were strewn with them; a true man would rather have been lying with the dead on the field of carnage, than here, among the craven and base. I came to a spring at last, and the stragglers surrounded it in levies. One of them gave me a cup to dip some of the crystal, and a prayerful feeling came over me as the cooling draught fell over my dry palate and parched throat. Regaining the road, I encountered reinforcements coming rapidly out of Culpeper, and among them was the 9th New York. My friend Lieutenant Draper recognized me, and called out that he should see me on the morrow, if he was not killed meantime. Culpeper was filling with fugitives when I passed up the main street, and they were sprinkled along the sidewalks, gossiping with each other. The wounded were being carried into some of the dwellings, and when I reached the Virginia Hotel, many of them lay upon the porch. I placed my blanket on a clean place, threw myself down exhaustedly, and dropped to sleep directly.

CHAPTER XXIV

Out with a Burying Party

———

W HEN I rose at ten o'clock on the morning of Sunday, August 10, the porch was covered with wounded people. Some fierce sunbeams were gliding under the roof, shining in the poor fellows' eyes, and they were stirring wearily, though asleep. Picking my way among the prostrate figures, I resorted to the pump in the rear of the tavern for the purpose of bathing my face. A soldier stood there on guard, and he refused to give me so much as a draught of water. The wounded needed every drop, and there were but a few wells in the town. I strolled through the main street, now crowded with unfortunates, and pausing at the courthouse, found the seat of justice transmuted to a headquarters for surgeons, where amputations were being performed. Continuing by a street to the left, I came to the depot, and here the ambulances were gathered with their scores of inmates. A tavern contiguous to the railway was also a hospital, but in the basement I found the transportation agents at breakfast, and they gave me a bountiful meal.

It was here arranged between myself and an old friend —a newspaper correspondent who had recently married and whose wife awaited him at Willard's in Washington— that he should proceed at once to New York with the outline of the fight, and that I should follow him next day (having, indeed, to report for duty and fresh orders at Headquarters of the army in Washington), with particulars and the lists of killed. I commenced my part of the labors at once, employing three persons to assist me, and we districted Culpeper, so that no one should interfere with the grounds of the other. My own part of the work embraced both hotel-hospitals, the names and statements of the prisoners of the courthouse loft, and interviews with some of the generals and colonels who lay at various private residences. The business was not a desirable one; for hot hospital rooms were now absolutely reeking, and many of the victims were asleep. It would be inhuman to awaken these; but in many cases those adjacent knew nothing, and with all assiduity the rolls must be imperfect. I found one man who had undergone a sort of mental paralysis and could not tell me his own name. However, I groped through the several chambers where the bleeding littered the bare floors. Some of them were eating voraciously, and buckets of ice-water were being carried to and fro that all might drink. Some male nurses were fanning the sleeping people with boughs of cedar; but the flies filled the ceiling, and, attracted by the wounds, they kept up a constant buzzing. I imagined that mortification would rapidly ensue in this broiling atmosphere. A couple of trains were being prepared below, to transport the sufferers to Washington, and from time to time individuals were carried into the air and deposited in common freight-cars upon the hard floors. Here they were compelled to wait till late in the evening, for no trains were allowed to leave the village during the day. At the Virginia Hotel, I visited, among others, the room in which I had lodged when I first came to Culpeper. Eight persons now occupied it, and three of them lay across the bed. I took the first man's name, and as the man next to him seemed to be asleep, I asked the first man to nudge him gently.

"I don't think he is alive," said the man; "he hasn't moved since midnight. I've spoken to him already."

I pulled a blanket from the head of the figure, and the tangled hair, yellow skin, and stiffened jaw told all the story. The other man looked uneasily into the face of the corpse and then lay down with his back toward it.

"I hope they'll take it out," said he, "I don't want to sleep beside it another night."

The guard at the courthouse allowed me to ascend to the loft, and the prisoners—forty of fifty in number—clustered around me. They had received, a short time before, their day's allotment of crackers and bread, and some of them were sitting in the cupola, with their bare legs hanging over the rails. They were anxious to have their names printed, and I learned from the less cautious the names of the brigades to which they belonged. Before I left the room I had obtained the number of regiments in Jackson's command and the names of his brigadier-generals. Some prisoners arrived while I was noting these matters. They had been sent to pick up arms, canteens, cartridge-boxes, etc., from the battle-field, and some of our cavalry had ridden them down and captured them. They were a little discomposed, but said, for the most part, that they were weary of the war and glad to be in custody. As a rule, Northern and Southern troops have the same general manners and appearances. These were more ragged than any Federals I had ever known, and their appetites were voracious.

I found General John White Geary, a Pennsylvania brigade commander, in the dwelling of a lady near the end of the town. He had received a bullet in the arm, and, I believe, submitted to amputation afterward. He was a tall, athletic man, upwards of six feet in height, and a citizen of one of the mountainous interior counties of the Quaker State. His life had been marked by much adventure, and he had been elevated to many important civil positions in various quarters of the Republic. He occupied a leading place in the Mexican War, and was afterward Mayor of San Francisco and Governor of Kansas. He acted with the Southern wing of the Democratic party, and was discreetly ambitious, promoting the agricultural interests of his commonwealth, and otherwise fulfilling useful civil functions. He was a fine exemplar of the American gentleman, preserving the better individualities of his countrymen, but discarding those grosser traits which have given us an unenviable name abroad. Geary could not do a mean thing, and his courage came so naturally to him that he did not consider it any cause of pride. The bias of party, which in America diseases the best natures, had in some degree affected the General. He was prone to go with his party in any event, when often, I think, his fine intelligence would have prompted him to an independent course. But I wish that all our leading men possessed his manliness, for then more dignity and self-respect, and less "smartness," might be apparent in our social and political organizations.

He was lying on his back, with his shattered arm bandaged, and resting on his breast. Twitches of keen pain shot across his face now and then, but he received me with a simple courtesy that made his patience thrice heroic. He did not speak of himself or his services, though I knew both to be eminent; but McDowell had insulted him, as he rode disabled from the field, and Geary felt the sting of the word more than the bullet. He had ventured to say to McDowell that the Reserves were badly needed in front, and the proud "regular" had answered the officious "volunteer," to the effect that he knew his own business. Not the least among the causes of the North's inefficiency will be found this ill feeling between the professional and civil soldiery. A regular contemns a volunteer; a volunteer hates a regular. I visited General Christopher C. Augur—badly wounded—in the drawing-room of the hotel, and paused a moment to watch Colonel Donnelly, mortally wounded, lying on a spread in the hall. The latter lingered a day in fearful agony; but he was a powerful man in physique, and he fought with death through a bloody sweat, never moaning nor complaining, till he fell into a blessed torpidity, and so yielded up his soul.

The shady little town was a sort of Golgotha now. Feverish eyes began to burn into one's heart, as he passed along the sidewalks. Red hospital flags hung like regalia from half the houses. A table for amputations was set up in the open air, and nakedness glared hideously upon the sun. How often have they brought out corpses in plain boxes of pine, and shut them away without sign, or ceremony, or tears, driving a long stake above the headboard. The ambulances came and went, till the line seemed stretching to the crack of doom; while, as in contemplation of further murder, the white-covered ammunition-teams creaked southward, and mounted provosts charged upon the skulkers, driving them to a pen, whence they were forwarded to their regiments. Old Mr. Paine, the landlord, tottered up to me, with a tear in his eye, and said:

"My good Lord, sir! Who is responsible for this?"

He did not mean to suggest argument. It was the language of a human heart pitying its brotherhood.

At twelve o'clock I started anew for the field, and fell in with Captain Chitty on the way. He stated that his courage during the fight surpassed his most heroic expectations, and added, in an undertone, that he was deliberating as to whether he should allow his name to be mentioned officially, since several military men were urging that honor upon him. I dissuaded Chitty from this intent, upon the ground that his reputation for modesty might be sacrificed. Chitty at once said that he would take my advice. We encountered Surgeon Ball, of Ohio, after a time, and he informed us that a day's armistice had been agreed upon, to allow for the burial of the dead. The work of interment was already commenced in front, and the surgeon had been ordered to see to the wounded, some of whom still lay on the places where they fell. He allowed us to accompany him in the capacity of cadets, but we first diverged a little from the road, that he might obtain his portmanteau of instruments. I fell into a little difficulty here, by unwittingly asking aloud of the 28th Pennsylvania regiment, if that was not the organization which hid itself during the fight? The 28th had been ordered, on the morning of Saturday, to occupy Telegraph Mountain, an elevation in the rear of Cedar Mountain, which was used for a Federal signal-post. Nobody having notified the 28th to return to camp, they remained on the mountain, passively witnessing the carnage, and came away in the night. But although my remark was jestingly said, the knot of soldiers who heard it were intensely excited. They spoke of taking me "off that hoss," and called me a New York "snob," who "wanted his head punched." This irate feeling may be attributed to the rivalry which exists between the "Empire" and the "Keystone" States, the latter being very jealous of the former, and claiming to have sent more troops to the war than any other commonwealth. The 28th volunteers doubtless expected a terrific onslaught from the next issue of the Philadelphia papers.

The reserves, which had lain some miles in the rear the previous evening, were now massed close to the field, but in the woods, that the enemy might not count their numbers from his high position. Stopping at times to chat with brother officers, at last I reached the meadow whence I had been driven the previous evening. I looked for my nag in vain. One soldier told me that he had seen him at daylight limping along the high road; but after sundry wild-goose chases, I gave up the idea of recovering him.

At last I passed the outlying batteries, with their black muzzles scanning the battle-ground, and ascending the clover field, came upon the site of the battery which had so discomfited us the previous night. A signal vengeance had overtaken it. Some splinters of wheel and an overturned caisson, with eight horses lying in a group—their hoofs extended like index boards, their necks elongated along the ground, and their bodies swollen—were the results of a single shell trained upon the battery by a cool artillerist. Beyond, the road and fields were strewn with knapsacks, haversacks, jackets, canteens, cartridge-boxes, shoes, bayonets, knives, buttons, belts, blankets, girths, and sabres. Now and then a mule or a horse lay at the roadside, with the clay saturated beneath him; and some of the tree-tops, in the depth of the woods, were scarred, split, and barked, as if the lightning had blasted them. Now passing a disabled wagon, now marking a dropped horseshoe, now turning a capsized ambulance, now regarding a perfect wilderness of old clothes, we emerged from the timber at last, and came to the place where I had slept on the eve of the battle. A hurricane had apparently swept the country here, and the fences had been transported bodily. Sometimes the ground looked, for limited areas, as if there had been a rain of kindling-wood;

and there were furrows in the clay, like those made by
some great mole which had ploughed into the bowels of
the earth. All the tree boles were pierced and perforated,
and boughs had been severed so that they littered the
way. Cedar Creek ran merrily across what had been the
road—the waters limpid and cool as before—and when I
passed beyond, I entered the region of dead men. Some
poisonous Upas had seemingly grown here, so that adventurers were prostrated by its exhalations. A tributary rivulet formed with the creek a triangular enclosure of ground,
where most of the Federals had fallen. To the left of the
road stood a cornfield; to the right a stubble-field, dotted
with stone heaps: deep woods formed the background to
these, and scrub-timber, irregularly disposed, the foreground. On the right of the stubble lay a great stretch of
"barren," spotted with dwarf cedars, and on the left of
the cornfield stood a white farm-house, with orchards and
outbuildings; beyond, the creek had hollowed a ravine
among the hills, and the far distance was bounded by the
mountains on the Rapidan. In the immediate front, towered Cedar Mountain, with woods at its base; and the roadway in which I stood, lost itself a little way on in the
mazes of the thicket. Looking down one of the rows of
corn, I saw the first corpse—the hands flung stiffly back,
the feet set stubbornly, the chin pointing upward, the
features losing their sharpness, the skin blackening, the
eyes great and white—"A heap of death—a chaos of cold
clay."

Turning into the cornfield, we came upon one man with
a spade, and another man lying at his feet. He was digging
a grave, and when we paused to note the operation, he
touched his cap—

"Pardner o' mine," he said, indicating the body; "him
and I fit side by side, and we agreed, if it could be done,
to bury each other. There ain't no sich man as that lost
out o' the army, private or officer—with all respect to you."

It was a eulogy that sounded as if more deserved, because it was homely. There are some that I have read,
much finer, but not as honest. At little distances we saw

parties of ten or twenty opening trenches; only the tributary brook dividing the Confederate and Federal fatigue
parties. Close to this brook, in the cornfield, lay a fallen
trunk of a tree, and four men sat upon it. Two of them
wore gray uniforms, two wore blue. The latter were Generals Benjamin S. Roberts and George L. Hartsuff of the
Federal army. They were waiting for Generals Stuart and
Early, of the Confederate army; and the four were to de-
fine the period of the armistice. The men in gray were Major Hintham of Mississippi, and Lieutenant Elliott Johnston of Maryland. Hintham was a lean, fiery, familiar man,
who wore the uniform of several field-marshals. An ostrich
feather was stuck in his soft hat and clasped by a silver
star upon a black velvet ground. A golden cord formed his
hat-band, and two tassels, as huge as those of drawing-
room curtains, fell upon his back. His collar was plentifully
embroidered as well as his coat-sleeves, and a black seam
ran down his trousers. He wore spurs of prodigious size,
and looked, in the main, like a tragedian about to appear
upon the stage. The other man was young, stout, and good
humored; and he talked sententiously, with a little vanity,
but much courtesy. The Federals had nothing to say to
these, they dealt only with equals in rank. It became a
matter of professional ambition, now, to obtain the greatest
amount of information from these Confederates, without
appearing to depart from any conventionality of the armistice. I got along very well till Chitty came up, and his in-
terrogatives were so pert and pointed that he very nearly
spoiled the entire labor. Young Johnston was a Balti-
morean, and wished his people to know something of him;
he gave me a card, stated that he was one of General
Thomas S. Garnett's aids, and had opened the armistice,
early in the day, by riding into the Federal lines with a
flag of truce. By detachments, new bodies of Confederate
officers joined us, most of them being young fellows in
gray suits; and at length General Jubal A. Early rode down
the hillside and nodded his head to our party.

It was the custom of our newspapers to publish, with its
narrative of each battle, a plan of the field; and in further-

ance of this object, having agreed to act for my absent friend, I moved a little way from the place of parley, and laying my paper on the pommel of my saddle proceeded to sketch the relative positions of road, brook, mountain, and woodland. While thus busily engaged, and congratulating myself upon the fine opportunities afforded me, a lithe, indurated, severe-looking horseman rode down the hill, and reining beside me, said—

"Are you making a sketch of our position?"

"Not for any military purpose."

"For what?"

"For a newspaper engraving."

"Umph!"

The man rode past me to the log, and when I had finished my transcript, I resumed my place at the group. The newcomer was Major General J. E. B. Stuart, one of the most famous cavalry leaders in the Confederate army. He was inquiring for General George L. Hartsuff, with whom he had been a fellow-cadet at West Point; but the Federal General had strolled off, and in the interval Stuart entered into familiar converse with the party. He described the Confederate uniform to me, and laughed over some reminiscences of his raid around McClellan's army.

"That performance gave me a major-generalcy, and my saddle cloth there, was sent from Baltimore as a reward, by a lady whom I never knew."

Stuart exhibited what is known in America as "airiness," and evidently loved to talk of his prowess. Directly General Hartsuff returned, and the forager rose, with a grim smile about his mouth—

"Hartsuff, God bless you, how-de-do?"

"Stuart, how are you?"

They took a quiet turn together, speaking of old school-days, perhaps; and when they came back to the log, Surgeon Ball produced a bottle of whiskey, out of which all the generals drank, wishing each other an early peace.

"Here's hoping you may fall into our hands," said Stuart; "we'll treat you well at Richmond!"

"The same to you!" said Hartsuff, and they all laughed.

It was a strange scene—this lull in the hurricane. Early was a North Carolinian, who lost nearly his whole brigade at Williamsburg. He wore a single star upon each shoulder, and in other respects resembled a homely farmer. He kept upon his horse, and had little to say. General Samuel Crawford was gray and mistrustful, calmly measuring Stuart with his eye, as if he intended to challenge him in a few minutes. Hartsuff was fair and burly, with a boyish face, and seemed a little ill at ease. Stuart sat upon a log, in careless posture, working his jaw till the sandy gray beard brushed his chin and became twisted in his teeth. Around, on foot and on horse, lounged idle officers of both armies; and the little rill that trickled behind us was choked in places with corpses. A pleasanter meeting could not have been held if this were a county training. The Surgeon told General Stuart that some of his relatives lived near the Confederate Capital, and as the General knew them, he related trifling occurrences happening in their neighborhoods, so that the meeting took the form of a roadside gossip, and Stuart might have been a plain farmer jaunting home from market. The General, who was called "Jeb" by his associates, so far relented finally as to give me leave to ride within the Confederate outer lines, and Lieutenant Johnston accompanied me. The corpses lay at frequent points, and some of the wounded who had not been gathered up remained at the spots where they had fallen. One of these, whose leg had been broken, was incapable of speaking, and could hardly be distinguished from the lifeless shapes around him. The number of those who had received their death wound on the edge of the brook, while in the act of leaping across was very great. I fancied that their faces retained the mingled ardor and agony of the endeavor and the pang. There seemed to be no system in the manner of interment, and many of the Federals had thrown down their shovels, and strolled across the boundary, to chaff and loiter with the "Butternuts." No one, whom I saw, exhibited any emotion at the strewn spectacles on every side, and the stories I had read of the stony-heartedness during the plague were more than ri-

valled by these charnel realities. Already corruption was
violating the "temples of the living God." The heat of the
day and the general demoralizing influences of the climate
were making havoc with the shapely men of yesterday,
and nature seemed hastening to reabsorb, and renew, by
her marvellous processes, what was now blistering and
burdening her surface.

Enough, however, of this. Satiated with the scenes of
war, my ambition now was to extend my observations to
the kingdoms of the Old World.

[Townsend left America with little money but with confidence that he possessed a commodity that foreigners
would readily buy—a first-hand knowledge of the Civil
War. He landed in Liverpool on October 1, 1862, and immediately set off on a lecture tour. Suffering from the lingering effects of the Chickahominy fever, and also from a
new ailment—stage fright—he spoke to half-filled audito-
riums, and frequently had to endure the heckling of Confederate sympathizers.

[He soon gave up lecturing and journeyed to London,
where he hoped to write for the newspapers. For a time
this second scheme succeeded little better than the first,
and Townsend experienced poverty and loneliness not
unlike that of which he had read in the novels of Dickens.
But gradually he began to sell some of his articles to London magazines, and by the time he left England, after a
residence of about nine months, he had attained a fair
amount of success. He travelled on the Continent for a
year after leaving England, and upon returning to the
United States became war correspondent for the New
York *World*. In Chapter XXV his war narrative recom-
mences with the Battle of Five Forks, fought on April 1,
1865.—Ed.]

The Battle of Five Forks

I COMMENCE my account on the battle-field, but must soon make the long and lonely ride to Humphrey's Station, where I shall continue it.

I am sitting by Major General Philip H. Sheridan's camp-fire, on the spot he has just signalized by the most individual and complete victory of the war. All his veterans are around him, stooping by knots over the bright fagots to talk together, or stretched upon the leaves of the forest, asleep, with the stains of powder yet upon their faces. There are dark masses of horses blackened into the gray background, and ambulances are creaking to and fro. I hear the sobs and howls of the weary, and note, afar off, among the pines, moving lights of burying parties, which are tumbling the slain into the trenches. A cowed and shivering silence has succeded the late burst of drums, trumpets, and cannon; the dead are at rest; the captives are quiet; the good cause has won again, and I shall try to tell you how.

Many months ago the Army of the Potomac stopped before Petersburg, driven out of its direct course to Richmond. It tried the Dutch Gap and the powder-ship, and shelled and shovelled till Sherman had cut five States in half, and only timid financiers, sutlers, and congressional excursionists paid the least attention to the armies on the James. We had fights without much purpose at our breastworks, and at Hatcher's Run, but the dashing achievements of Sheridan in the Shenandoah Valley overtopped all our dull infantry endeavors, and he shared with Sherman the entire applause of the country. No one knows but that behind these actors stood the invisible prompter, Grant; yet prompters, however assiduous, never divide applauses with the *dramatis personæ*; and, therefore, when Sheridan the other day, by one of those slashing adventures which hold us breathless, appeared on the Pamunkey and crossed the peninsula to City Point, even the armies of the Potomac and James were agitated. The personality of the man, not less than his renown, affected people. A very Punch of soldiers, a sort of Rip Van Winkle in regimentals, it astonished folks that with so jolly and grotesque a guise, he held within him energies like lightning, the bolts of which had splintered the fairest parts of the border. But nobody credited General Sheridan with higher genius than activity; we expected to hear of him scouring the Carolina boundary, with the usual destruction of railways and mills, and therefore said at once that Sheridan would cut the great Southside road. But in this last chapter Sheridan must take rank as one of the finest military men of our century. The battle of Five Forks was, perhaps, the most ingeniously conceived and skilfully executed that we have ever had on this continent. It matches in secretiveness and shrewdness the cleverest efforts of Napoleon, and shows also much of that soldier's broadness of intellect and capacity for great occasions.

Sheridan had scarcely time to change his horses' shoes before he was off, and after him much of our infantry also moved to the left. We passed our ancient breastworks at Hatcher's Run, and extended our lines southwestward till they touched Dinwiddie Court House, thirty miles from City Point. The Rebels fell back with but little skirmishing, until we faced northward and reached out toward their idolized Southside Railway; then they grew uneasy, and, as a hint of their opposition, fought us the sharp battle of Quaker Road on Thursday. Still, we reached farther and farther, marvelling to find that, with his depleted army, Lee always overmatched us at every point of attack; but on Friday we quitted our intrenchments on the Boydtown plank-road, and made a bold push for the White Oak road. This is one of the series of parallel public ways running east and west, south of the Southside, the Vaughan road being the first, the Boydtown plank-road the second, and the old Court House road the third. It became evident to the Rebels that we had two direct objects in view: the severing of their railways, and the occupation of Five Forks. The latter is a magnificent strategic point. Five good roads meet in the edge of a dry, high, well-watered forest, three of them radiating to the railway, and their tributaries unlocking all the country. Farther south, their defences had been paltry, but they fortified this empty solitude as if it had been their capital. Upon its principal road, the White Oak, aforenamed, they had a ditched breastwork with embrasures of logs and earth, reaching east and west three miles, and this was covered eastward and southeastward by rifle-pits, masked works, and felled timber; the bridges approaching it were broken; all the roads picketed, and a desperate resolve to hold to it averred. This point of Five Forks may be as much as eight miles from Dinwiddie Court House, four from the Southside road, and eighteen from Humphrey's, the nearest of our military railway stations. A crooked stream called Gravelly Run, which, with Hatcher's, forms Rowanty Creek, and goes off to feed the Chowan in North Carolina, rises near Five Forks, and gives the name of Gravelly Run Church to a little Methodist meeting-house, built in the forest a mile distant. That meeting-house is a hospital tonight, running blood, and at Five Forks a victor's battle-flags are flying.

The Fifth Army Corps of General Gouverneur K. Warren has had all of the flank fighting of the week to do. It lost five or six hundred men in its victory of Thursday, and on Friday rested along the Boydtown plank-road, at the house of one Butler, chiefly, which is about seven miles from Five Forks. On Friday morning, General Romeyn B. Ayres took the advance with one of its three divisions, and marched three-quarters of a mile beyond the plank-road, through a woody country, following the road, but crossing the ubiquitous Gravelly Run, till he struck the enemy in strong force a mile and a half below White Oak road. They lay in the edge of a wood, with a thick curtain of timber in their front, a battery of field-pieces to the right, mounted in a bastioned earthwork, and on the left the woods drew near, encircling a little farm-land and Negro-buildings. General Ayres's skirmish-line being fired upon, did not stand, but fell back upon his main column, which advanced at the order. Straightway the enemy charged headlong, while their battery opened a cross fire, and their skirmishers on our left, creeping down through the woods, picked us off in flank. They charged with a whole division, making their memorable yell, and soon doubled up Ayres's line of battle, so that it was forced in tolerable disorder back upon General Samuel Crawford, who commanded the next division. Crawford's men do not seem to have retrieved the character of their predecessors, but made a feint to go in, and, falling by dozens beneath the murderous fire, gave up the ground. Griffin's division, past which the fugitives ran, halted awhile before taking the doubtful way; the whole corps was now back to the Boydtown plank-road, and nothing had been done to anybody's credit particularly.

General Griffin rode up to General J. L. Chamberlain in this extremity. Chamberlain is a young and anxious officer, who resigned the professorship of modern languages in Bowdoin College to embrace a soldier's career. He had been wounded the day before, but was zealous to try death again.

"Chamberlain," said Griffin, "can't you save the honor of the Fifth corps?"

The young General formed his men at once—they had tasted powder before—the 185th New York and the 198th Pennsylvania. Down they went into the creek waist deep, up the slope and into the clearing, muskets to the left of them, muskets in front of them, cannon to the right of them; but their pace was swift, like their resolve; many of them were cut down, yet they kept ahead, and the Rebels, who seemed astonished at their own previous success, drew off and gave up the field. Almost two hours had elapsed between the loss and the recovery of the ground. The battle might be called Dabney's Farm, or more generally the fight of Gravelly Run. The brigades of Generals Joseph J. Bartlett and Edgar M. Gregory rendered material assistance in the pleasanter finale of the day. An order was soon after issued to hasten the burial of the dead and quit the spot, but Chamberlain petitioned for leave to charge the Rebel earthwork in the rear, and the enthusiasm of his brigade bore down General Warren's more prudent doubt. In brief, Griffin's division charged the fort, drove the Rebels out of it, and took position on the White Oak road, far east of Five Forks. While Griffin's division must be credited with this result, it may be said that their luck was due as much to the time as the manner of their appearance; the Rebel divisions of Pickett and Bushrod Johnson were, in the main, by the time Griffin came up, on their way westward to attack Sheridan's cavalry. Ayres and Crawford had charged as one to four, but the forces were quite equalized when Chamberlain pushed on. The corps probably lost twelve hundred men. In this action, the Rebels for the first time for many weeks exhibited all their traditional irresistibility and confidence. The merit of the affair, I am inclined to think, should be awarded to them; but a terrible retribution remained for them in the succeeding day's decrees.

The ill success of the earlier efforts of Sheridan shows conclusively the insufficiency of ever so good cavalry to resist well organized and resolute infantry. Concentrating at Dinwiddie Court House, he proceeded to scour so much of the country that he almost baffled conjecture as to where his quarters really were. As many thousand cavalry as constitute his powerful force seem magnified, thus mounted and ever moving here and there, to an incredible number. The Court House, where he remained fittingly for a couple of days, is a cross-road's patch, numbering about twelve scattered buildings, with a delightful prospect on every side of sterile and monotonous pines. This is, I believe, the largest village in the district, though Dinwiddie stands fourth in population among Virginia counties.

At present there is almost as great a population underground as the ancient county carried on its census. Indeed, one is perplexed at every point to know whence the South draws its prodigious armies. Some English officers have been visiting Dinwiddie during the week, and one of them said, curtly, "Blast the country! it isn't worth such a row, you know. A very good place to be exiled, to be sure, but what can you ever make of it!"

This soulless Briton had never read any of the poems about the "boundless continent," and had no distinct conception of "size."

From Dinwiddie fields, Sheridan's men went galloping, by the aid of maps and cross-examination, into every byroad; but it was soon apparent that the Rebel infantry meant to give them a push. This came about on Friday, with a foretaste on Thursday.

Little Five Forks is a cross-road not far from Dinwiddie Court House, in the direction of Petersburg. Big Five Forks, which, it must be borne in mind, gives name to the great battle of Saturday, is farther out by many miles, and does not lie within our lines. But, if the left of the army be at Dinwiddie, and the right at Petersburg, Little Five Forks will be first on the front line, though when Sheridan fought there, it was neutral ground, picketed but not possessed. Very early in the week, when the Rebels became aware of the extension of our lines, they added to the regular force which encamped upon our flank line at least a division of troops. These were directed to avoid an infantry fight, but to seek out the cavalry, and, by getting it at a disadvantage, rid the region both of the harmfulness of Sheridan, and that prestige of his name, so terrifying to the Virginia housewife. So long as Sheridan remained upon the far left, the Southside road was unsafe, and the rapidity with which his command could be transferred from point to point rendered it a formidable balance of power. The Rebels knew the country well, and the peculiar course of the highways gave them every advantage. The cavalry of Sheridan's army proper is divided into two corps, commanded by Generals Thomas C. Devin and

George A. Custer; the cavalry of the Potomac is commanded by General Crook; Mackenzie has control of the
cavalry of the James. On Friday, these were under separate orders, and the result was confusion. The infantry
was beaten at Gravelly Run, and the cavalry, met in flank
and front by overwhelming numbers, executed some
movements not laid down in the manual. The centre of
the battle was Little Five Forks, though the Rebels struck
us closer to Dinwiddie Court House, and drove us pell
mell up the road into the woods, and out the old Court
House road to Gravelly Run. We rallied several times, and
charged them into the woods, but they lay concealed in
copses, and could go where sabres were useless. The plan
of this battlefield will show a series of irregular advances
to puzzle anybody but a cavalry-man. The full division of
Bushrod Johnson and General George E. Pickett were developed against us, with spare brigades from other corps.
Our cavalry loss during the day was eight hundred in
killed and wounded; but we pushed the Rebels so hard
that they gave us the field, falling back toward Big Five
Forks, and we intrenched immediately. Two thousand
men comprise our losses of Friday in Warren's corps and
Sheridan's command, including many valuable officers.
We shall see how, under a single guidance, splendid results were next day obtained with half the sacrifice.

On Friday night General Grant, dissatisfied, like most
observers, with the day's business, placed General Sheridan in the supreme command of the whole of Warren's
corps and all the cavalry. General Warren reported to him
at nightfall, and the little army was thus composed:

General Sheridan's Forces, Saturday April 1, 1865.
Three divisions of infantry, under Generals Griffin,
Ayres, and Crawford.
Two divisions of cavalry, formerly constituting the army
of the Shenandoah, now commanded by General Wesley
Merritt, under Generals Devin and Custer.
One division cavalry of the Army of the Potomac, under
General George Crook.

Brigade or more cavalry Army of the James, under General Ronald S. Mackenzie.

In this composition the infantry was to the cavalry in the proportion of about two to one, and the entire force a considerable army, far up in the teens. Sheridan was absolute, and his oddly-shaped body began to bob up and down straightway; he visited every part of his line, though it stretched from Dinwiddie Court House to the Quaker road, along the Boydtown Plank and its adjuncts. At daybreak on Saturday he fired four signal-guns, to admonish Warren he was off; and his cavalry, by diverging roads, struck their camps. Just south of Culpeper is a certain Stony Creek, the tributaries to which wind northward and control the roads. Over Stony Creek went Crook, making the longest detour. Custer took a bottom called Chamberlain's Bed; and Devin advanced from Little Five Forks, the whole driving the Rebels toward the left of their works on White Oak road.

We must start with the supposition that our own men far outnumbered the Rebels. The latter were widely separated from their comrades before Petersburg, and the adjustment of our infantry as well as the great movable force at Sheridan's disposal, renders it doubtful that they could have returned. At any rate they did not do so, whether from choice or necessity, and it was a part of our scheme to push them back into their intrenchments. This work was delegated to the cavalry entirely, but, as I have said before, mounted carbineers are no match for stubborn, bayoneted infantry. So when the horsemen were close up to the Rebels, they were dismounted, and acted as infantry to all intents. A portion of them, under Gregg and Mackenzie, still adhered to the saddle, that they might be put in rapid motion for flanking and charging purposes; but fully five thousand indurated men, who had seen service in the Shenandoah and elsewhere, were formed in line of battle on foot, and by charge and deploy essayed the difficult work of pressing back the entire Rebel column. This they were to do so evenly and ingeniously, that the Rebels should go no farther than their works, either to escape eastward or to discover the whereabouts of Warren's forces, which were already forming. Had they espied the latter they might have become so discouraged as to break and take to the woods; and Sheridan's object was to capture them as well as to rout them. So, all the afternoon, the cavalry pushed them hard, and the strife went on uninterruptedly and terrifically. I have no space in this hurried despatch to advert either to individual losses or to the many thrilling episodes of the fight. It was fought at so close quarters that our carbines were never out of range; for had this been otherwise, the long rifles of the enemy would have given them every advantage. With their horses within call, the cavalry-men, in line of battle, stood together like walls of stone, swelling onward like those gradually elevating ridges of which Lyell speaks. Now and then a detachment of Rebels would charge down upon us, swaying the lines and threatening to annihilate us; for at no part of the action, till its crisis, did the Southern men exhibit either doubt or dismay, but fought up to the standard of the most valiant treason the world has ever had, and here and there showing some of those wonderful feats of individual courage which are the miracles of the time.

A colonel with a shattered regiment came down upon us in a charge. The bayonets were fixed; the men came on with a yell; their gray uniforms seemed black amidst the smoke; their preserved colors, torn by grape and ball, waved yet defiantly; twice they halted, and poured in volleys, but came on again like the surge from the fog, depleted, but determined; yet, in the hot faces of the carbineers, they read a purpose as resolute, but more calm, and, while they pressed along, swept all the while by scathing volleys, a group of horsemen took them in flank. It was an awful instant; the horses recoiled; the charging column trembled like a single thing, but at once the Rebels, with rare organization, fell into a hollow square, and with solid sheets of steel defied our centaurs. The horsemen rode around them in vain; no charge could break the shining squares, until our dismounted carbineers poured in their volleys afresh, making gaps in the spent ranks, and then in their wavering time the cavalry thundered down. The Rebels could stand no more; they reeled and swayed, and fell back broken and beaten. And on the ground their colonel lay, sealing his devotion with his life.

Through wood and brake and swamp, across field and trench, we pushed the fighting defenders steadily. For a part of the time, Sheridan himself was there, short and broad, and active, waving his hat, giving orders, seldom out of fire, but never stationary, and close by fell the long yellow locks of Custer, sabre extended, fighting like a Viking, though he was worn and haggard with much work. At four o'clock the Rebels were behind their wooden walls at Five Forks, and still the cavalry pressed them hard, in feint rather than solemn effort, while a battalion dismounted, charged squarely upon the face of their breastworks which lay in the main on the north side of the White Oak road. Then, while the cavalry worked round toward the rear, the infantry of Warren, though commanded by Sheridan, prepared to take part in the battle.

The genius of Sheridan's movement lay in his disposition of the infantry. The skill with which he arranged it, and the difficult manœuvres he projected and so well executed, should place him as high in infantry tactics as he has heretofore shown himself superior in cavalry. The infantry which had marched at 2:30 P. M. from the house of Boisseau, on the Boydtown plank-road, was drawn up in four battle lines, a mile or more in length, and in the beginning facing the White Oak road obliquely; the left or pivot was the division of General Ayres, Crawford had the center and Griffin the right. These advanced from the Boydtown plank-road, at ten o'clock, while Sheridan was thundering away with the cavalry, mounted and dismounted, and deluding the Rebels with the idea that he was the sole attacking party; they lay concealed in the woods behind the Gravelly Run meeting-house, but their left was not a half-mile distant from the Rebel works, though their right reached so far off that a novice would have criticized the position sharply. Little by little, Sheridan, extending his lines, drove the whole Rebel force into their breastworks; then he dismounted the mass of his cavalry and charged the works straight in the front, still thundering on their flank. At last, every Rebel was safe behind his intrenchments. Then the signal was given, and the concealed infantry, many thousand strong, sprang up and advanced by echelon to the right. Imagine a great barn door shutting to, and you have the movement, if you can also imagine the door itself, hinge and all, moving forward also. This was the door:

AYRES—CRAWFORD—GRIFFIN

Stick a pin through Ayres and turn Griffin and Crawford forward as you would a spoke in a wheel, but move your pin up also a very little. In this way Ayres will advance, say half a mile, and Griffin, to describe a quarter revolution, will move through a radius of four miles. But to complicate this movement by echelon, we must imagine the right when half way advanced cutting across the centre and reforming, while Crawford became the right and Griffin the middle of the line of battle. Warren was with Crawford on this march. Edgar M. Gregory commanded the skirmishers. Ayres was so close to the Rebel left that he might be said to hinge upon it; and at 6 o'clock the whole corps column came crash upon the full flank of the astonished Rebels. Now came the pitch of the battle.

We were already on the Rebel right in force, and thinly in their rear. Our carbineers were making feint to charge in direct front, and our infantry, four deep, hemmed in their entire left. All this they did not for an instant note, so thorough was their confusion; but seeing it directly, they, so far from giving up, concentrated all their energy and fought like fiends. They had a battery in position, which belched incessantly, and over the breastworks their musketry made one unbroken roll, while against Sheridan's prowlers on their left, by skirmish and sortie, they stuck to their sinking fortunes, so as to win unwilling applause from mouths of wisest censure.

It was just at the coming up of the infantry that Sheridan's little band was pushed the hardest. At one time, indeed, they seemed about to undergo extermination; not that they wavered, but that they were so vastly overpowered. It will remain to the latest time a matter of marvel that so paltry a cavalry force could press back sixteen thousand infantry; but when the infantry blew like a great barn door—the simile best applicable—upon the enemy's left, the victory that was to come had passed the region of strategy and resolved to an affair of personal courage. We had met the enemy; were they to be ours? To expedite this consummation every officer fought as if he were the forlorn hope. Mounted on his black pony, the same which he rode at Winchester, Sheridan galloped everywhere, his flushed face all the redder, and his plethoric but nervous figure all the more ubiquitous. He galloped once straight down the Rebel front, with but a handful of his staff. A dozen bullets whistled for him together; one grazed his arm, at which a faithful orderly rode; the black pony leaped high, in fright, and Sheridan was untouched, but the orderly lay dead in the field, and the saddle dashed afar, empty. General Warren rode with Crawford most of the afternoon, mounted likewise, and making two or three narrow escapes. He was dark, dashing, and individual as ever, but for some reason or other was relieved of his command after the battle, and Charles Griffin was instated in his place. General Sheridan ordered Warren to report to General Grant's headquarters, sending the order by an aide. Warren, on his own hook, did not meet on Friday with his general success, and on Saturday Sheridan was the master-spirit; but Warren is a general as well as a gentleman, and is only overshadowed by a greater genius—not obliterated. Ayres, accounted the best soldier in the Fifth corps, but too quietly modest for his own favor, fought like a lion in this pitch of battle, making all the faint-hearted around him ashamed to do ill with such an example contiguous. General Bartlett, keen-faced and active like a fiery scimitar, was leading his division as if he were an immortal! He was closest at hand in the most gallant episodes, and held at nightfall a bundle of captured battle-flags. But Griffin, tall and slight, was the master-genius of the Fifth corps, to which by right he has temporarily succeeded. He led the charge on the flank, and was the first to mount the parapet with his horse, riding over the gunners as May did at Cerro Gordo, and cutting them down. Bartlett's brigade, behind him, finished the business, and the last cannon was fired for the day against the conquering Federals. General Crawford fulfilled his full share of duties throughout the day, amply sustained by such splendid brigade commanders as Henry Baxter, Richard Coulter, and John A. Kellogg, while James Gwyn and Richard N. Boweryman were at hand in the division of General Ayres; not to omit the fallen Winthrop, who died to save a friend and win a new laurel. What shall I say for Chamberlain, who, beyond all question, is the first of our brigade commanders, having been the hero of both Quaker Road and Gravelly Run, and in this action of Five Forks making the air ring with the applauding huzzas of his soldiers, who love him? His is one of the names that will survive the common wreck of shoulder-straps after the war.

But I am individualizing; the fight, as we closed upon the Rebels, was singularly free from great losses on our side, though desperate as any contest ever fought on the continent. One prolonged roar of rifle shook the afternoon; we carried no artillery, and the Rebel battery, until its capture, raked us like an irrepressible demon, and at every foot of the intrenchments a true man fought both in front and behind. The birds of the forest fled afar; the smoke ascended to heaven; locked in so mad frenzy, none saw the sequel of the closing day. Now Richmond rocked in her high towers to watch the impending issue, but soon the day began to look gray, and a pale moon came tremulously out to watch the meeting squadrons. Imagine along a line of a full mile, thirty thousand men struggling for life and prestige; the woods gathering about them—but yesterday the home of hermit hawks and chipmunks— now ablaze with bursting shells, and showing in the dusk the curl of flames in the tangled grass, and, rising up the boles of the pine trees, the scaling, scorching tongues. Seven hours this terrible spectacle had been enacted, but the finale of it had almost come.

It was by all acounts in this hour of victory when the modest and brave General Frederick Winthrop of the first brigade, Ayres' division, was mortally wounded. He was riding along the breastworks, and in the act as I am assured, of saving a friend's life, was shot through to the left lung. He fell at once, and his men, who loved him, gathered around and took him tenderly to the rear, where he died before the stretcher on which he lay could be deposited beside the meeting-house door. On the way from the field to the hospital he wandered in mind at times, crying out, "Captain Weaver, how is that line? Has the attack succeeded?", etc. When he had been resuscitated for a pause he said: "Doctor, I am done for." His last words were: "Straighten the line!" And he died peacefully. He was a cousin of Major Theodore Winthrop, the author of *Cecil Dreeme*. He was twenty-seven years of age. I had talked with him before going into action, as he sat at the side of General Ayres, and was permitted by the guard of honor to uncover his face and look upon it. He was pale and beautiful, marble rather than corpse, and the uniform cut away from his bosom showed how white and fresh was the body, so pulseless now.

General Griffin said to me: "This victory is not worth Winthrop's life."

Winthrop went into the service as a simple color-bearer. He died a brevet brigadier.

At seven o'clock the Rebels came to the conclusion that they were outflanked and whipped. They had been so busily engaged that they were a long time finding out how desperate were their circumstances; but now, wearied with persistent assaults in front, they fell back to the left, only to see four close lines of battle waiting to drive them across the field, decimated. At the right the horsemen charged them in their vain attempt to fight "out," and in the rear, straggling foot and cavalry began also to assemble. Slant fire, cross fire, and direct fire, by file and volley, rolled in perpetually, cutting down their bravest officers and strewing the fields with bleeding men. Groans resounded in the intervals of exploding powder, and to add to their terror and despair, their own artillery, captured from them, threw into their own ranks, from its old position, ungrateful grape and canister, enfilading their breastworks, whizzing and plunging by air line and ricochet; and at last bodies of cavalry fairly mounted their intrenchments, and charged down the parapet, slashing and trampling them, and producing inexplicable confusion. They had no commanders, at least no orders, and looked in vain for some guiding hand to lead them out of a toil into which they had fallen so bravely and so blindly. A few more volleys, a new and irresistible charge, a shrill and warning command to die or surrender, and, with a sullen and tearful impulse, five thousand muskets are flung upon the ground, and five thousand hot, exhausted, and impotent men are Sheridan's prisoners of war.

Acting with his usual decision, Sheridan placed his captives in care of a provost-guard, and sent them at once to the rear. Those which escaped, he ordered the fiery Custer to pursue with brand and vengeance; and they were pressed far into the desolate forest, spent and hungry, many falling by the way of wounds or exhaustion, many pressed down by hoof or sabre-stroke, and many picked up in mercy and sent back to rejoin their brethren in bonds. We captured in all fully six thousand prisoners. General Sheridan estimated them modestly at five thousand, but the provost-marshal assured me that he had a line four abreast a full mile long. I entirely bear him out, having ridden for forty minutes in a direction opposite to that they were taking, and growing weary at last of counting or of seeing them. They were fine, hearty fellows, almost all Virginians, and seemed to take their capture not unkindly. They wore the gray and not very attractive uniform of the Confederacy, but looked to be warm and fat, and passing along in the night, under the fir-trees, conveyed at most a romantic idea of grief and tribulation. They were put in a huge pen, midway between Big and

Little Five Forks, for the night, the officers sharing the same fare with the soldiers, from whom, indeed, they were undistinguishable.

Thus ended the splendid victory of Five Forks, the least bloody to us, but the most successful, proportionate to numbers engaged, that has been fought during the war. One man out of every three engaged took a prisoner. We captured four cannon, an ambulance train and baggage-teams, eight thousand muskets, and twenty-eight battle-flags. General James Longstreet, it is thought, commanded. Neither he nor Pickett nor Bushrod Johnston, division commanders, were taken; they were wise enough to see that the day was lost, and imitated Bonaparte after Water-loo.

I attribute this victory almost entirely to Sheridan; it was won by strategy and persistence, and in great part by men who would not stand fire the day before. The happy distribution of duties between cavalry and infantry excited a fine rivalry, and the consciousness of Sheridan's guidance inspired confidence. Has any battle so successful ever been fought in Virginia, or, indeed, in the East? I think not. It has opened to us the enemy's flank, so that we can sweep down upon the Appomattox and inside of his breastworks, enabling us to shorten our lines of intrenchments one half, if no more, and putting out of Lee's service fifteen thousand of his choicest troops. And all this, General Sheridan tells me, has cost him personally no more than eight hundred men, and the service no more than fifteen hundred. Compare this with Chancellorsville, Williamsburg, the Wilderness, Bull Run, and what shall we say? The enemy must have lost in this fight three thousand in killed and wounded.

The scene at Gravelly Run meeting-house at 8 and at 10 o'clock on Saturday night is one of the solemn contrasts of the war, and, I hope, the last of them. A little frame church, planted among the pines, and painted white, with cool, green window-shutters, holds at its foot a gallery for the Negroes, and at the head a varnished pulpit. I found its pews moved to the green plain over the threshold, and on its bare floors the screaming wounded. Blood ran in little rills across the planks, and, human feet treading in them, had made indelible prints in every direction; the pulpit-lamps were doing duty, not to shed holy light upon holy pages, but to show the pale and dusty faces of the beseeching; and as they moved in and out, the groans and curses of the suffering replace the gush of peaceful hymns and the deep responses to the preacher's prayers. Federal and Confederate lay together, the bitterness of noon assuaged in the common tribulation of the night, and all the while came in the dripping stretchers, to place in this golgotha new recruits for death and sorrow. I asked the name of the church, but no one knew any more than if it had been the site of some obsolete heathen worship. At last, a grinning sergeant smacked his thumbs as if the first idea of his life had occurred to him, and led me to the pulpit. Beneath some torn blankets and rent officers' garments, rested the hymn book and Bible, which he produced. Last Sunday these doled out the praises of God, and the frightened congregation worshipped at their dictation. Now they only served by their fly leaves to give me my whereabouts, and said:

Presented to Gravelly Run Meeting House by the Ladies.

Over the portal, the scenes within were reiterated, except that the greatness of a starry night replaced the close and terrible arena of the church. Beneath the trees—where the Methodist circuit-rider had tied his horse, and the urchins during class-meeting had wandered away to cast stones at the squirrels and measure strength at vaulting and running—the gashed and fevered lay irregularly, some soul going out at each whiff of the breeze in the fir-tops; and the teams and surgeons, and straggling soldiers, and galloping orderlies passed all the night beneath the old and gibbous moon and the hushed stars, and by the trickle of Gravelly Run stealing off, afeared. But the wounded had no thought that night; the victory absorbed all hearts; we had no losses to notice where so much was won.

A mile past the church, going away from headquarters all the time, lies Five Forks, the object and name of the battle. A large open field of perhaps thirty acres interposes between the church and the commencement of the Rebel works. Their left is only some rails and logs to mask marksmen, but the work proper is a very long stretch of all obstructions of a man's height in relief.

The White Oak road runs directly in front of these intrenchments, and was, at the time I passed, the general highway for infantry returning from the field and cavalrymen concentrating at General Sheridan's bivouac. Riding a mile I came upon the Five Forks proper, and just to the left, at the foot of some pines, the victor and his assistants were congregated. Sheridan sat by some fagots, examining a topographical map of the country he had so well traversed; possibly with a view to design further aggressive movements in the morning. He is opposite me now as I pen these paragraphs by the imperfect blaze of his bivouac fire. He is good humored and talkative, like all men conscious of having achieved a great work, and has been good enough to sketch for me the plan of the day's operations, from which I have compiled much of the statement above. Close by lies Custer, trying to sleep, his long yellow hair covering his face; and General Griffin, now commanding the Fifth corps, goes here and there issuing orders, while aides and orderlies ride in and out, bearing further fresh messages of deeds consummated or proposed. We shall have a hot night no doubt, for away off to the right, continue volleys of musketry and discharges of artillery, intermixed with what seem to be thunderbolts of our men-at-war at anchor in the Appomattox and James—if such can be heard at this great distance—which tell us that the lines are in motion.

CHAPTER XXVI

Richmond Desolate

THE scenes of entering the doomed stronghold, when Grant had burst its gates, ought to be made vivid as the spectacle of death. With my good and talented associate, Mr. Jerome B. Stillson, I hold the Spotswood Hotel, and from this caravansary of the late capital as thoroughly identified with Rebellion as the inn at Bethlehem with the gospel, we date our joint paragraphs upon the condition of the city. A week cannot have exhausted the curiosity of the North to learn the exact appearance of a city which has stood longer, more frequent, and more persistent sieges, than any in Christendom. This town is the Rebellion; it is all that we have directly striven for; quitting it, the Confederate leaders have quitted their sheet-anchor, their roof-tree, their abiding hope. Its history is the epitome of the whole contest, and to us, shivering our thunderbolts against it for more than four years, Richmond is still a mystery.

Know then, that, whether coming from Washington or Baltimore, the two points of embarkation, all bound hitherward must rendezvous at Fortress Monroe; thence, in such excellent steamers as the *Dictator*, start up the broad James River. To own a country-house upon the "Jeems" river is the Virginia gentleman's ultimate aspiration. There, with a tobacco-farm, and wide wheatlands, his feet on his front-porch rails, a Havana cigar between his teeth, and a colored person to bring him frequent juleps, the Virginia gentleman, confident in the divinity of slavery, hopes in his natural, refined idleness, to watch the little family graveyard close up to his threshold, till it shall kindly open and give him sepulture.

Elsewhere men aim to be successful, or enterprising, or eloquent, or scholarly, but that nobleness of hospitality, high spirit, dignity, and affability which constitute our idea of chivalry is everywhere save here an exotic. We say that chivalry is "played out," and that the prestige of "first families" is gone with the hurried retreat before Grant's salamanders. Not so. Secession as a cause is past the range of possibilities. But no people in their subjugation wear a better front than these brave old spirits, whose lives are not their own. Fire has ravaged their beautiful city, soldiers of the color of their servants guard the crossings and pace the pavement with bayoneted muskets. But gentlemen they are still, in every pace, and inch, and syllable—such men as we were wont to call brothers and countrymen. However, the James River, at which we commenced, has not a town upon it between the sea and the head of navigation. It is a strong commentary upon this patriarchal civilization, judged by our gregarious tastes, that one of the noblest streams in the world should show to the traveller only here and there a pleasant mansion, flanked by Negro cabins, but nowhere a church-spire nor a steam-mill. All that we see from Fortress Monroe to City Point are ridges of breastworks, rifle-pits, and forts, lying bare, yellow, and deserted, to defend its passage, excepting at James Island, where the solitary and broken tower of the ancient colony holds guard over some bramble and ruin. Here Smith founded the celebrated settlement, which wooed to its threshold the gentle Pocahontas, and fell to fragments at the behest of the fiery Bacon. The ramparts on the James will remain forever; great as they are, they would hardly hold the bones of the slain in the capture and defence. Four hours from Fortress Monroe we pass Harrison's Landing, where two grand armies, *beaten* aside from Richmond, sought the shelter of the river, and at City Point quit our large craft, to be transferred to a light draught vessel, which is to carry the first mail going to

Richmond under the national flag since the beginning of the war.

City Point is still a populous place, and the millions of mules upon it bray hoarsely; but we leave all these behind, as well as the national standard, which flaunts over General Grant's late headquarters, and steam past the mouth of the Appomattox to go through the enemy's lines.

Henceforward every foot of the way is freshly interesting. The Rebel ram *Atlanta* in tow of a couple of tugs, goes past us with a torpedo boat at the rear. She is raking, slant, and formidable; but "old glory" is waving on her. Directly our own leviathan, the *Roanoke* drifts up, and all her storm-throated tars cheer like the belch of her guns. We see to the right the tip of Malvern Hill, ever sorrowful and sacred, and soon a great unfinished ram careens by, which never grew to battle-size; the true colors shine above her bulwarks like a flower growing in a carcass. Then at little intervals there are frequent prizes from the docks of Richmond, tugs, transports, barges, some of which show under our beautiful banner the Rebel cross, pale and contemptible. These malcontents committed as great crime against good taste in substituting for our starry emblem this artistic abomination, as against law and policy in changing the configuration of the Union. There is another flag, however, which we see, half exultantly, half vindictively—the cross of St. George—flying from a British cutter.

By and by we come to our intrenchments upon the upper James and at Bermuda Hundred. Now they are very listless and half empty. The boys have gone off to tread on Lee's shanks. Only a few vessels stand at the landings, and the few remnants have laid down the rifle, and taken up the fishing-pole. One should come up this river to get a conception of our splendid navy. Sharp-pointed gunboats, with bullet-proof crows' nests and swivels that are the gentlest murderers ever polished; monitors through whose eyeholes a ball a big as a cook-stove squints from a Columbiad socket; ferry-boats which are speckled with brass cannon, and all sorts of craft that can float and manœuvre, provided they look at us through deadly muzzles, are there to the number of fifty or sixty, as many as make the entire navies of all other American nations. After the war we must have a great naval review, and invite all the crowned heads to attend it. Soon we reach Dutch Gap, where lies Butler's canal, or "Butler's gut," as the sailors call it. The river at this point is so crooked that Butler must have laid it out by the aid of his wrong eye. The canal is meant to cut on a long elbow; but being almost at right angles to the course of the river, only the most obliging tide would run through it. As a consequence, it is a sort of a sluice merely, of insufficient width, and as a "sight" very disappointing to great expectations. Between the points of debouch of this canal crosses a drawbridge of pontoons, for the use of our troops, and just beyond it Aiken's Landing, where the flag of truce boat stopped. A fine brick mansion stands in shore, with a wharf abreast it. The banks around it are trodden here with many feet. These are the traces of the poor prisoners who reached here, fevered, and starving and naked, to catch for the first time the sight of cool waters and friends, and the bright flag which they had followed to the edge of the grave. How they threw up their hats, and cheered to the feeblest, and wept, and danced, and laughed. Long be the place remembered, as holy, neutral ground, where death never trod, and multitudes passed from suffering to freedom and home. Beyond this point, the most formidable Rebel works we have seen, line the high bluffs and ridges. They are monuments of patient labor, and make of themselves hills as great as nature's. But the siege pieces, which often bellowed upon them like thunderbolts along the mountain-tops, are gone now, and only straggling, meddling fellows pass them at all. The highest of these works commands both ends of the Dutch Gap canal, and while our lads were digging they often hid themselves in caves which they dug in the cliff-sides.

We reach the first torpedo at length; a little red flag marks it, by which the boat slips tremulously, though another and another are before, at the sight of which our nervous folks are agitated. Here is a monitor with a drag behind it, which has just fished up one; and the sequel is told by a bloody and motionless figure upon the deck. These torpedoes are the true dragon teeth of Cadmus, which spring up armed men.

Happily for us, the Rebels have sown but few of them, and the position of these was pointed out by one of their captains who deserted to our side. In the midst of these lie the obstructions. Great hulks of vessels and chained spars, and tree-tops which reach quite across the river, except where our pioneers have hewn a little gap to let the steamer through. Upon these obstructions a hundred cannon bear from the cliffs before us, and as we go further we see the whole river-bed sprinkled with strange contrivances to keep back our thunder-bearers. We think it absolutely impossible, under any circumstances, that our fleet could have got to Richmond so long as the Rebels contested the passage; each step forward finds new and greater obstacles. The channel is as narrow as Harlem River and as crooked as a walk in the ramble of Central Park. Each elbow of the stream is muscular with snag and snare wherever the swift stream swoops around abruptly. Jagged abatis, driven piles, and artificial lumber, bar the way before us. To the right of us, to the left of us, behind us, stand up the bare parapets, crowned with airy lookout towers, where, at the coming of a nautilus, the whole horizon and foreground would rain crossfires of shell and iron bolts, to sweep into annihilation the tiniest or the staunchest opposition from the earth's surface, and under the earth and above the earth death waited to leap up and draw the daring to its bosom. Not one, nor two, nor three lines of defences frowned down as we cautiously steamed along, but every precipice was bristling with defiance, as if the deep subterranean fires underlying our race had burst here fitfully and frequently, heaving up the swells of the hills till they lay hard and barren for human ingenuity to garnish them with anxious artillery. All along were the deep funnel-shaped cases of the torpedoes just disentombed. But at nightfall Drury's Bluff flitted by like the battlemented wall of a city, and then we saw no more.

The band that greeted us from a distance stops playing as the boat nears the wharf.

There is a stillness, in the midst of which Richmond, with her ruins, her spectral roof, afar, and her unchanging spires, rests beneath a ghastly, fitful glare—the night stain which a great conflagration leaves behind it for weeks—struggling silently with colossal shadows along the foreground, two hideous walls alone arise in front, shutting these gleams. They are the Libby Prison and Castle Thunder. Right and left, and far in the moonlighted perspective beyond, there is a soft glitter upon cornices and domes. A haggard glow of candles faintly defines the thoroughfares that have not suffered ruin; while massive, and upon a height overlooking all, stands the Capitol, flying its black shadow from the sinking moon across a hundred crumbling walls, until its edges touch the windows of the Libby.

But over its massive roof, dimly seen through the mists of the river, and, as before, "through the mists of the deep," the banner of the Union, banished for four years, is shaken out again, broad and beautiful, by the breath of an April night. Upon the face of every leaning figure on the steamer's deck, in sight of that radiant signal, is the same half-melancholy, half-triumphant smile.

The thought of the battle which has passed, of the army, which, after struggling through years for this majestic procession, has swept by and beyond without the view for which its straining eyes have yearned, is sad and strange. There comes back dimly suggestive, a story of Iran and his host, thundering at the gates of Tupelo, for the possession of a wondrous jewel, and awakening once upon a dawn to learn that Tupelo was an empty casket—to turn back longing, "wondering eyes upon the city, and to hunt the fleeing prize afar." Yet unto those legions of the republic which have emptied Richmond of a prize which yet they may have easily clutched, there go out reverence and blessing even larger than might be bestowed upon them resting in camp, upon these overlooking hills. That true allegiance, that calm and stern self-sacrifice which impels an army forward past the sweet applauses and rewarding calms to which great victories might entitle it, are the purest sources of its glory and its fame. God bless the army that has permitted us to consummate this journey and to gaze upon this spectacle, while it does not impress us too proudly, too triumphantly. Both pride and triumph have, of course, a place in the tumultuous feeling that surges through the hearts of all; yet as in every true man is born an instinct of compassion for a fallen foe, we prefer that the shout should go up in honor of our victory alone, and not because these have suffered.

The boat touches the shore at Rockett's, the foot of Richmond. A few minutes' walk and we tread the pavements of the capital. There are no noisy and no beseeching runners; there is no sound of life, but the stillness of a catacomb, only as our footsteps fall dull on the deserted sidewalk, and a funeral troop of echoes bump their elfin heads against the dead walls and closed shutters in reply, and this is Richmond. Says a melancholy voice: "And this is Richmond."

We are under the shadow of ruins. From the pavements where we walk far off into the gradual curtain of the night, stretches a vista of desolation. The hundreds of fabrics, the millions of wealth, that crumbled less than a week ago beneath one fiery kiss, here topple and moulder into rest. A white smoke-wreath rising occasionally, enwraps a shattered wall as in a shroud. A gleam of flame shoots a grotesque picture of broken arches and ragged chimneys into the brain. Huge piles of debris begin to encumber the sidewalks, and even the pavements, as we go on. The streets in some places are quite choked up from walking. We are among the ruins of half a city. The wreck, the loneliness, seem interminable. The memory of lights in houses above, beheld while upon the steamer, alone keeps despondency from a victory over hope; and although the continued existence of the Spotswood Hotel is vouched for by authority, my lodge in such a wilderness seems next to impossible. Away to the right, above the waste of blackened walls, around the phantom-looking flag upon the capitol—the only sign betwixt heaven and earth, or upon the earth, that Richmond is not wholly deserted—beyond and out of the ruins, we walk past one of two open doorways where the moon serves as candle to a group of talking Negroes. The gas works, injured by fire, are not working, and "ile" has nót been struck in the Confederacy. Not a white man appears until we reach the Spotswood—there before the entrance is a conclave of officers—then, at last, entering, we stand in that most famous of Southern hotels, the interior of which is filled with the very aroma of the Rebellion. A thankful yielding up of carpet-bags and valises to the indignant Negro waiters, and then a brief moonlight stroll toward the capitol.

Within the gates of the Square, that swing on their hinges silent as the hour we pass alone, before us stands the magnificent monument crowned with Crawford's equestrian statue of Washington. The right hand of the rider, lifted against the sky, points a prophetic finger toward the southwest. Dark, and motionless, and grand, it is the one symbol belonging solely to the Union, which they have not dared to desecrate; which they have strangely chosen to consider neither as an insult nor a rebuke.

Gazing beyond at the capitol itself, and back again at the figure which overlooks the building, it is not hard to imagine that, while the noisy debates of a congress of traitors to the Union that he founded were in progress, those bronze lips sometimes smiled in scorn.

Leaving Richmond proper, and descending into the low, squalid portion of the town known as Rocketts, one sees among the many large warehouses, used without exception for the storage of tobacco, a certain one more irregular than the rest. An archway leads into it, and upon the outside of the second story windows runs a long ledge or footway, whereupon sentries used to stride, guarding the miserable people within. This is the jail of Castle Thunder, and it was the civil or State prison of the capital. Ill as were the accommodations of prisoners of war, the treatment of their own unoffending citizens by the Rebel government was ten times more infamous. We could not repress indignation, nor by any philosophic or charitable effort excuse the atrocious tyranny which here lashed, chained, handcuffed, tortured, shot, and hung, hundreds of people whom it could not stultify or impress. We may grant that the Confederacy had become a government; that, in its perilous incipiency, it had apology for severity and rigor with all malcontents; that, in its own struggle for death or life, it might, in self-defence, absorb all private liberty; but even thus the terrible testimony of this Castle Thunder is an everlasting stigma upon the Southern cause. We entered its strong portal, and there in the new commandant's room lay the record left behind by the Confederates. Its pages made one shudder.

These are some of the entries:

"George Barton,—giving food to Federal prisoners of war; forty lashes upon the bare back. Approved. Sentence carried into effect July 2.

"Peter B. Innis,—passing forged government notes; chain and ball for twelve months; forty lashes a day. Approved.

"Arthur Wright,—attempting to desert to the enemy; sentenced to be shot. Approved. Carried into effect, March 26.

"John Morton,—communicating with the enemy; to be hung. Approved. Carried into effect, March 26."

In an inner room are some fifty pairs of balls and chains, with anklets and handcuffs upon them, which have bent the spirit and body of many a resisting heart. Within are two condemned cells, perfectly dark—a faded flap over the window peep-hole—the smell from which would knock a strong man down.

For in their centre lies the sink, ever open, and the floors are sappy with uncleanliness. To the right of these, a door leads to a walled yard not forty feet long, nor fifteen wide, overlooked by the barred windows of the main prison rooms, and by sentry boxes upon the wall-top. Here the wretched were shot and hung in sight of their trembling comrades. The brick wall at the foot of the yard

is scarred and crushed by balls and bullets which first
passed through some human heart and wrote here their
damning testimony. The gallows had been suspended from
a wing in the ledge, and in mid-air the impotent captive
swung, none daring or willing to say a good word for
him; and not for any offence against God's law, not for
wronging his neighbor, or shedding blood, or making his
kind miserable, but for standing in the way of an upstart
organization, which his impulse and his judgment alike
impelled him to oppose. This little yard, bullet-marked,
close, and shut from all sympathy, is to us the ghastliest
spot in the world. Can Mr. Davis visit it, and pray as he
does so devoutly afterward? When men plead the justice
of the South, and arguments are prompt to favor them, let
this prison yard rise up and say that no such crimes in
liberty's name have ever been committed, on this continent, at least. Upstairs in Castle Thunder, there are two or
three large rooms, barred and dimly lit, and two or three
series of condemned cells, pent-up and pitchy, where, by
a refinement of cruelty, the ceiling has been built low so
that no man can stand upright. Here fifteen or twenty
were crowded together, and, in the burning atmosphere,
they stripped themselves stark naked, so that when in the
morning the cell-doors were opened, they came forth as
from the grave, begging for death. There are women's cells
too; for this great and valiant government recognized
women as belligerents, and locked them up close to a
sentry's cartridge, so that, in the bitterness of solitude,
they were unsexed, and railed, and blasphemed, like wan-
ton things. On the pavements before the jail were hidden
numberless guards, who shot at every rag fluttering from
the cages, and all this little circle of death and terror was
enacted close to the bright river, and airy pediment of
that high capitol, where bold men hoped by war to wring
from a reluctant Union, acknowledgment of arrogant independence to rein civilization as it pleased, and warp the
destinies of our race.

CHAPTER XXVII

The Ruins Of The Rebellion

———

WHEN Richmond was a plain city, a county seat, and the residence of a governor and commonwealth legislature, its enterprise was as gradual, as its hospitality and private probity were steadfast. It was always a fierce political arena, and its two great journals, the *Whig* and *Enquirer*, were not more violently partisan than its hustings. In the latter its debaters were wide-famed. No such "stump" has ever existed in America, commencing with Patrick Henry, whose eloquence was as intense and telling as his statesmanship was errant and inconsistent, and passing through the shrill and bitter apostrophes of John Randolph down to the latest era of Henry A. Wise, the most sufferable and interminable campaign orator extant, and John Minor Botts, scarcely his inferior. With us, out of door rhetoric is dry, studied, and argumentative; here an inspiration, based upon feeling rather than reason, and so earnest that it knew no personal friendship where its political affinities stopped. Whig and Democrat were not men of the same race or family in Richmond; they passed each other on the sidewalk with a sneer or a scowl, and knew no coalition even in the house of God. Even when the Whig party as an organization deceased, the Whigs, as individuals, retained their traditional antipathy, and the advent of secession was decried by these, not because they loved the Union more, but the triumphant Democracy the less. Separation was a feature of the hated faith, and no good could come out of Nazareth. The Union men of Richmond who have hungered in Castle Thunder, and been driven, needy and naked, from the South, were all old line Whigs, distrusting the North, but disliking Democracy. However, the war burst at last, heralded by that mysterious lunatic who appeared like a warning giant in the twilight day of the Union—old John Brown; and as the Gulf States wheeled into line and pulled down the old colors, the Old Dominion, Southern and slaveholding, was too impulsive not to follow the whirlwind. She did not go for policy's sake, nor for principle's sake, but for emotion's sake. How wild and jubilant, and confident, were those Richmond mass meetings, at which separation was counselled! How awful seems their levity at this distance, with the city conquered and in ruins! On the Capitol Hill the mad orators inveighed; within the Capitol met the disunion assembly in secret and prolonged session; before the American, the Exchange, and the Spotswood hotels, visiting commissioners harangued the crowd; the people went to ballot on the day of State suicide, with laughing and wagging, and at the decree that Virginia and her people had resolved to quit the fabric of their fathers, bonfires and illuminations lit up the river and the sky.

Done, these were the men to stand fast. Done in dream, the first acts were mirages rather than comprehensible events. They marched upon Harper's Ferry; they suppressed the Unionists in their midst; they erased the sacred mottoes of amity and unity from their monuments, and won to the new cause they so blindly embraced every inch of their soil except Old Point, where Fortress Monroe still stood defiant, to be in the end the source of their downfall. Gayly went the populace of Richmond, and splendid parties made the nights lustrous. When they heard that their town was mentioned, among many others, as the probable Confederate capital, they threw their hearts into the suggestion and offered lands and edifices as free gifts for the honor of being the centre of the South. A few, more interested, beheld in the coming of the seat of government higher rents and increased patronage, crowded hotels, and railway stock at a premium; but the mass, with the enthu-

siasm of women or children, thought only of their beloved
city growing in rank and power; the home of legislators,
orators, and savants; the seat of all rank and the depository
of archives. At last the good news came; Richmond was
the capital of a great nation; that courtesy bound all grateful Virginian hearts to the common cause forever; the hey-
day and gratulation were renewed; the new President, and
the reverend senators appeared on Richmond streets; the
citizens were proud and happy.

There was no spectre of the mighty North, slowly rising
from lethargy like those Medicean figures of Michael An-
gelo, which leap from stone to avengers. There was no
mutter of coming storm, no clank of coming sabres and
bayonets, no creak of great wheels rolling southward, and
war in its extremest and most deadly phase. Richmond and
Virginia laughed at these, flushed in the present, and in-
vincible in the past. They only held high heads—and trade,
with vanity, grew strong, till every citizen wondered why
all this glory had been so long delayed, and despised the
ten years preceding the rupture, if not, indeed, the whole
past of the Union.

The President of the United States proclaimed war; an
army marched upon the city. Not until the battle of Bull
Run, when the dead and mangled came by hundreds into
the town, did any one discover the consequences of Richmond's new distinction; but by this time the Rebel government had absorbed Virginia, and was master of the city.
Thenceforward Richmond was the scene of all terrors, the
prey of all fears and passions. Campaign after campaign
was directed against her; she lived in the perpetual thunder of cannon; raiders pressed to her gates; she was a great
garrison and hospital only, besieged and cut off from her
own provinces; armies passed through her to the sound of
drums, and returned to the creak of ambulances. She lost
her social prestige, and became a barrack-city, filled with
sutlers, adventurers, and refugees, till, bearing bravely up
amid domestic riot and horrible demoralization—a jail, a
navy-yard, a base of operations—she grew pinched, and
base, and haggard, and, at last, deserted. Given over to

sack and fire, the wretches who used her retreated in the night, and the enemies she had provoked marched over her defences, and laid her—spent, degenerate, and disgraced—under martial law.

The outline of the scenes immediately associated with the evacuation of Richmond has been told by telegraph. Now that the stupefied citizens have recovered reason and memory so well as to tell us the story, it seems the most dramatic and fearful of the war. On Saturday the city was calm and trusting; Lee, its idol, held Grant, at Petersburg, fast; the daily journals came out as usual, filled with soothing accounts; that night came vague rumors of reverses; in the morning vaguer rumors of evacuation; by Sunday night the public records were burned in the streets, and the only remaining railway carried off the specie of the banks; before daylight on Monday, the explosions of bridges and half-built ships of war shook the houses; in the imperfect day, women, and old men, and children began to sway and surge before the guarded depot, which refused to admit them; then the town fell afire; no remonstrance could pacify the incendiaries; the spring wind carried the flame from the burning boats on the canal to the great Galligo Mills, to files of massive warehouses groaning with tobacco, into the heart of the town, where stores, and vaults, and banks, and factories lined the wide, undulating streets; it filled the gray concave with flame till the stars of the dawn shrank to pale invisibility in the advancing glare, and the crackle of hot roofs and beams, and the crash of walls and timbers, drowned the cries of the frightened and bankrupt, who beheld their fortunes wither in an hour, and the inheritance of their children fall to ashes. By the red, consuming light, poured past the straggling Confederate soldiers, dead to the acknowledgment of private rights, and sacking shop and home with curses and ribaldry; the suburban citizens and the menial Negroes adopted their examples; carrying off whatever came next their hands, and with arms full of "swag," dropping it in the highway, lured by some dearer plunder. Negroes, with baskets of stolen champagne and rare jars of tamarinds, sought their dusky quarters to swill and carouse; and whites of the middle, and even of the higher class, lent themselves to theft, who, before this debased era, would have died before so surrendering their honor. All was peril, terror, and license; all who had nothing to lose were thieves; all who had anything left to lose were cowards. The conflagration swept through the densest, proudest blocks, driving off, not only the resident worthy, but the resident corrupt. Where were the lewd contractors, who had hoarded Confederate scrip by the basest exactions? With the fall of the capital their dollars dwindled to dust; four years of crime had resulted in beggary; still, with grasping palms, they adhered to their valueless paper, bearing it away. But of all the wretched, the Cyprians were the foremost. These inhabited the dense and business part of the town, where their houses were serried and compact; and, driven forth by the fire, they sought the street in their plumes and calicoes, to spend a cold and shivering bivouac in the square of the Capitol. From afar, the rich men of Sunday watched the flames of Monday sweeping on in terrible impetuosity, knowing that every tongue of light which leaped on high carried with it the competence they had sinned to acquire. And behind all, plunderer, incendiary, and straggler, came the one vague, overlapping, dreadful fear of—the enemy. Would they finish what friends had commenced—the sack, the desolation, the slaughter of the place? Richmond had cost them half a million of lives, a mountain of blood and wealth, four years of deadly struggle; would they not complete its ruin?

The morning came; the Confederates were gone; cavalry in blue galloped up the streets; a brigade of white infantry filed after them; then came the detested Negroes. Behold! the victors, the subjugators, assist to quench the flames—and Richmond is captured, but secure!

Many of the churches were open on the Sunday of April 9, 1865, and were thinly attended by the more adventurous of the citizens, with a sprinkling of soldiers and Northern civilians. Mr. Woodbridge, at the Monument Church,

built on the site of a famous burnt theatre, prayed for "all
in authority," and held his tongue upon dangerous topics.
The First Baptist Negro Church has been occupied all
the week by Massachusetts chaplains, and Northern Negro
preachers, who have talked the gospel of John Brown to
gaping audiences of wool, white-eyeball, and ivory, telling
them that the day of deliverance has come, and that they
have only to possess the land which the Lord by the bayonet has given them. Today, Mr. Allen, the regular white
preacher, occupied the pulpit, and told the Negroes that
slavery was a divine institution, which would continue forever, and that the duty of every good servant was to stay
at home and mind his master. Half of the enlightened
Africans got up midway of the discourse and left; the rest
were in doubt, and two or three black class-leaders, whom
the parson had wheeled over, prayed lustily that the Lord
would keep Old Virginny from new ideas and all Yankee
salvations; so that in the end the population were quite
tangled up, as much so as if they had read the book of
Revelation. I attended Saint Paul's, the fashionable Epis-
copalian church, where Lee, Davis, Meminger, and the
rest had been communicants, and heard Doctor Minne-
gerode discourse. He was one of the Prussian refugees of
1848, and, though a hot Jacobin there, became a more bitter secessionist here. He is learned, fluent, and thoughtful,
but speaks with a slight Teutonic accent. Jeff Davis's pew
was occupied by nobody, the door thereof being shut. Jeff
was a very devout man, but not so much so as Lee, who
made all the responses fervently, and knelt at every re-
quirement. This church is capable of "seating" fifteen hundred persons, has galleries running entirely around it, and
is sustained at the roof within by composite pilasters of
plaster, and at the pulpit by columns of mongrel Co-
rinthian; the *tout ensemble* is very excellent; a darky sex-
ton gave us a pew, and there were some handsome ladies
present, dark Richmond beauties, haughty and thinly
clothed, with only here and there a jockey-feathered hat,
or a velvet mantilla, to tell of long siege and privation. We
saw that those who dressed the shabbiest had yet pre-

served some little article of jewelry—a finger-ring, a
brooch, a bracelet, showing how the last thing in woman to
die is her vanity. Poor, proud souls! Last Sunday many of
them were heiresses; now many of them could not pay the
expenses of their own funerals. There were some Confederate officers in the house. They reminded me of the captive Jews holding worship in their gutted Temple. Some
ruffians broke into this church after the occupation, and
wrote ribaldry in the Bible and hymn-book. Dr. Minne-
gerode dared not pray for the Confederate States, and his
sermon was trite, based upon the text of the eleventh
chapter of the Acts—"The disciples were first called
Christians in Antioch." In the opening lesson, however, he
aimed poison at the North, selecting the forty-fourth and
following Psalms, commencing, "We have heard with our
ears, O God! our fathers have told us, what work Thou
didst in their days, in the times of old." Then it spoke of
the heathen being driven out and the chosen people
planted; afflicted by God's disfavor, the forefathers held
the territory, and the generation extant would yet rout its
enemies. But now the old stock were put to shame, a re-
proach to their neighbors and those that dwelt round
about them. "Thou hast broken us in the place of dragons,
and covered us with the shadow of death," going not forth
with our armies, bowing our souls to the dust till our bellies cleave unto the earth; we are killed all the day long,
and counted as sheep for the slaughter.

Let all who would drink the essence of sorrow and anguish, read this wonderful Psalm, to learn how after this
recapitulation, the parson said aloud the thrilling invocation.

"Arise! for our help, and redeem us for thy mercies'
sake."

Then came the next Psalm, light and tripping, full of
praise for the king and his bride, coming to the nuptials
with her virgin train: "instead of thy fathers, shall be thy
children, whom thou mayst make princes in all the earth."
A poetic parallel might be drawn between all this and the

early hopes of Richmond; but the third Psalm came in like a beautiful peroration.

"God is our refuge and strength, a very present help in trouble,—the Lord of Hosts is with us, the God of Jacob is our refuge. Selah! He maketh wars to cease unto the end of the earth; he breaketh the bow and cutteth the spear in sunder; he burneth the chariot in the fire."

Clear, direct, and in meaning monotone, the captive high-priest read all this, so fearfully applicable to the subjugated and ruined town, and then the organ threw its tender music into the half-empty concave, sobbing like a far voice of multitudes, until the sweet singing of Madame Ruhl, the chorister, swept into the moan of pipes, and rose to a grand peal, quivering and trilling, like a nightingale wounded, making more tears than the sublimest operatic effort and the house reeled and trembled, as if Miriam and her chanting virgins were lifting praises to God in the midst of the desert.

That part of the New Testament read, by some strange fatuity, touches also the despair of the city. It told of Christ betrayed by Iscariot, deserted by his disciples, saying to his few trusty ones: "I will smite the shepherd, and the sheep of the flock shall be scattered abroad." "Can ye not watch with me one hour?" he says to the timid and sleeping; and turning to his conquerors, avers that the Son of Man shall return to Jerusalem, "sitting on the right hand of power, and coming in the clouds of heaven." All this, of course, was the prescribed lesson for the Sunday before Easter, which today happened to be; but had the pastor searched it out to meet the exigencies of the place and time, it could not have been more *apropos*. He read also from Daniel, where the king's dream was interpreted; his realm, like a tree worn down to the root, and the king himself making his dwelling with the wild asses, but in the end "thy kingdom shall be sure unto thee, after that thou shalt have known that the heavens do rule."

Again the organ rang, and the wonderful voice of the choristers alternated with deep religious prayers, whose refrain was, "Have mercy upon us."

Only one Sunday gone by, the church was densely packed with Rebel officers and people; Mrs. Lee was there, and the President, in his high and whitened hairs. Midway of the discourse a telegram came up the aisle, borne by a rapid orderly. The President read it, and strode away; the preacher read it, and faltered, and turned pale. It said:

My lines are broken; Richmond must be evacuated by midnight.   ROBERT E. LEE

Ill news travels without words; the whole house felt that the great calamity had come; they broke for the doors, and left the rector, alone and frightened, to finish the solemn services.

Now the enemy is here; the music and the prayer are not interrupted. God is over all, whether Davis or Lincoln be uppermost.

This campaign, so gloriously and promptly finished, has consumed just eleven days. It took three to flank the Rebel army, one to capture Petersburg, one to occupy Richmond, and six to pursue, overtake, and capture the Army of Northern Virginia. No such memorable fighting has ever been known on our continent, and it parallels the Italian, the Austerlitz, and the Jena campaigns; in breadth of conception, it outrivals them all; it took less men to do it than the last two; it shows equal sagacity with any of them, but none of their brilliant episodes; and, unlike them, we cannot trace its full credit to any single personality. It has made the army immortal, but the lustre of it is diffused, not concentrating upon any single head. Grant must be credited with most of the combinations; yet without the genius and activity of Sheridan, the bewildering rapidity of Sherman, and the steadfastness of such reliable men as Wright, Parke, and Griffin, these combinations would have fallen apart. It is said that Stoneman and Sheridan were to have joined their separate cavalry commands at Lynchburg, and effect a simultaneous junction with the Army of the Potomac. This failed, through a miscalculation of distance or time; but had they succeeded, we should have been less than three days in turning Lee's right, and so made the campaign even more concise. But Grant's talent has been marked and signal. He is the long-expected "coming man." None can be lukewarm in surveying the nice adjustment of so many separate and converging routes to a grand series of victories. Sherman leaves the Rebellion no Gulf city to inhabit, and cuts off Lee's retreat while he absorbs Johnston; the navy closes the last seaport; Sheridan severs all communication with Richmond, and swells the central forces; then the Rebels are lured from their lines and scattered on their right; the same night the intrenchments of Petersburg are stormed, Richmond falls as this prop is removed, being already hungry-hearted, and the flushed army falls upon Lee and finishes the war. Is not this work for gratulation? Glory to the army, perfect at last, and to Grant, to Sheridan, to each of its commanders!

Let us not do injustice to Lee. His tactics at the close of his career were as brilliant as necessity would permit. He could not feed Richmond, even though its impregnable works were behind him to retire to. So he gave his government time to evacuate, and, with his thinned and famishing ranks, made a bold push to join Johnston, some of whose battalions had already reinforced him; overtaken on the way, and punished anew, he did as any great and humane commander would do—stopped the useless effusion of blood, and gave up his sword.

Unless Davis has been captured, we would think it improbable that he had given up the Rebel cause. He was born to revolutionize, containing within himself all the elements of a Rebel leader, and too proud to yield, even when, like Macbeth, pursued to his castle-keep. I am assured by those who know him best that he has been, throughout, the absolute master of the Confederacy, overawing Lee, who, from the first, was a reluctant Rebel; and his design was, until abandoned by his army, to hold Richmond, even through starvation, making, behind its tremendous fortifications, a defense like that of Leyden or Genoa.

There is no more faith in the Rebellion; it will be a long

time before the United States is greatly beloved, but it will be always obeyed. Our soldiers look well, most of them being newly uniformed, and behave like gentlemen. Courtesy will conquer all that bayonets have not won. The burnt district is still hideously yawning in the heart of the town, a monument to the sternness of those bold revolutionists who are being hunted to their last quarry. Despotism, under the plea of necessity, has met with its end here as it must everywhere. We shall have no more experiments for liberty out of the Union, if the new Union will grant all that it gave before. Yesterday, when our splendid levies were paraded in the street, with foot, cavalry, and cannon, in admirable order, and kindly-eyed men in command, I looked across at their cleanly lines, tipped with bayonets, to the Capitol they had won, bearing at last the tri-color we all love and honor, as the symbol of our homes and the hope of the world, and thought how more grandly, even in her ruin, Richmond stood in the light of its crowding stars, rather than the den of a desperate cabal, whose banner was known in no city nor sea, but as the ensign of corsairs, and hailed only by fustian peers, now rent in the grip of our eagle, and without a fane or an abiding-place. Let us go on, not conquerors, but Republicans, battering down only to rebuild more gloriously—not narrowing the path of any man, but opening to high and low a broader destiny and a purer patriotism.

Index

Index

(Unless otherwise indicated, place names are for Virginia)